The Personal Creed Project and a New Vision of Learning

For Peter —

Brother on the long
universe learning
highway.

With Love and
Thanks for
standing up for
better angels —

John Creger 11/23/2021

Loaves and Fishes

This is not
the age of information.

This is *not*
the age of information.

Forget the news,
and the radio,
and the blurred screen.

This is the time
of loaves
and fishes.

People are hungry,
and one good word is bread
for a thousand.

—*David Whyte*

The Personal Creed Project and a New Vision of Learning

Teaching the Universe of Meaning
In & Beyond the Classroom

John Creger

HEINEMANN
Portsmouth, NH

Heinemann
A division of Reed Elsevier Inc.
361 Hanover Street
Portsmouth, NH 03801–3912
www.heinemann.com

Offices and agents throughout the world

The author and publisher wish to thank those who have generously given permission to reprint borrowed material:

Excerpt from "The Dream That Must Be Interpreted" by Rumi from *The Essential Rumi* translated by Coleman Barks. Copyright © 1995 by Coleman Barks. Published by HarperCollins, New York. Reprinted by permission of the translator.

"Loaves and Fishes" from *The House of Belonging* by David Whyte. Copyright © 1997 by David Whyte. Used by permission of the author and Many Rivers Press, *www.davidwhyte.com*.

Library of Congress Cataloging-in-Publication Data
Creger, John.
The personal creed project and a new vision of learning : teaching the universe of meaning in and beyond the classroom / John Creger.
    p. cm.
  Includes bibliographical references and index.
  ISBN 0-325-00666-0 (alk. paper)
    1. Active learning—United States. 2. Experiential learning—United States. 3. Project method in teaching—United States. I. Title.

LB1027.23.C73 2004
371.39—dc22   2003023010

Editor: Lisa Luedeke
Production coordinator: Elizabeth Valway
Production service: Matrix Productions
Cover design: Joni Doherty
Front cover photo: Student Trevor Carrier presenting his Personal Creed. Trevor intends his presentation poster, a map of California highways, to represent his journey through life. In his presentation, Trevor shares his reflections on who and what have influenced his past, explains what he stands for in the present, and outlines his vision for his future life.
Composition: Tom Allen, Pear Graphic Design
Manufacturing: Steve Bernier

Printed in the United States of America on acid-free paper
08 07 06 05 04 VP 1 2 3 4 5

This book is dedicated to the children
of the twenty-first century.
Become parents and grandparents
whose children and grandchildren prize
the loving designs of a learning universe.

A Beginning Model of Twenty-First-Century Learning

GOALS FOR TEACHING AND LEARNING PRACTICES

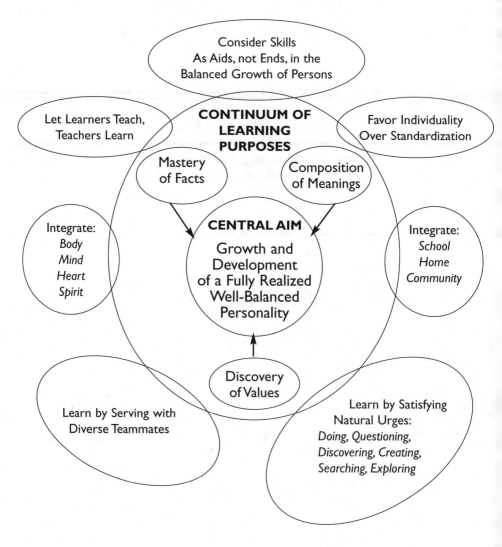

Consider Skills
As Aids, not Ends, in the
Balanced Growth of Persons

Let Learners Teach,
Teachers Learn

**CONTINUUM OF
LEARNING
PURPOSES**

Favor Individuality
Over Standardization

Mastery
of Facts

Composition
of Meanings

Integrate:
*Body
Mind
Heart
Spirit*

CENTRAL AIM

Growth and
Development
of a Fully Realized
Well-Balanced
Personality

Integrate:
*School
Home
Community*

Discovery
of Values

Learn by Serving with
Diverse Teammates

Learn by Satisfying
Natural Urges:
*Doing, Questioning,
Discovering, Creating,
Searching, Exploring*

Cross Section of 21st Century English Curriculum

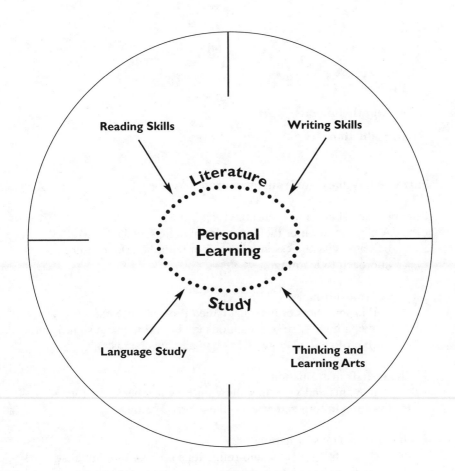

 Contents

instructions for students, annotated for teachers. Includes
graphics, rubric, and student responses.

What follows are the site contents as of the publication of this book. Additional materials and features will be added to the site as time goes on.

Web Resources
www.universeWired.com

For the Creed Project
  Complete Instructions for Step I to IV Reflections
    Semester-Long Version (with sample cover)
    Mid-Length Version
    Workshop Version (for adults)
  Sample Step V Reflective Essays
    Eddie's Creed Essay
    Natalie's Creed Essay
    Jennifer's Creed Essay

For Weaving Personal Learning Through the Year
  Sample Two-Legged Writings
    Danielle's Spring Final Exam Essay
    Matt's Spring Final Exam Essay
    Melissa's Spring Final Exam Essay
    Anthony's Spring Final Exam Essay
  Cosmos-Friendly Themes
  Student Statements on the Value of Meditation
    Tatiana's Moment That Mattered
    Marissa's Moment That Mattered

Other Web Resources
"Zora Neale Hurston's Janie: Pointing the Way to Two-Legged Curriculum," by John Creger, reprinted from *California English*, February 2002.

 # Preface

To a Teacher-Learner Mover-Shaper

Since you have chosen to pick up this book, you are most likely a teacher. You may teach in a classroom or a home, in a workplace, church, mosque, temple, or on the street. If you are the better kind of teacher, you are also a learner. Wherever and whomever you truly teach, you are a mover and a shaper. More than the political leaders and entertainment personalities who love to be filmed at the helm of the world, or the more elusive ones who grip lower on the wheel in corporate and strategic boardrooms, this book assumes it is true teachers and true learners, by dint of wisdom and insight mined at daily discovery in rich, many-stranded veins of learning, who are meant to steer civilization. While in its specifics this book may speak of a classroom setting, this is a guidebook for teachers and learners everywhere who are willing to commit to, conceive, and build a century when more human beings will discover new ways to listen to the voice inside themselves and, hearing, bring cool water for a world that thirsts for the learning beyond knowledge.

Acknowledgements

To my visionary friends with NCTE's Assembly for Expanded Perspectives on Learning who showed me I wasn't the only wild-eye willing to go to the edges to find things and bring them back: to Bruce Novak for your sweet drunkenness on human wine; Susan Allenbaugh for your clear voice and encouragement; Leah Johnson for your wise and soulful partnering across the college divide. To Byron Belitsos for twenty years of friendship and for steering me back from misty dreams to my own actual audience. And to all my other Teaching Mission homefolks.

To my thinking partners: Duron Aldredge for sharing your friendship, your family, and a mind as filled with truth and beauty as your heart is with goodness; David Xu for sharing the bumps in your road and the visions in your mind; Huda Shreim for your fearless love of God and the daring clarity of your spirit.

To my teachers: Charles Muscatine for my first conscious model of a teacher's power and joyful serving; Ojars Kratins for your loyalty to what you saw inside me; to Herb and Velma Kennedy for showing me how teachers listen and live; to Terri Tinsley for taking an ungainly recruit under your wise wing; Jo Keroes for pure teaching inspiration; to all my unseen mentors for getting me this far.

To my AHS Creed Partners: Sharron Harris for lending smarts and heart and dignity wherever you go, and for believing in me; Aileen Tsujimoto for taking a chance and raising the level of the waters with the love you inspire in your students; Brett Nelson for helping put the project on a bigger map; Patty Baca for brainy energy and openness to the new and strange; Mikila McCart for pulling the galaxy together with a thinking smile; and to Connie White who keeps the angels laughing and the school humming—and still finds time to be principal.

To Nacho Ice (Luis T. Nava) for passionate devotion to the souls of your students; to many nameless strangers who lit up on hearing of these things—you refilled my sails in slack moments.

To my editors: Lois Bridges for welcoming me in so warmly; Lisa Luedeke for handing me the torch and helping me learn to run with it.

To the students who found your way into this book: Should anyone find anything of value between its covers, it will have been your words, your thoughts and experiences, and your generous willingness to share them, that made it possible. To *all* my students: all the words that climb the pages of this book don't begin to describe the light you leave behind you in the classroom.

James Moffett: this book is intended to play a role in the further uncovering of the learning universe you so faithfully and cogently represented among us. You have left behind dirt rich enough to keep generations of sharp minds digging for jewels. May this book be one of many arising in your footsteps to help us realize and live the deeper spiritual understanding the founders of democracy knew was the only hope of securing its continuance.

To my parents William and Nancy: my first teachers more than I know.

My wife Meilan and our daughters Rebecca and Hana: Without your patience and your loving support, this book would still be in my dreams. I only hope I've brought back something worthy of the beauty of your souls.

Introduction

Something central and indispensable is missing from what we have called education over the past two centuries. No matter how well or poorly educated, each of us is marked by this lack. In my own case, from my high school interactions with teachers I have no memory of a single conversation that mattered to me. By the time my stiff legs carried me to the parking lot after that last class, I had grown so hungry for *whatever* experience waited for me beyond the school fence that the thought of attending my graduation ceremony never came to mind long enough to visualize. Eventually, in the life story I began mentally to write and rewrite, my first day of real life began the morning *after* my last day of high school.

Admittedly, this was 1969. "Tuning in and dropping out" was fashionable. Teachers, in our generation's youthful quest for a better world, were a part of the problem, a part many felt it was time we escaped, an easy part to dismiss while we tuned in to whatever solutions presented themselves. I survived coming of age in the confusing confluence of late sixties excesses by tuning in to the freeing stretch of highways, the beckoning songs of my guitar, the independent gifts of a trade, the soothing sanities of New England woods and ponds. But today the counterculture that supported those choices no longer exists. Legions of us boomers, ourselves now teachers and administrators, spend our days putting our shoulders to the wheel of school change. Working together and going it alone, we do impressive things. And we will continue to. Still, for most students and many teachers, whether or not we are recognized as successes on our respective sides of the teacher's desk, school—especially middle and high school—continues to be chronically unsatisfying.

In this guidebook I describe a project that has grown out of a conversation my sophomores and I have been having over the past ten years or so in the classrooms we've shared at American High School in Fremont, California. The book also looks beyond this project, toward certain larger ideas about learning I have come quite recently to notice standing in the background, behind my students' experiences in the project. The book attempts to show how these larger perceptions about learning explain a universal enthusiasm that immediately grips students in high school, college, and middle school, teachers at all levels who are exposed to this project, even strangers on the street who simply hear of it. This enthusiasm stands out in sharp relief against the chronic dissatisfaction I knew and know so well.

Juniors and seniors stop me in the hall early every spring, peer earnestly, and ask me if this year's sophomores have started the Creed Project yet. Students who graduated five, even eight years ago, dropping by to visit, ask the same question. Looking through the bins in a Berkeley frame store, I hear a voice behind me: "Excuse me, aren't you a teacher?" Turning around, I see a young man I don't recognize at first. "Mr. Creger, right? The Personal Creed Project!" Tim long ago graduated, finished college, has now moved for graduate school to the town where I live. But when he recognizes me—nine years later and thirty-five miles from Fremont—this project is the first thing to come to mind.

The Personal Creed Project as my students and I have developed it over more than a decade is a classroom-based personal rite of passage for high school sophomores. By "personal rite of passage" I mean an accumulating series of personal reflections on life and purpose, a journey of self-discovery of a scope few sophomores have undertaken. My observations in fifteen years of teaching and learning with sophomores make it clear to me that at some point between the ages of fifteen and sixteen in the teenage mind a developmental readiness for such personal reflection kicks in. Few sophomores at the beginning of the year seem ready to stand outside themselves, look selfward, and take stock of what they see. But when the end of the year rolls around, surprisingly, most of mine are ready, even *hungry* for this kind of reflection.

Though the Creed Project is evolving, with other teachers and their students in classrooms around the country creating adaptations and variations, from upper elementary to lower division in college, to my knowledge all versions continue to consist of a series of interwoven reflections (Steps I through IV), and culminate in a presentation (Step V) in the final week or weeks of the year. In the presentations, students share a creative work that has grown from their reflections—their choice from a growing array of presentation options—or a reflective essay. Standing with this creation before her peers and teacher during a Creed presentation, a student shares what the project has helped her realize about herself and her life, emphasizing in the manner of her choosing the following basic elements:

- This is who and what have influenced and inspired me to be the person I am today, and of them these are the influences and inspirations I most and least value or admire (Steps I and II).

- These are the values, principles, or ideals I feel committed to enough to say I stand for at this point in my life, and this is why I persist in holding them (Steps III and IV).

• This is the kind of *person* (not career) I want to become in ten years, and this is how I might want to be serving, helping, or influencing others at that point (Step V).

In this book, through my students' observations borrowed from their project reflections, portfolios, and course evaluations, you can begin to sample the enthusiasm that comes with the chance to do this kind of thinking about one's own life. You can think along with me as I narrate my attempts over the past several years to more deeply hear and more fully understand my students' responses to the project. In my role as guide, I take you through some of the same experiences that continue to help me see and think more clearly about what happens in my classroom during what I have come to call Creed season.

Weaving together the student insights mentioned above with my own vignettes of key moments in the classroom, I try to re-create for you the impact of the Personal Creed presentations, the most powerfully affecting classroom experiences I have witnessed in the decade and a half since I became a teacher. You will see how our school is showing signs of embracing these Creed presentations as a mid-high school tradition, and how this past year a steady stream of student visitors came to my classes to be on hand for their friends who were "presenting their creeds." You can sample the reflective essays some students use to prepare for these presentations. Rounding out the picture, teachers and learners fresh from the creed experience at a number of "creed sites," classrooms and departments around the country where teachers and students have begun their own experiments with the project, contribute their own observations and insights. I hope this cross section of perspectives conveys the broad reception for the project and sheds light on the effects on one's life of the reflections the Creed experience allows one to undertake. What forms do these reflections themselves take?

At various points in the project, learners reflect on the connections among their pasts, presents, and futures, think back on their influences and inspirations, contemplate what they now stand for, and imagine the kinds of lives they wish to lead in ten years. They reflect on the deeper parts of their lives, their value systems in particular, considering which values appear stable and pondering which may change over time. And, most exciting for satisfying learning and growth I'm finding, they reflect on how the *facts*, *meanings*, and *values* of their lives can become interrelated, interdependent phases of their learning. Though it probably doesn't sound earthshaking at this point, this realization—of the interdependence of facts, meanings, and values in satisfying learning—may become the major contribution of this book.

If you are drawn to experiment, I help you create your own version of the Personal Creed Project for, and with, your students. If you should choose to create a coming-of-age version of the project with your own child (as I am currently attempting with my thirteen-year-old daughter)—or, as one colleague and a recent workshop participant plan to do, a version with your own adult self—with a little creative adaptation, perhaps this book can also help.

To discover that learning can be deeply satisfying, and in a classroom of all places, *excites* students. They call for more. Indeed, students' enthusiasm, and now colleagues' enthusiasm in places across the nation, excites me. Contemplating this enthusiasm, I have been convinced that the kind of learning that is available through the Creed Project is a window on a deeper awareness of the nature of learning. I have just read the first two years of student evaluations from the first "creed site" beyond my classroom, the freshman composition classes at American University in Washington, D.C., where Professor Leah Johnson and her colleague Cindy Bair VanDam work with their students to create their own adaptations of the project. Their insights, as you'll see, echo those of our high school sophomores and, I predict, will parallel those of another creed site colleague's fifth graders next year.

American University freshmen of Leah Johnson and her colleague the past three years on the east coast, fifteen sections of American High School sophomores among four English colleagues the past two years on the west coast, many more in my own ten years of experimentation, and every teacher I know of in upper elementary, middle, high school and college who has adapted the project for students—all seem to agree: Two, even four weeks, are not enough time for this project. I am beginning to see outlines of why.

Surveying my students in a variety of ways over the past six years, I find that they hanker for serious *personal learning*. With what I do not exaggerate to describe as increasing fervor, they want it not only at the end of the year but at the beginning and all the way through. I am convinced that students' yearning for personal meaning is intensifying. It is growing, I believe, in direct proportion to the pressure we apply on them to produce academically, while we continue failing to offer them carefully conceived sets of learning experiences that satisfy their needs to discover who they are as individuals and how they fit in all the various communities to which they belong and will one day grow into.

The message from all these quarters is this: Students want education as much devoted to learning about themselves and how to connect themselves more fully to others and to the whole of experience, as it is intended to equip them with knowledge and skills. "Show us how what we do in class relates to the rest of our lives," they seem to shout silently, "and we'll show you what real learning looks like!" This book offers some suggestions for class activities, and course and program designs that help create this kind of personal learning.

Part One of this book opens with a chapter in which I attempt to concisely articulate the central problem we face, the root of the chronic dissatisfaction with school. Anyone who knows me will tell you what a challenge whittling down my thoughts to a concise form poses to me. And so throughout the book I call in help from thinkers more adept at such operations, including numbers of my students. In the remaining three chapters in Part One you find verbal snapshots of Personal Creed presentations, pictures I hope adequately capture and pass along to you the power of these presentations to create surprising alterations in the normal disgruntlements of classroom life. You will see for yourself the unusual effects of these presentations on students, on teachers, and on the magic alchemies of class "chemistry."

Part Two then invites you to join me in examining more deeply the learning experiences behind the excitement and commitment the Creed presentations tend to generate, and to consider how these experiences point the way to what may be new insights into the nature of learning. These insights, I believe, explain *why* the Creed Project "works."

In Part Three you learn *how* it works. You find the nuts and bolts—instructions for students, annotations for teachers to save time and anticipate questions—everything teachers need to create step-by-step adaptations of the Creed Project for their own students and classrooms. In a final chapter, you can explore how what the Creed Project teaches us about learning can inform course and program design. The design approach I am calling Two-Legged Learning begins with the intention to balance the academic and the personal at every stage of classroom and curricular planning. Throughout the book, I connect you with continuing support and networking possibilities through my website, www.universeWired.com.

I've chosen to begin with the verbal snapshots and commentary in Part One (Chapters Two through Four), the vignettes and reflections from a West Coast high school and an East Coast university, because I hope they will help you take your own inductive pulsebeat of the Creed Project experience, and begin making your own intuitive sense of it. If, however, you're the type who needs the nuts and bolts first, feel free to sequence to your own taste, and go directly to Part Three. If you're somewhere in between, you may want to flip back and forth.

My continuing experiences creating the Creed Project with my students, and the experiences of increasing numbers of students, colleagues, friends and acquaintances around the country who encounter or have come through it, are a cool mouthful in a dry time. They tell me that this project can play a role in bringing us a fuller, more deeply satisfying kind of learning. This is the kind of refreshing water that we teachers, in classroom, home, workplace, street, and yes, boardroom, can and should begin offering our students, as we who shepherd the most powerful human act—learning—set ourselves to defy history and design a more deep and satisfying kind of century.

John Creger
August 2003
Berkeley CA

Part One

Witness to Transformation

Humankind is being led along an evolving course,
through this migration of intelligences,
and though we seem to be sleeping,
there is an inner wakefulness
that directs the dream,

and that will eventually startle us back
to the truth of who we are.

—Rumi (Persia/Afghanistan, 1207-1273)

My eagerness to leap that fence around my high school once and for all may have helped propel me into life. I certainly wasted no time looking back: Only once have I revisited that scene from before my "life began" thirty-five years ago. And I have no desire to put in another appearance. This permanently sour taste in my memory, and similar distaste etched in the memories of countless others before and since me, are symptoms of the "central and indispensable" lack I mentioned in the Introduction. In his final book, a far-reaching blueprint for twenty-first-century education called *The Universal Schoolhouse,* pioneer literacy educator James Moffett tuned his insightful mind on the enduring symptoms of this lack. I invite you to join me in thinking along with Moffett as he articulates some of these symptoms, and goes on to identify precisely the problem at the center of our present system of learning. One of my favorite young minds joins us on the way through this first chapter. In the remaining chapters of Part One you see and hear from students, teachers, and whole classes during the culminating presentations of the Personal Creed Project, when the thing that is normally so absent shows up in class as the central focus of learning.

 # CHAPTER ONE

The Central and Indispensable Lack
(or I Hope You Don't Mind Me Saying This, But . . .)

> If the only tool you have is a hammer, it is tempting to treat
> everything as if it were a nail.
>
> —Abraham Maslow

Why do I and so many others rarely think back on our experiences in
school without a feeling of almost physical discomfort? Moffett illuminates one key source of my continued reluctance to revisit my high
school and similar aversions in many:

> Years of being treated as an object of testing, of being measured and
> monitored by external standards, of having one's worth constantly
> questioned have taught low self-esteem and anxiety. Most of the adult
> populace retains this feeling of being perpetually on probation. (58)

This assertion's truth is highlighted by the fact that the feeling of per-
petual probation is not limited to those the system fails to serve, but is
more prevalent the higher one travels in academia. The more one suc-
ceeds in our learning system, the more probationary one is made to
feel, publishing if fortune smiles, perishing if not. Indications are that
care of yet-to-be-tenured faculty is a thriving sub-specialty of psychi-
atry. As further evidence on the trail to the essential problem with
school, Moffett points to our willingness to violate the freedom of children's wills in the interest of providing citizens for the state:

> The truth is, our school system violates children's civil rights so seri-
> ously that it plays a major role in their negative plight. No govern-
> ment or public institution has the right to compel its citizens—chil-
> dren or adults—to spend most of their waking life for years on end in
> conditions over which they have very little control and where their

behavior is programmed by bureaucratic forces for reasons of state. The fact that we take for granted this appalling subjection to institutions shows how little our understanding matches our declarations of freedom and democracy. Human beings are not here to be molded by the state. (57–8)

This begs the question: If we are not here to be molded in our learning by the state, for what purpose are human beings here to learn? Today's answer, by default for the most part because we have not yet begun to seriously ask this question in our societal conversation, is that we go to school to gain skills and knowledge to equip us to play our roles as productive and responsible citizens. But this, we see in the rest of this book, is no longer a usable conception of learning. Indeed, it is becoming more and more evident that our current system fails to meet even this limited objective.

Our system fails, Moffett argues, not because of a lack of rigor, or a failure of accountability (though these may be *effects* of the problem), but because it devotes itself so thoroughly to *ranking* students and schools against one another that it pays mostly lip service to serving *even so limited a notion of the purpose of learning* as preparing productive and responsible citizens. Citizens productive and responsible for what ends? If the question appears murky, it is because we have too long failed to ask it.

This excessive emphasis on competitive ranking in schooling is grounded, incidentally, in a misunderstanding of Darwin's notion of natural selection, a process Darwin himself understood as more relevant in *biological* evolution (as we'll see in a brief foray in Part Two into what Darwin actually thought), than in the more sophisticated processes involved in *human* evolution. This misunderstanding results in Darwin's notion of the survival-of-the-biologically-fittest being misapplied to processes on a higher evolutionary level. The processes involved in the survival of the biologically fittest, we'll see, are only the starting point in understanding the vastly more complex operations of *human beings learning and growing in human society*—operations that for only one major difference incorporate the variable of conscious *choice*, a variable much less in evidence in the processes of pure biological evolution.

This resulting misapplication of the survival-of-the-fittest notion leads logically, inexorably, and tragically to a system of schooling whose most basic assumptions spotlight learners who come out on top, and wrap in shadow those who do not. Both for those who would be winners, anxious that they may in fact not succeed in reaching the coveted spotlight, and those who become de facto losers, resigned to invisibility in the academic shadows, in its day-to-day realities such a system is essentially *fear-driven*.

This is not a rationale from sour grapes. In a recent essay, thinker and writer David Kantor offers one possible context in which to consider this situation. Kantor describes a spectrum of four generalized attitudes a given individual can feel toward life in a given moment. At one end of this spectrum is *despair;* at the other end is *faith.* (In this discussion, "faith" does not necessarily denote a religious attitude, but could also encompass the person's faith in himself or herself, in the person's family, friends, culture, nation, or in humanity, as it could faith in some spiritual reality.) In the spectrum's central positions are *doubt,* in a position next to despair, and *hope,* in the place next to faith. The range of this given person's general attitudes toward life in a given moment, then, goes: *despair-doubt-hope-faith.* Most of us, according to Kantor, spend the majority of our time in the center of the spectrum, hovering between the attitudes of *hope* and *doubt.* Two other forces, Kantor continues, play the activating roles in this model. (See figure in Appendix I or on website.)

One of these forces, *fear,* tends to propel us toward attitudes of *doubt* and, when fear is in enough supply, toward *despair.* What force, then, moves us toward the *hope* and *faith* portion of the spectrum? In Kantor's spectrum it is *ideals.* It is what we deeply desire for ourselves, for our families or for the world that gives us the capacity to shift our attitudes in the moment from doubt to hope, or, when hope moves toward certainty, to faith (Kantor 1). Ideals can even move us out of despair. It was vestiges of ideals that gave Elie Wiesel the wherewithal to survive and begin to recover from the despair of Auschwitz, and that enabled Chinese labor camp survivor Harry Wu to survive nineteen years in the Chinese Gulag and later expose to the world history's largest system of forced labor prisons. Is our learning system driven more by fear, or by ideals?

To whatever extent our learning system is designed to reward "winners" at the expense of "losers," to that extent it is fear-driven. And here's the rub. A fear-driven system of learning erodes our commitment to democratic values—which are ideal-driven—and leads us inevitably along Kantor's spectrum away from hope to doubt and, ultimately, as is evident in many schools, despair. This background dynamic may be more in evidence than we realize.

Hannah Arendt, a Jewish refugee from Nazi Germany, observed, "The fundamental contradiction of the United States is political freedom coupled with social slavery." Perhaps the root of the challenge facing American democracy is the collision of an ideals-driven model of government with an educational system that, for all its well-intentioned reform remains fundamentally fear-driven. Can a fear-based education system, more intended to prepare children to compete for economic advantage than to nourish their vision of a just and democratic society, inspire citizens in large enough numbers to develop the ideals of selfless public service?

More than five years before the "high stakes" version of standardized testing began to hit schools, and a decade before the second President Bush ordered the attack on Iraq called Iraqi Freedom, James Moffett described the damaging, far-reaching effects of this contradiction:

> Schooling as we know it breeds rigidity and neurosis in the lucky and despair and fury in the unlucky. This is not how a democratic state keeps hale and whole. Years of forced competition for scores and grades have taught that you set yourself up by putting others down, that selfishness and secrecy hold the key to success. Conflict and war will seem natural. (58)

Despite this fundamental flaw, however, for reasons we will explore in Part Two, school is the natural vehicle for society to improve and even re-create itself. It is a symptom of the deepest problem with school, then, that we not only fail to recognize this opportunity but allow school to incubate and exacerbate other societal problems. After a quarter century as a tireless pioneer of literacy reforms, Moffett reveals his own frustrations with the problems he faced in his work:

> School . . . is so stupefying and ungratifying that it sets up addiction to drugs and television, so dehumanizing and infuriating that it helps engender crime and violence. The natural reaction to all this is enormous resentment, which individuals act out toward each other and the society. The dysfunctional family can generate more resentment and usually does far more damage to children than school does, because its closer relationships intensify feeling, but wouldn't it be good if public education could, instead of reinforcing other traumas, offset them? (58)

Insightful students understand these things more than we realize. I had the pleasure for a year and a half of commuting to school with one of my favorite student thinking partners, Duron Aldredge. A promising education theorist even at sixteen, possessed of a surprisingly mature mind, Duron greatly enjoys thinking about learning. In one of our continuing conversations about education as it ought to be, one March afternoon on the way home up the freeway Duron lit up with a truth. "Mr. Creger," he began gently, "I hope you don't mind me saying this, but . . ."

. . . you know the General Motors plant in south Fremont? Well, at one end of the plant they put a chassis on the assembly line. It moves along the line, and the doors, fenders, bumpers, seats, dash, engine and transmission get bolted or welded on. At the other end of the plant, the car comes off the line, and a printout listing everything that's been attached gets taped to the windshield." With his forefinger, Duron traced the empty rectangle where this paper would sit on my windshield. "Well, Mr. Creger . . ." I noticed a tired patience in his eyes as he concluded, "that printout's pretty much the same thing as our transcripts when we graduate."

Duron Aldredge, March 2001

I can think of few of our conversations that did not leave me impressed with Duron's knowledge of the world and how it works, or teach me something, particularly about science. But Duron's greatest accomplishments in school are not recorded on his transcripts. As the school's most distinguished conflict mediator, a key student player in reducing school violence through the gang risk intervention program, a trusted listener to anyone needing to be heard in or out of the peer counseling program, and a particularly effective president of the Black Students' Union, Duron has left a serious leadership vacuum behind him since he graduated. The fact that such evidences of *personal mastery* are not deemed important enough to recognize in a student's official record is certainly another symptom of the essential problem with school.

True, unlike most of his low-performing cohorts, Duron was honored for these accomplishments. True, unlike some of them, after a senior year on the brink of failure, laboring day and night spring semester under a load of *nine* classes he *had* to pass, in the end he did graduate, and with some impressive awards to hang on the wall for his family and friends to see. But why didn't the overwhelming portion of his time in school, the time he spent in classes and so often spent again in summer school (yes, even for my class), the "seattime" that shows on his transcripts, why didn't those classes call up Duron's commitment? He admits to laziness as part of the problem. But why had his school experience been such that during his sleep-starved last semester this deep-thinking young man confided in me one morning on the freeway, "Since my sophomore year I haven't much thought about learning. I only think about getting things done so I can graduate and leave."

In our conversations, Duron offered some key insights into this problem. He had entered high school in 1998, just as the standards movement sparked by progressive educators was being commandeered by government and business forces for motives that did not include helping students grow as persons while they acquire skills and knowledge. Without a clear knowledge of all these forces per se, Duron noticed the increasing emphasis on holding him and his peers accountable to standards, and the decreased interest in helping them unfold themselves as learning human beings. Despite a love of learning that is native to his nature, Duron's disaffection with school had begun with his transition to middle school. This was when he suddenly lost the consistency in the one-classroom learning situation and the close working relationships with his teachers and classmates, the things that had nourished his love of learning in elementary school. Impossible with seven teachers and seven classrooms in middle school, these nourishing things had evaporated. And as standards began to morph into high stakes testing across the country, making school even less about learning and growing as a person, he could see where this was going. Quietly to himself during his freshman year, he made some predictions.

Commuting together half his junior year and his entire senior year, Duron and I talked regularly until he graduated in 2002. In the four years since he had entered high school, state tests on the standards had become a curricular reality, the school's curriculum had been "aligned" with those tests, and the California High School Exit Exam loomed over the heads of the class two years behind his. From my side of the teacher's desk, I too was noticing some changes.

One morning on the way to school during Duron's senior year, I confided in him that I was seeing what I thought could be a significant deterioration in the maturity of my incoming sophomores over the past two years. Beginning with his graduating class when they were sophomores, I had observed that students were having a markedly more difficult time sitting still in class, keeping a class discussion focussed without side-chatting, and rising above the general level of goofiness I had observed in student-teaching eighth grade a decade earlier. The school as a whole was making encouraging progress (thanks to efforts Duron contributed to) in reducing previous levels of gang-related violence, and the overall school climate was clearly improving. Paradoxically, the classroom behavior, other teachers tended to agree, seemed on the decline. Though for the most part nice, well-meaning kids, sophomores were coming in with eighth-grade classroom behavior.

Why, I wondered aloud at the wheel, would this be happening? Again Duron lit up, surprised by the force of a realization. "Mr. Creger," he said, "you're not going to believe this but this is what I predicted was going to happen. When I was a freshman I used to think about this all the time. As they raise the academic expectations higher and higher, I was thinking, students aren't going to be happy about it, and it will show up in their behavior." As I write today, a year and a half after this conversation, it seems completely obvious, but then it was a minor aha for me: The more we raise the bar academically *without making learning more personally rewarding—indeed, actually making it less so*—the fewer the students who will be able to engage school learning happily. Kids are spending more and more time doing less meaningful schoolwork, and less and less time growing up. School becomes more and more like the factory in Duron's image.

Duron's image of a meaningless education assembly line leads us eloquently back to the "central and indispensible lack" I brought up in the Introduction. What, then, is at the root of the problem? When all is said and done, what *is* the tragic flaw in our understanding of learning? What failure of concept allows us to take something so fundamental and precious as learning and create a system of education so open to the charges Moffett levels and Duron's image implies? James Moffett believes that education's "largest single problem," and what most needs to be corrected, is "the *depersonalization* of schooling" (122).

I could not agree more wholeheartedly. And in Part Two we will look into precisely what Moffett means by this phrase.

I did not come into agreement with Moffett's analysis, however, only by considering symptoms such as those we've examined so far. I arrived by having caught a glimpse of what it will look like to celebrate *personal* learning at the center of what we do in school. I've seen it in the writings and faces, and heard it in the voices of students and colleagues who have participated in the Personal Creed Project.

CHAPTER TWO

Class Transformations

> The present is the moment when the past can be transformed
> and the future lit with radiance.
>
> —Thomas Cahill

About Testimonials

Several who have read drafts of this book wondered whether the testimonials in the chapters you are about to read rightly belong in a book intended (if not exclusively) for classroom teachers. Will these often emotional statements from students and teachers who have experienced the Creed Project seem "touchy-feely"? Might readers question whether such emotional confessions are appropriate classroom activities? Might they ask if teachers are qualified to handle such sensitive issues anyway? Perhaps. If at any point you find yourself uncomfortable with the testimonials or their use questionable, I invite you to skip ahead to pages 31 to 32 (beginning with the paragraph starting with "Some may ask . . ."), where I offer a defense of using these student statements and argue for taking them seriously.

Though no one has raised it yet, another possible objection to using statements from my students as the largest part of the evidence in this book comes to mind. Teachers in our society, especially secondary English teachers, as a national survey of our spouses would reveal, spend an enormous portion of our allotted hours on earth laboring in stacks of student papers for the uplift of the species. Many of us receive only rare appreciation from our students or their parents, our colleagues or our principals. Against this lukewarm background, the kind of glowing enthusiasm you will read in most of the student statements in this book can be heady, even intoxicating. To publish inordinate numbers of glowing testimonials could be a not-so-subtle way of grandstanding: *Hey! Look what my students say about my class!* Let me be honest. One reason I collect student statements is precisely that they often make me feel good about my teaching. In my near-exhaustion at the end of a year of teaching full-time English, I even bundle a set of course evaluations at the bottom of each set of final exam essays to cheer me on and keep me reading to the end of the set. Indeed, one of my reasons for assigning course evaluations is to support myself through the endless labors of my job.

But I collect students' insights on their learning in my classes for reasons beyond helping myself to feel good and survive. Some statements I share in this book disturb and even shock me. Others help me understand what isn't working. Still others validate the inklings that have led me to develop this project and the teaching ideas and practices it points me toward. All such statements help me more deeply understand my students' learning experiences so I can find ways to help make their learning more effective and rewarding. I believe the testimonials in this book also demonstrate the capacity of young adults to honestly and truthfully assess their own lives. This makes me feel good about my teaching at deeper levels than simple validation.

I hope the ideas and practices in this book lead you to glowing statements from your own students! Feeling good about our teaching is, after all, a good thing. It isn't, of course, our main purpose as teachers, but more a kind of by-product of creating a good learning climate. A teacher's teaching is only one component, if a crucial one, in the kinds of learning that can go on in a classroom, as I hope this book shows. The statements from students I include in this book give me what I have come to believe are important lessons about how my students, how all of us, learn best.

As much as any group in the past several years, Jennifer Morgan and her entire class persuaded me that something unusual was happening. The Personal Creed presentations in this fourth-period class were so, well, extraordinary that I realized I needed to listen more carefully to what students were telling me between the lines, during and after the Creed Project.

Since the early 1990s when I experimented with early versions of the project, my breath had been taken away each year by the power of the presentations. I saw so much in so short a time—as many as 120 often emotional presentations in a single week before finals each year—that the specifics tended to blur in my memory. The only adult to witness all this, I had no one but understandably skeptical colleagues and a busy wife to sputter to about what I was seeing happen.

Only after a two-year leave of absence in graduate school had given me time to *reflect* on what happens in my classroom did I think to invite other adults to witness the presentations. It wasn't until the 2000–2001 school year, then—the year I began paying closer attention, taking notes and keeping journals—that other adults began to see what it was I had been sputtering about.

The main thing this fourth-period class led me to realize was that during Creed presentations I nearly always witness surprising and often profound transformations. Mulling it over, I've realized these changes come in various kinds. The first kind consists of alterations in the climate, the chemistry, of a class. Jennifer's presentation, one of the most memorable I've seen in ten years, is a good place to begin exploring this kind of transformation.

Most students prefer to stand before their peers with a visual aid—photo gallery, collage, PowerPoint, or any in a range of creed presentation choices. When her moment came, Jennifer sat down empty-handed in front of the class and smiled. Retaining her smile throughout, her tone and facial expression empty of judgment or anger, she simply told her truth without fear or hesitation:

> When my mother was my age she was basically a whore. She got pregnant and had an abortion, got pregnant and had an abortion, got pregnant and had an abortion, and then when she got pregnant again her mother told her it was unhealthy to have another abortion, so I was born.
>
> Still in high school, my mother took care of me for a while until one night when my father, he was still a teenager himself, came into a room where my mother was the only girl in a roomful of guys drinking and doing drugs. I was on the bed in diapers that hadn't been changed in long enough that they were full of poop and whatever else. My dad took me out of there and has been trying his best to raise me ever since. Now he's thirty and I'm fifteen.
>
> A while ago I ran away from home and was acting wild until my father sat me down. He told me I was acting very much like someone he once knew, someone we had seen only once since he took me out of that room: When I was eight my dad and I were eating in a Lyon's restaurant one night when a waitress came up and gave me a big hug and left before I could say anything. I asked my dad who she was. "That's your mom," he answered.
>
> That's when I started to realize that I was heading down the same road as my mother, and knew that wasn't where I wanted to go.

Part of Jennifer's personal creed, she went on to explain, included making wiser choices than her mother had made. What does this have to do with a transformation of class climate? In her course evaluation the following week Jennifer chose to write about the Creed Project. She offered some clear insights not only on her own experience while presenting but on the effect of the experience on the class as a whole:

> This project totally opened up my eyes to myself and everyone in my class. I have a new level of respect for everyone who presented. It was good for me because I was able to express a hurt and bruised side to a group of people that I normally would not. The audience was awed by everything everyone said. Everyone was respectful because all the walls were open, from the moment the first person started talking to the end everyone respected and loved everyone at that moment.
>
> —Jennifer Morgan, June 2001

Few who frequent high school classrooms or have clear memories of their own experiences in them would say that Jennifer's last sentence above describes a day, let alone five minutes, in a typical one. In no way, I assure you, does her description remotely reflect the climate in this fourth period class for most of the 2000–2001 school year. The truth is that this was one of the most unruly groups I can recall in fifteen years of teaching. Teaching? There were days when this class felt like chair-and-cane work better left to a lion keeper! Yet Jennifer's observations on the change that came over this class during the Creed presentations are corroborated by the perceptions of several of her classmates.

Norah, a shy student from a very traditional Hindu family, was overtaken in her presentation by an unscripted moment of truth. Before she knew it, Norah was confessing to us that she had recently attempted suicide by the alarming practice among certain groups of teen girls of regaining the repressed ability to feel emotions by making cuts in the wrists and elsewhere with a razor blade until the physical evidence of blood and pain restores the sense of being emotionally alive. Disturbing? Yes! (I referred her to the counselor, who later advised me that she appeared to be out of danger.) For a selection in her end-of-year portfolio we call the "Moment That Mattered," Norah chose to write about the presentations:

> My moment that mattered would have to be the Creed presentations because everyone just listened and did not judge you or say something that might have discouraged you they were all there to support you and listen to what you had to say about your life and what you stand for. I really enjoyed the presentations because of this I especially like to listen to everyone else's because I learned things about him or her that I would never have known. Through all the tears and

laughter I learned more about my classmates and myself as well. I have never known my classmates as I know them today. I always thought that we were all so different but now I know we are only different in appearance but mostly we all stand for the same things.

—Norah Chaudhary, June 2001

Especially sensitive and quiet, Norah had failed first semester, and was in the midst of a steady and ultimately successful effort to pass this time. Even though I had witnessed her presentation itself, it was a surprise to read this outpouring of feeling in her later reflection, and Norah helped me further understand the change in class climate. What might be the elements of this change?

A sense of *relief* is evident in Norah's "everyone just listened and did not judge you or say something that might have discouraged you they were all there to support you and listen to what you had to say about your life and what you stand for." Relief is present too in Jennifer's "It was good for me because I was able to express a hurt and bruised side to a group of people that I normally would not." But don't teenage girls simply tend to be more ready for this kind of sharing? What about the boys in the class?

Dave had been quiet most of the year, unless he was chatting it up with his neighbors when he should have been giving his attention to the person recognized to speak. Dave's body language, like mine thirty-five years before, was calculated to send the message that, hey, if it's school, Dave isn't buying any. Do what's needed to get by, but little more. By the end of the year as he began the Creed Project, this attitude was changing. With the presentations behind him, Dave wrote in his course evaluation:

The biggest jump I took in this class emotionally happened only a few days ago when I watched all of my classmates get in front of the class and present their creed. Now when I see all of those classmates in the hallways walking by it feels like I KNOW them and that I could sit with them for hours and just talk. I have a greater respect for the people in my fourth period class than any of my other classes.

—Dave Simpson, June 2001

Again relief is in evidence, if less explicit in Dave's statement than in Jennifer's or Norah's. For Dave and others, male and female alike as we'll see, relief seems associated with an enhanced feeling of *connection* to his classmates. An awareness of a heightened state of relationship to others during these presentations, then, appears to be a second quality of the transformed class climate.

Indeed, relief stemming from a pronounced connectedness is common to the statements from all three students. Each writes about this sense when describing the heightened *respect* in the classroom during and even after the presentations. Norah enjoys the surprise of learning how the students "mostly . . . all stand for the same things." Fremont, in the news in the wake of September 11 as an example of a community dealing with complex cultural issues, has been accurately described as a "global suburb." With a blend of whites, Hispanics, blacks, and a large and varied Asian population, including Sikh, Hindu, and the largest Afghan American community in the United States, Fremont is known for tolerance among its cultural groups, and Norah had probably experienced little overt discrimination growing up in this community. Still, tolerance does not necessarily mean *understanding*, and it was a relief to Norah to learn how, despite their differing appearances, her classmates' value systems overlapped her own. This deepened *understanding*, then, is something else I think sets the classroom climate during Creed presentations apart from the norm. Dave, who comes from a more mainstream background, shares Norah's relief and wants to find out more about these people he has so recently seen in ways he had never seen them before. For Jennifer, the entire experience went further, imparting an awe, even love.

A note of sobriety here. There is always the possibility that "affective data" such as these statements become skewed by lazy or otherwise unproductive hopes of students that their teacher, emotionally affected by a bit of "creative writing" in such statements, might be moved to "donate" a passing grade. However, given the yearlong lack of regard for grades in this particular class, this seems unlikely. The class *average* of this "college prep" class often dipped below the 60 percent minimum passing mark, and I wondered what was wrong with my teaching or the course as long stretches passed with no student earning an A and few pulling B's. By the time students had written these statements, those who were failing had already secured berths in summer school, and an unusually high number of class members had grades too low to even bother working on my sympathies. To make this altogether unlikely as a motivation for some of these statements, a number of the more moving insights into the Creed experience come from the most hopelessly failing students, and this seems to have been true for all three years since I began taking notes. Testimonials from such students, who have nothing to gain from writing them, shed a special light on the transformation of the classroom and I think they deserve a special ear in this narrative.

John Vroman, a highly gifted student who had lost both parents to illness and accident in the previous several years, had serious and compound motivation problems in school. While occasionally brimming with ambitious plans to resurrect his English grade, a project for which I was as open for business as John was capable, he never managed to follow through with his plans. Even victory over his English teacher in a bowling match one afternoon couldn't help him break the pattern, and he was falling more and more permanently behind.

John rose to the occasion for the Creed Project, however. Standing before his classmates, improvising unabashedly, John trusted us to hear him and proceeded to lay his true situation in life before us. Later, in his course evaluation, his relief was still almost palpable:

> The Personal Creed Project is one of the best things a school could have. I enjoyed looking into myself and finding out what I stand for. *Creed Proj: This is a must for all schools!*
>
> —John Vroman, June 2001

John's last sentence, scrawled dramatically in yellow highlighter at the bottom of his course evaluation, sounds adamant, almost authoritative. This tone suggests that he understood very well the opportunity this project was presenting him to develop himself personally. His exuberance hints at how brilliantly he used the occasion of an unusually supportive audience of peers to help him come to grips with the tragically changed realities of his life. An atmosphere of enhanced *trust*, then, is another quality of this altered class climate. John's trust in his classmates and me must have figured among the forces that spurred him to rise to the occasion with no hope of passing the class. Would more regular opportunities to relate his real-life situation to his learning in school affect John's motivation to succeed?

Lorena and I might have met in my reading class, had it not been for the district's unfortunate decision that year to abolish all basic and remedial English classes with no viable plan to support the students who would have been in them. As it was, struggling with residual second-language issues, Lorena found the pace in the college prep class too rapid, and struggled all year to keep up. Still, choosing to mention the project in her course evaluation, she wrote:

> My creed project was my favorite from them all and I'm thankful we did it because it was easy and touching.
>
> —Lorena Romero, June 2001

Challenged as she was in the academics, it is interesting to consider that when it came to the *personal learning* Lorena was on an equal footing with her classmates. And why should *all* of the learning in school be based on competition? If personal learning were more in evidence in this class, would Lorena see an uptick in her confidence and therefore her motivation and performance? So an *equal chance to succeed* was a further characteristic of the class climate that made the Creed Project work for Lorena.

Jordan in second period, despite good skills and excellent literary insight, failed all year. But Jordan's *insight*, though not in itself sufficient to enable him to pass without doing the required work, does inform his comment below, one of many that year that spurred me to think more pointedly about the picture I now see emerging through the window of the Creed Project:

> I think next year you should do a little of the Creed Project at the beginning of the year to see what the kids stand for at the start of the year and then at the end of the year you should see what they stand for.
>
> —Jordan Francis, June 2001

In order to graduate, Norah, John, Lorena, and Jordan must repeat at least a semester of sophomore English. Yet each speaks with conviction and appreciation about this project. Why do the course essays, the literature program, the reading and vocabulary activities I offer fail to claim these students' allegiance when this project evokes such commitment from them? Why do the two most hopelessly failing students go *beyond* personal observations to offer insightful suggestions—even demands—for incorporating more personal learning into the course? Jordan's suggestion, in fact, belongs to a chorus. Marcos and Matt add their voices:

> One word, creed. This project was the best project I have ever done. It was the first one I actually enjoyed. I love this project, you should have one in the beginning and one at the end to see how it has changed.
>
> —Marcos Diaz, June 2001

> The creed project was the best part of the year, but I think it should be done twice. It would be cool if we did it during the first semester also so we could compare how we changed throuout [sic] the year.
>
> —Matt Vivian, June 2001

The voices of two articulate college freshmen representing Professor Johnson's classes at American University in Washington, D.C., deepen the chorus:

> The problem for me was that I could have, conceivably, spent an entire semester on this project. I was frustrated by the time constraints because I don't feel as though I was able to fully express the nuance and circumstantial relativity of my views.

> I enjoyed the Creed Project; it was a good way to take a guided look at myself and learn new things. Although it seemed tedious at the time, in retrospect I wish there was another part.
>
> —both unsigned, June 2002

These sentiments, Leah Johnson confirms in a recent letter, were widely shared:

On the teacher evaluations I received at the end of the semester, many students suggested spending much more time on the project. We spent about four weeks on it, but they wanted longer. So next spring, I'm going to block out a good six weeks.

—Prof. Leah Johnson, July 2002

Back on the West Coast, another series of unexpectedly deep presentations at American High School in June 2002 before surprisingly respectful sophomore audiences—including another especially restive fourth period—led me to a conjecture: The more unruly the class, the more profound the potential transformation to the class climate during the Creed presentations. Of course, this could be partly a matter of perception: Such a change in such a class travels a greater behavioral distance than a similar change in a more willing group, and I would naturally be more impressed by it. But it is also true that students are unruly for personal reasons as much or more than for academic ones. Learning that is designed to honor personal learning and that actually assists students to understand themselves more deeply might naturally reduce unruliness. My hunch is that such experiences as periodic phases of students' learning will lead ultimately to greater academic achievement. Social and emotional learning expert James Comer has observed pointedly, "It is a child's overall development—not simply cognitive or intellectual development—that makes academic learning possible."

The following, then, are some of the qualities that seem to characterize the changed climate in Personal Creed presentations:

- an increased sense of connection to others
- a greater awareness of equality
- the relevance of insight in learning
- a more pronounced level of trust
- all resulting in relief, even awe and love

Could a regular supply of such qualities in our classrooms make "academic learning possible," as James Comer puts it, to a degree we may never have imagined? And if the Creed presentations affect groups of students in these ways, how do they affect *teachers*?

CHAPTER THREE

Teacher Transformations

Our students learn much more from our learning than they'll ever pick up from our teaching.

—Polly Berands

West Coast Home Fires

After years of polite interest from colleagues, my hopes of finding teacher allies at school to work in a serious way with students to build personal learning into our program were growing dim. Then, all at once last year two other sophomore English teachers at AHS were jumping in and taking their students through the Creed Project. Suddenly, the project was on the map, and not only at the other creed sites around the country, but right here where it started, at American High School. One of the main surprises for me in all this was the degree to which my colleagues were affected by the experience.

It is the week of the presentations. Aileen Tsujimoto, an energetic and respected thirty-five-year veteran English teacher, well-loved in the classroom, in the department, and around the district, sweeps into the faculty lunchroom. I can see right away that she is moved, and she approaches me bubbling with the urge to talk about it. "I wasn't sure how this was going to turn out, my first time through and all," she begins.

> Every single presentation today was wonderful! Each one just a little bit different. At one point most of us were weeping. They took risks! In fact, a couple of kids who aren't usually into school were really into it. One of them wants a second chance to present because he feels he didn't go deeply enough the first time! Another interesting situation, a popular cheerleader, inspired by others who presented, wanted

19

me to help her take greater risks than she was used to and to share what she found out about herself.

—Aileen Tsujimoto, June 2002

A few days before the presentations, Aileen had been so excited about her students' response to the written portion of the project that she had mailed her twenty-nine-year-old daughter a set of the project instructions. A graduate of a highly regarded college, she still seemed uncertain of her priorities and was having difficulty making decisions about what to do with her life. Aileen felt that the Creed experience might help her daughter engage in some further reflection. This has given me the idea to create a version with my own thirteen-year-old daughter. (See website.)

Sharron Harris, another thirty-five-year veteran who, as English Department chair, successfully herded a collection of iconoclastic teaching cats closer to the day when we might put together a program designed to equip us not merely to teach but to satisfy learners, arrives a little nervously the day she plans to begin the Creed Project with her reading class. Opening the class with this often unmotivated, sometimes surly group, she exerts her usual classroom controls, as teachers all learn to do in order to survive the span of our careers. At a certain point early in the class, though, Sharron realizes it won't do. With this assignment, she'll just have to let go and stop "being the teacher." They need her to help them find *their* understanding and establish *their* pace. Once the students sense that Sharron really wants them to engage the project in their own way—and that, as one disengaged student in my class put it, looking sharply up a moment from his customary head-in-arms-on-desk-reverie, "Huh? We can write about *people*!?"—things change. One of her students is asking to sit in the hall so he can concentrate. Now Sharron is coaching another student, a boy who lives in a group home, to reflect on who and what have influenced him in his life so far. Soon three of her classes have gone through the Creed experience. That day we talk in the lunchroom.

Glowing, Sharron is full of ideas for how she'll do things differently next year. For one thing, she'll allow the project more time (as her students requested), and for another . . .

"But Sharron," I remind her gently, "aren't you retiring after first semester next year?"

She looks back at me sheepishly. "Yeah, huh?" she murmurs quietly. "But unless some capable hands come along to take my kids through this project," she comes back, her tone rising jauntily and eyes widening wildly, "I just might have to stick it out another semester." I am not sure whether Sharron's experience with the project did more to kindle her ongoing passion for teaching or enhance her capacity to forget time and place.

Brett Nelson is big, brash, and a self-described "kid with a tie." He's twenty-seven and sometimes catches himself behaving a little more like his World History students than he will as he comes into his teaching stride. Bright, creative, and hardworking, Brett teaches history for a particularly personal reason, and his story intersects the Creed Project story. Perhaps a student could tell it as well or better than I could:

> My World History teacher Mr. Nelson is standing in front of my English classroom. Today he and Mr. Creger, my English teacher, are making the first two Creed presentations. (We'll be making ours next week. I hope mine'll be ready!) Anyway, Mr. Creger just told us that when Mr. Nelson found out Mr. Creger was planning to make the first of these presentations about our personal creeds—or what we think we stand for I think—Mr. Nelson asked whether he could present too. He has this sort of wheel hung up on the whiteboard, and now he's telling us that it's made of willow branches that he cut himself in the woods down in Big Sur and twined together to make that large circle. It's maybe three feet across. When he made it five years ago for his coming of age ceremony—Hey, Mr. Nelson's a member of a California Indian tribe!—he stretched this piece of leather hide across it and now he's telling us what those things mean that he hung on it. Let's see. The one in the center of the wheel, that represents his wife, since that's the most important thing in Mr. Nelson's life. Then the two hawk feathers represent his father, whose name is Soaring Hawk. And the shark's tooth, that reminds him of who he is and where he comes from, since his tribe lived mostly on seafood from the Monterrey Bay and the ocean.
>
> Before he started talking about the medicine wheel, he gave us a little history lesson about his people. Two hundred and fifty years ago, there were even more languages spoken in California than there are today—except they were all Native American languages. I guess even then everyone wanted to come to California. But most of the Indians were killed by diseases the Europeans brought or they were hunted down and killed, or the women were raped or forced to marry white settlers. Mr. Nelson says there are only 237 of his tribe

members left. When Mr. Creger asked how many of his tribe were of mixed race, Mr. Nelson said 100 percent. The last person able to speak the Esselén language died in 1950. The most interesting thing to me was that one of the main reasons Mr. Nelson became a history teacher was so that he could help keep the story of his people alive. His Indian name is Koltolá. So I guess all this was kind of what he stands for. This is cool!

It looks like Mr. Creger's getting his presentation ready for us now.

                                                    "composite" student, June 2002

When he turned twenty, his father and other adult members of the Esselén tribe of California natives from the Big Sur region where Brett Nelson grew up guided him in his creation of the traditional tribal medicine wheel. The idea is to update it every few years. He'd added nothing since he made it, and wanted to keep the process current in his mind. So he couldn't let me share my personal creed without sharing the wheel with his students. Resourcefully, he managed to get sub coverage and make his presentation for each of my five classes. At one point, we moved to a double-sized room so Sharron Harris and her students could join us in kicking off that year's Creed season at American High School.

To model the classroom rite of passage we are creating here for our students who come to us from cultures all over the world, Brett shared what I would call a traditional Native Californian version of the Creed Project. This gave us one way to approach a Creed presentation: Numbers of students chose to use Brett's medicine wheel motif, or the Plains Indian quadrant version, for their visual aids (as I have done for several figures in this book). Brett also modeled for us in three noteworthy ways. First, he clearly laid out a part of what he stands for (his creed)—preserving Native Californian history and culture. But he went beyond simply *telling* us about his creed. In giving us the history lesson and sharing his personal story, Brett also modeled *standing up for* his creed.

Finally, Brett's presentation is an example of the blending of personal and academic learning this book will go on to advocate. Whether or not many realized it, his students caught a glimpse of the connections between Brett's *personal* (and cultural) history and his *academic* (and professional) life. Seeing how Mr. Nelson keeps the personal element in his learning alive may inspire students to similar efforts—despite the current high stakes demands for person-less academics. Perhaps Native American traditions of personal learning will offer us more food for thought in the work of balancing academic learning with personal learning at our school. I wonder, twenty or thirty years from now, how Brett will view the impact on his career as an educator of having shared his medicine wheel with his students in his first few years of teaching. Thanks to Brett, Aileen, and Sharron, the first year we took the project beyond my classroom at the school, at least half the sophomore class went with us. The following spring, thanks to first year teacher Patty Baca, we had slightly more.

East Coast Kindlings

Two Januarys ago in Washington, D.C., during Leah Johnson's winter break, she emailed me, ruminating as she prepared to bring her American University freshmen composition students through the Creed Project for the second year. She wrote:

> I'm about to fine tune the Creed Project for spring. The challenge, I think, will be to create the rhythm and energy that will keep it going until it culminates in the presentation. So far, this is the only assign-ment I'm excited about.
>
> —Leah Johnson, January 2002

A little more than a year later, in the weeks before America's first war widely regarded as a war of aggression, Leah posted an email of another sort:

> We are not sleeping well here. My husband is a defense analyst; sometimes it's not so good to know more than other people. Today I put a sign on our front door that says, "Still Praying for Peace." We're feeling desperate.
>
> A very bright light on the bleak horizon is the Creed Project. I just skimmed some of the Step I papers that came in today, and I'm blown away by them. This is the best writing these kids have done all year. Honest, soulful, deep. One student told me that it's forcing/allowing him to face some demons and that he suspects the next step in the healing process will be his presentation. As usual, I'm invigorated by this project.
>
> —Leah Johnson, March 2003

From our chance meeting at a summer conference, Leah seems to have discovered a new, more fulfilling and energizing avenue of her teaching.

Midwest Ruminations

By the end of last year, I had been contacted by a teacher who rounds out Leah's reflections on the Creed Project as it takes shape in urban college classrooms on the East Coast and my accounts of its manifestations

among West Coast suburban teenagers with plans to adapt the project for
her own high school sophomores on the rural northern plains. I emailed
her for the school's whereabouts. She posted back:

> Wagner is located in the south central portion of South Dakota, near
> the Missouri River . . . I live at North Wheeler—about 45 miles from
> Wagner. Yes, I drive that far every day—7 miles on a winding
> gravel/mud road leading from the river bottom to the plains via lots
> of reservation land. Very sparsely populated. We're a rather quiet,
> unattended part of the plains out here. I like that. Because my days are
> spent with all the noise and hustle of teenagers, I value the quiet of
> the river's edge even more. It's my way of achieving balance. That's
> probably why your Creed Project appealed so much to me. I think we
> have something spiritual to open up to our students—whether it's
> internal spiritual recognition or the recognition of the spirit of place.
>
> —Sue Morrell, May 2002

Will a "creed site" spring up on the northern plains? I wonder.

My Own Creed Story

All this began for me somewhere in the middle of my second year of
teaching.

> It's lunchtime, and I am enjoying a conversation with Alex Rybkin, a
> bright student recently emigrated with his family from what was still
> known as Leningrad. The topic of our conversation I do not recall. I
> think I remember we are standing in the area we call the Faculty
> Commons, but this, too, is hazy. What comes back to me clear as
> noon, though, is something Alex says with a musical Russian accent
> in response to whatever I have said perhaps jokingly. Smiling, he
> rejoins:
>
> ***But Mr. Creger, that would not be in step with my creed.***
> Something right away is different. I see the word *creed* imprinting
> itself in my brain, as if the gray matter were being branded with a hot
> iron. My entire awareness becomes a question: A fifteen- or sixteen-
> year-old can have a *creed*? What does this *mean*?

A thought had never fascinated me so quickly and completely. A first
draft of the Creed Project came along at the end of that year.

Eight or ten years later, returning to teach at American after two
years in graduate school, I met Michael Febo, a good-humored, per-
sonable student in my sixth-period class who became a friend. Despite
his natural brightness, school for Michael consisted of a continuous
flow of failure notices. It was Michael, a week or two into the Creed

Project, drumming his fingers on his desk, who blurted out a little mischievously, "Hey, Mr. Creger, you're having us do all this thinking about who we are and what we stand for, right? So, uh, what's *your* creed, Mr. Creger?" Michael's classmates echoed his question, falling silent then and gazing at me with amused interest. Sitting on the corner of the teacher's desk, fingers to my chin, I began to stutter out my long, rambling answer. That night I went home and typed up my creed. I wouldn't get caught like this again.

Every year since then I revise my presentation a little. Now it's on PowerPoint with music behind it; and it has kicked off Creed season the past three years, if not to acclaim from students at least to polite approval (see Appendix I). Some students this past year even appeared to use my presentation as a jumping-off place for their own far more sophisticated PowerPoint offerings.

I may be a kind of midwife to this project. But being a midwife is not the same as giving birth to one's own baby. Thanks to Michael Febo and his classmates, I am now an actual participant with my students in this project. I keep my reflections current on what forces have molded me, what I now stand for, and what kind of person I wish to become. Every spring, wanting to kick off the Creed Project with something honest and current, I take another look at these things and update my presentation if need be. Though I am a fairly reflective type, and do naturally tend toward this kind of thought, before Michael and his classmates came along, I had no regular incentive to rethink and refresh my understanding of these things. Perhaps keeping as clear as I can about what I stand for and the kind of person I wish to become is even a good way to increase my chances of becoming that person. And so not only is this project the most consistently rewarding, most continuously surprising and renewing experience in my career as a teacher; it has become a major help in my journey as a person.

Yet transform my teaching it has too, and this may be a good place to explain how I come up with ideas and practices such as those in this book.

A Note on Method

My "process" (some might call it a research method) seems to form a loop starting with inklings or hunches or simply strong impressions such as that moment in my conversation with Alex when I heard him say *creed*. Trusting these inklings and others that come later in the loop, and trusting that I'll find a way to follow them well enough, I seem to create learning experiences such as the Creed Project, the Wisdom Project, the Thought Log, and the Two-Legged approach (more in Chapters Ten and Fourteen on these last three). Usually, however, despite a certain confidence that they will ultimately lead in good directions, I'm far from certain how these activities, sometimes initiated by only a momentary insight, will really affect students.

So, in order to gather a sense of how these learning experiences actually work for students, I regularly provide open-ended opportunities for them to comment on projects or other elements of the course. Here are some of these opportunities:

- Semester and year-end written course evaluations
- "Two-Legged" writings (writing designed for both academic and personal purposes)
    Final exam essays
    Personal Creed Project reflections and reflective essays
    Journal writings
    Other Two-Legged writings
- Student portfolio pieces
    Preface
    Moment That Mattered
    Self-Assessment Essay

As I read through these assignments over the year, I keep a weather eye out for student statements that offer perspectives on elements of the course or the course as a whole I can learn from. My new copier at home now allows me to "capture" especially insightful comments without having to type them in or write them down on index cards. Periodically, after one of these writings that has taught me something, we'll follow up with a class discussion that helps me gain more understanding of my students' learning experiences. When something irresistible comes up in a discussion, I might make a note on an index card, which then goes into my system.

Meanwhile, I continue my habit of collecting quotes from the far corners of the universe, a number of forthcoming friends from other planets offering their generous assistance, and from my personal spiritual studies on issues related to the course themes and learning experiences, and to life in general. My growing collection of quotes also includes quite a few snippets of wisdom from the mouths, pens, and browsers of my students. We use quotes from this collection in a popular activity called the Thought Log, which not only keeps these issues in our conversations but provides regular reading and thinking workouts (See Chapters Ten and Fourteen). Through the year, as more inklings and hunches pop into my mind (and, as time goes on, into the minds of my students), I think them over in the shower or on the drive to and from work, make notes, and create new or refine existing learning experiences.

Probably the most stimulating and rewarding part of this loop is my practice of cultivating relationships with special student "thinking partners." These are students who for one reason or another, usually having to do with frustrations unusually bright yet unorthodox thinkers face with learning in school as it now exists, fall into an ongoing one-on-one conversation with me about the nature of learning—and how school could come closer to honoring truer understandings of learning. Many of the notes I make during and after these conversations have worked their way into this book as ideas or vignettes. These thinking partners have included unusual students like Huda, a brilliant Palestinian you'll meet in the next chapter, and Yama, a deep-thinking Afghan American whose revealing Creed presentation you can read about in Chapter Thirteen and whose essay you can find on the website. Conversations with two of the most exceptional thinkers among my student thinking partners continued for two years or more, and developed into deep friendships. Duron Aldredge and David Xu have both graduated, and I'm wondering what bright student minds will come along to replace them. We heard from Duron in the last chapter; you will meet David in Part Two.

For a final thought on my "process," another quick word on the validity of the student-written evidence I use in this book. I've mentioned the possibility of students, in hopes of merciful grading, falling to the temptation of "tempering" their written comments about the course. Since all the assignments I pull comments from are graded (some of the course evaluations are for extra credit, which might always make for some sweeter-than-real responses), I can make no claims that the student insights I have relied on in the thinking described in this book are completely objective.

I do hope my students believe me, though, when I tell them that I do not expect them to believe what I say simply because I'm the teacher, and that their job, as I see it, is to learn to think for themselves. And I hope students soon realize I mean this, and that I especially appreciate—and will reward—students who disagree with me on an issue *and* depart from the current White House practice by providing solid evidence.

As explained earlier, to establish the project's credibility, in Part One I use comments from students *least* likely to write to please a teacher. In Part Three, the step-by-step guide for you to create your version of the project with your students, I offer student comments to help illuminate each step. A significant portion of the comment mix in Part Three will consist of comments from the honors classes that for the first time since the early days of the Creed Project became a part of my teaching day this past year. While I had forgotten, and was somewhat surprised to realize once again, that students in honors classes are far more likely to "B.S." for grades, I also was impressed that they are capable of articulating especially valuable insights. This, then, with these caveats, is the process I use in this book.

So far, you have seen snapshots of how the project experience can orchestrate class transformations, and have heard how six teachers have been affected, some even changed by the experience. Let's move now to some pictures that suggest what the Creed Project experience can mean to individual students. Here I'll start mixing in some of my favorite insights from known (and some not-so-known) thinkers and writers on learning.

CHAPTER FOUR

Individual Transformations

> Someone who thinks well of himself is said to have a healthy
> self-concept and is envied. Someone who thinks well of his
> country is called a patriot and is applauded. Someone who
> thinks well of his species is regarded as hopelessly naïve and
> is dismissed.
>
> —Alfie Kohn (1990, 3)

It may seem as if the snapshots I've shared so far have all been from
teens whose lives are a bit more than usually dislocated. There may be
some accuracy to this perception. But the more we work with teens, the
more we discover that there is little about most of their lives that is
smooth or easy. According to a recent estimate, 50 percent of teens
struggle with some form of serious mental or emotional disturbance.
However, in the majority of presentations I've seen students choose
not to lay it all on the line, opting instead to play it a little safe. Most
choose to use the presentation as a way to publicly honor the support
systems of family and friends they are lucky enough to have, and then
go on to share what they've found they value in their lives enough to
stand for.

An accomplished dancer, Katrina brings promo photos of her performances to dramatize her belief in artistic expression as part of her
creed, and honors her single mother for supporting her years of lessons
and performances. In her junior year she is invited to apply to Julliard
School of the Arts, the nation's premier school for aspiring dancers.
Brian, a skateboarder, shows video clips of his skating and, giving
credit to pro skater Tony Hawk for inspiration, relates his skating to his
growing ability to believe in his abilities and rise to challenges.
Alexandra shares pictures of her cheerleading squad's trials as an
example of the importance of practice and the emotional support of

working with a team, and dedicates the presentation to all her squad-mates. Steve, a talented quarterback, shows PowerPoint slides of plays and personal and team statistics to suggest the value of hard work and discipline, and pays tribute to his father for being a good role model. Such presentations, while they may entail less risk than some of the more dramatic ones, have great value, as we'll explore in Part Three.

In this section on personal transformations, however, I include examples that illustrate the power of this project to promote deepened insight into oneself and celebrate noteworthy change and transforma-tion. Let's start with Hewan's.

> A cappella except for her friend's live "beatbox" accompaniment, Hewan sings a soulful song she has written specially for her presen-tation, on the theme of succeeding in school and making her parents proud. Dramatized by the amazing range and clarity of percussive sounds her "beatbox" accompanist makes with her mouth and lungs, Hewan's song honors her hardworking Ethiopian immigrant parents and celebrates moving forward in her vision with the improvement she has brought about in her academic performance this year.
>
> —June 2002

Though she works very hard on her academics, and was aggressive enough to play varsity basketball as a sophomore, in class Hewan is for the most part a shy person, and took large risks in this performance. (She received, by the way, off-the-hook applause from the class and an over-the-top presentation grade from me. For more on her change, see Hewan's Moment That Mattered in Chapter Thirteen and her essay on the website.)

Melissa had spoken in her presentation of being coerced to take the drug ecstasy at a party, and arriving home to get caught by her parents:

> The moment that mattered most to me and will stay with me for prob-ably the rest of my life is my Creed presentation. This presentation let me talk about myself and helped me let people take a look inside of me (which I rarely let happen). I had never shared some of those things with anyone before and it was very difficult for me to share. Once I talked about those things it felt like so much weight was lifted off my shoulders and I felt that I could actually breathe.
>
> —Melissa Townsend, June 2001

Melissa's last sentence, like one of Jennifer's in the previous chapter on classroom transformation, sheds a special light on the cathartic value of speaking truths about our lives in a trust-dominated classroom climate such as described earlier. When I cross paths with Melissa in the halls more than a year later, in my overactive imagination at least, she *still* appears relieved.

Some may ask whether teachers have any business engineering opportunities for such emotional purging in the classroom. Are teachers qualified to deal with such situations? My answer would be that if we aren't, then it's time we become qualified. Even if more widespread *academic* success alone were a sufficient goal of school change—or, for that matter, of learning—that goal will never be achieved until more weight is lifted off the shoulders of more students.

Can we simply disregard the weight teens carry, passing it along to overburdened counselors? Yes, we can. But not if we expect them to devote themselves to learning in our classrooms. More teenagers than not in our society must deal today with the aftermath of parental divorce, while most teens settle for less guidance than they need from adults who work more hours than ever before. Manipulated by the most powerful commercial forces in human history, teens in the United States assume with the rest of us that they are the rightful recipients of the computers, audio systems, cars, and other amenities that come to so many of them. Little do they know that only 1 percent of human beings we share the planet with own a computer. Or that it is no longer possible to pretend that the majority of the world's teenagers don't watch their economies crippled and their environments compromised in their nations' efforts to continue supplying U.S. appetites for energy and materials. Or that the West consumes so unequal a share of world resources that raising consumption throughout the world to Western levels would require the resources of *four planet earths* by the year 2100 (Davis 2). And no wonder.

The same forces of self-interest that keep us in daily ignorance of the lives of people in the rest of the world keep teens' ears filled with sounds created more for commercial gain than for artistic or social expression, their eyes tracking images on television, computer, and video game screens that have little to do with helping them understand their lives, and their bodies sporting logos that have everything to do with corporate bottom lines. In the face of all these less-than-nurturing forces, more than ever teens need sets of learning experiences in a learning environment that permits them to create an ongoing inventory of themselves and how they fit in the world and universe. School could play a counterbalancing role, applying research in creative ways to nourish students' lives.

Yet instead of helping them with these needs, their schools have stepped aside to let the big-shoed, deep-pocketed forces of commerce and government sweep importantly through the nation's classrooms. What are we "holding students accountable" for? Simply *more* of the same kind of learning schools have for too long insisted students confine themselves to. But this limited form of learning isn't enough to satisfy them. James Moffett, to whose 1994 *The Universal Schoolhouse* this book and my classroom owe enormous debts, saw this coming:

> Consciously or not, the man in the street [and girl in her seat] cries for meaning and purpose and will seek it in trivial or destructive ways if no framework exists through which to give significance to daily life. (31 my addition)

What, then, keeps school learning for most students so shallow of meaning? In Chapter One, James Moffett helped us see that the "central and indispensable" lack I mention earlier is the *depersonalizing* of learning. In Part Two, on the level of ideas, we'll further develop this point from what may be some new perspectives on learning. Considering it now on the level of feeling, what indispensable human emotion in the current de facto philosophy of learning is not considered? One teacher points in a helpful direction:

> Education is a difficult enough process under any circumstances, because educational effort is primarily an expression of hope on the part of the students.

> —T. Ham

Left out of the equation in the flurry of bar-raising and accountability is the importance of *hope* in finding and sustaining the motivation to learn. Those of us who have witnessed Creed presentations have seen changes in classroom chemistry that surfaced emotions like trust, respect, connection, and affection. Such a changed climate can prepare the ground for hope.

Three months before September 11, 2001, during the June Creed presentations in the same fourth period you are acquainted with, Huda, a dynamic Palestinian student new to the school, had spoken passionately and articulately of having lost close relatives in the fighting at home, the recent conflict being then almost a year old. In moving terms, she spoke of her desire to return home to fight and die for her people. Even in the explosion of media coverage *since* September 11, 2001, few teens in the United States have been exposed to teens from the Arab and Muslim world, let alone to the personal stories of Palestinian teens. But *pre*-9/11, to the average American teenager Huda's story and the depth of her commitment to her people—her willingness to *die* for them—seemed inexplicable, completely out of the blue. Yet Marcos Diaz was powerfully impressed enough by Huda's presentation to choose it as his Moment That Mattered in his sophomore portfolio:

I chose this moment to remember because when Huda told her story
I actually felt a piece of her pain. When my eyes began to tear I was
surprised, I was expecting something totally different. I will always
remember this because it was the first time I actually felt emotional
towards someone I don't really know very well.

—Marcos Diaz, June 2001

Huda's presentation gave her comparatively sheltered Fremont classmates the opportunity to be exposed to experiences and perspectives
from a people and part of the world they would not ordinarily
encounter. It gave Huda the chance to share her story with a group of
peers influenced by the unusually open class climate during the presentations, some of whom, like Marcos, might be mature enough to rise to
the occasion and honor her despite the natural discomfort of hearing a
classmate speak of her readiness to give her life. Thankfully for me,
the following fall Huda volunteered not for such service, but to be my
teaching assistant. And so we had the opportunity to experience
September 11 together.

Two weeks before the attacks Huda asked me what my background
was. I explained that though technically half Jewish on my father's
side (and therefore not considered Jewish by traditional Jews), I
identified myself as a Jew. By this time I had already met her father and
sister and felt the beginnings of a good friendship with the family. This
pleased me a great deal, given the escalating conflict between Israelis
and Palestinians. And, Jewish teacher or not, Huda had seemed to have
a good experience in my class the previous spring. Before coming to
Fremont, she had lived in Jordan and had never actually met a Jewish
person. Knowing Israelis only as those whose government's actions
could be explained in no other way than by a clear intention to kill and
displace her people, Huda had understandably assumed that all Jews
were bad people. "But," she said, smiling with the marvelous freshness
and openness that are unique to teenagers, "you're a good person!"

To what extent goodwill or hope from the Creed experience the
previous spring helped encourage such interactions I do not know. But
these pleasant interchanges continued: Within three weeks of the
September 11 attacks, during the charged aftermath of the probably
falsified images broadcast around the world of Palestinians cheering
the news of the downed towers, Huda made a special trip to my classroom after school. This poised and exuberant Palestinian teenager
with her head covered in the scarf she chooses to wear, this activist
who had been speaking in the confused days after the attacks at our
lunchtime gatherings for Muslim students concerned with how these
attacks were changing their lives, urging them to be proud of their
Muslim identities and tolerant of the misunderstandings they were

encountering in school and the community, this young Muslim had come specially to my classroom after school—to wish me a Happy Rosh Hashana. Tears came to my eyes.

How in the world would I reciprocate? As luck would have it, in a few days a former student, an Afghan American, emailed to say hi. I asked Wahida how she'd suggest I repay Huda's kindness. A week or two later, on the first day of the Muslim holy month of Ramadan, Wahida came to the school with a plate of dates she had stuffed by hand with blanched almonds, a traditional Ramadan food. I then had the pleasure of presenting them to Huda and her family. Huda later told me that this year for some reason her mother had not managed to make the dates, and so the gift enabled Huda to provide them for the family. Thank God, I thought, for a global suburb in this post 9/11 world!

How does this relate to the Creed Project? I include Huda's presentation in this section on individual transformations because Marcos's statement suggests that he may not have been the only one of her classmates to have experienced such emotional bridge-building, and grown from it. Huda certainly helped me grow in my perceptions of the dignity of the Palestinians, growth that has since helped me better serve other Palestinian students and their families. And I hope the opportunity to be heard in an unusually receptive room gave her a small taste of the attention and respect that too rarely come to her people. All this hardly served to reduce tensions in the Middle East. But given the opportunities, many around the United States today have to experience the people of the world in our local communities—relatively free of political, corporate, and media spin—the fourth-period Creed presentations may have sown some hope in Fremont. And, as you may recall from Chapter One, according to Kantor's spectrum, hope always stems from *ideals,* from our desire for and a commitment to a better future. Hope, then, always transforms. As we'll see in Part Three, the Creed Project is a way to introduce teens today, who may never have considered such a possibility, to the notion and function of ideals.

> Driven by anxiety, we build prisons. Driven by hope, we build schools.
>
> —NPR report

But we needn't look only to immigrants from the embattled Middle East to find students whose learning experience could transform dramatically with an increase in hope. James Ikande is a bright, thoughtful young man. Comfortable enough in class by the end of the year to be the voice in our third-period discussions I could most often depend on for an intelligent opening remark or an insightful and relevant comment to get us back on track, James was always respectful and on task in class. Though he is able to write an excellent essay, however, James missed due dates consistently, on homework and major assignments alike, and earned grades that don't yet reflect the caliber of his mind, his academic potentials, or his skills. James is his own person with his own mind. But his pattern is part of the pattern of underachievement among black students in our society. Most educators have been exposed to the discouraging statistics. In *The Dreamkeepers: Successful Teachers of African American Children*, education professor Gloria Ladson-Billings reminds us:

> African American children are three times as likely to drop out of school as white children are and twice as likely to be suspended from school . . . African American students make up only about 17 percent of the public school population but 41 percent of the special-education population. These dismal statistics hold despite two waves of educational reform initiated in the 1980s. (2)

These statistics do not derive from a vacuum. Ladson-Billings goes on to fill in some of the social and economic background to these facts:

> Nearly one out of two African American children is poor. African American children . . . are four times as likely [as white children] to live with neither parent . . . and twice as likely to live in substandard housing. More young African American males are under the control of the criminal justice system than in college. Indeed, an African American boy who was born in California in 1988 is three times more likely to be murdered than admitted to the University of California. (2)

Whether or not James is abreast of these unhopeful statistics per se, I doubt they would surprise him, as some of these social and economic facts are likely true in his life. Numbers such as these are important to keep before us so we don't fall into the dreamworld of leveled playing fields. But numbers aren't what might bring hopeful fuel to James's efforts to use his clear mind and reap the benefits in his life.

I recently attended a seminar called Beyond Diversity: A Strategy for De-Institutionalizing Racism and Improving Student Achievement. To achieve a seminar conversation that confronts fears concerning race and enables participants to break new ground in their understandings of how race conditions the lives of our nonwhite students in the United States, Beyond Diversity creator Glenn Singleton puts forward Four Norms of Effective, Courageous Racial Discourse (see website). One of these, "Speak Your Truth," rang a bell somewhere deep in my brain. Thinking back, I realized that even though African American students do tend, like James, to be strong participants in spoken activities in my classes, I could recall fewer examples than I would like to recall of black students really making the Creed presentation a special event for themselves. In fact, as I thought about it, suddenly my impression was that African American students over the years may have struck me as slightly uncomfortable making Creed presentations. Perhaps something was missing in the instructions and guidelines for the project.

Inspired by the Beyond Diversity seminar, I consulted several student friends, one of them Duron Aldredge, my thinking partner and president of the Black Students' Union, which I serve as co-adviser. In this year's Creed Project instructions I decided to include an invitation to students to explore to what extent race or ethnicity might be influences on their lives. I also made a point of using certain Beyond Diversity tools during second semester to incorporate conversation about race and ethnicity into our class discussions. While no one was *expected* to grapple with this issue in their projects, I wanted students for whom race was a distinct part of their daily experience to feel free to speak this part of their truths in their presentations. We see in Part Three that race can distinctly condition daily experience for students of all racial backgrounds.

It was James who rose to this occasion. In the course of his presentation, he recounted two recent incidents. In one, he and his young stepbrother are waiting at a bus stop for a bus home, when a car pulls alongside, a window rolls down, and an Asian man puts his head out the window and yells racially offensive names at the two boys. The man is a total stranger. Uncomfortable for their safety, James takes his brother with him into the store next to the bus stop, and asks to use the phone behind the counter to call home for a ride. Looking dubiously at James and his brother, the man at the counter tells them the phone is for employees only, and points to the pay phone on the sidewalk outside. James explains the problem of a hostile man out there. Still the man does not allow him to use the phone. More upset than ever, James is unsure what to do. But by this time the man in the car has driven off and the bus has arrived. James takes his brother aboard and gets home safely. The second incident involved being followed in a store and unfairly suspected of shoplifting.

These incidents did not occur in a small southern town, but in one of the most racially and culturally mixed cities in the United States, and James was upset about it. The Creed presentation gave him the chance to share not only his unhappiness about these incidents themselves, but his disappointment at the injustice of such things happening on a routine basis to him and others with dark skin. The Beyond Diversity seminar had made me aware of the tendency of most white people to resist absorbing the truth that daily experience for nonwhites in our society is far different than for those of us who are white. Had my own resistance to acknowledging the pervasiveness of these experiences not been reduced dramatically recently in the Beyond Diversity seminar, I may not myself have been as open to hearing of James's experience without suspecting him of some intention to play upon his anger or my sympathy.

This was not about being politically correct. It was about respecting my student and supporting his opportunity to tell us a truth about his life. In a project that asked him to explore circumstances and events that shaped his life, James had summoned the courage to share this circumstance of his real life with us. His unhappiness with the situation was clear, and I hope he felt his audience was sympathetic and responsive to his truth. I hope sharing this part of his life helped lift some weight from James's shoulders and put some hope in his heart. And, if indeed this was an important moment for him, when the opportunity arises again I hope James feels free to speak his truth about how race impacts his life. If the opportunity is long in coming, I hope he remembers once when this part of his real life became the learning for his entire English class sophomore year. Would James, like John Vroman, be a different kind of student if school gave him more opportunities to bring his real life to his learning?

> Truth can be heard best when surrounded and protected by love.
>
> —T. Olfana

Nuri Lundy's Creed presentation came together unexpectedly. A sharply independent thinker and talented writer and poet, Nuri was not fond of school. He resented the amount of time teachers expect students to apply themselves to assignments that rarely were meaningful or satisfying or empowered students to use their creative gifts. His poems allowed his gifts to surface, and his mind to wrestle with life. "American Me," his hard-hitting poem questioning the use of the hyphenated term "African-American," was read before the entire student body at our Black History Month rally his senior year. Because the Creed Project sounded different, Nuri did sit down with it a few times and tried to write. But try as he might, he just couldn't manage to wrap his mind around the assignment. "Write about who and what have influenced or inspired me in my life? Decide which influence I most and least admire? And then write about what *I* stand for? Nope. I'm not ready for this! That's *too* hard."

"Yes, it's challenging alright," I agreed. "But why not try stretching yourself a little and see what happens?"

Nuri sat on the tall grey metal stool at the front of the class. He had just finished explaining to us that he'd given this a shot, but this was the hardest assignment he'd ever been asked to do, a great assignment maybe, but nothing had come to him. He was about to step down. "Hang on a second," I said. I was getting some kind of inspiration. "If you want," I continued, "you might try asking your classmates what *they* feel you stand for." Not missing a beat (he's a poet, hey), Nuri was back on the stool asking his classmates for their help, rather humbly it seemed to me. "I'm clueless," he admitted. "If you all have any ideas what I'm about, I'm all ears."

Slowly hands began coming up. A friend who had known Nuri as far back as elementary school made an observation: "You don't say things you don't mean." Pausing to reflect, a shy Denzel smile on his dark face, Nuri commented thoughtfully. Another spoke, "What you do say, you say with some thought behind you. And you stand behind it." One after another, classmates mirrored back to him what they perceived of what he stood for. And Nuri responded to their perceptions. This was a character-appreciation fest, coming to a classroom as naturally as leaves appear on a tree, students of racial and cultural backgrounds as varied as one can imagine, in different ways commending one of their own for his personal and intellectual integrity.

The message came across plainly, as did his classmates' affection and admiration for him. What began as an admission of failure turned into a conversation like none I had ever witnessed in a classroom. How did this experience affect Nuri? Was this an occasion he'll remember forever or not at all? Did the experience bring any change in Nuri's outlook on life? Unfortunately, this was two years before I began making regular notes from students' course evaluations and portfolios, and I have no statement from him. True, news of Nuri's bold improvisation quickly traveled around campus, creating quite a stir and adding to his already considerable poetic (and romantic) mystique around the school. True, he did establish a new Creed presentation option for the brave of heart (the "On the Spot" approach). But Nuri was the kind of student whose life, like mine, could well have begun the day *after* graduation. And, though I and many of his classmates may never forget it, it's likely that for him the entire experience has already evaporated.

Recalling Nuri's presentation, back in June 1999, causes me to reflect. What might have caused him to "block" as he tried to write? What factors might have been involved that he didn't mention? A little conversation, as the impromptu interchange between Nuri and his classmates shows, can go a long way. How easily we teachers forget to invite students to simply talk to each other at *all* stages of learning. Would talking things through ahead of time with peers or me have helped Nuri rise more fully to the challenge the Creed Project presented him? Having no definitive answer, I have tried since Nuri's presentation to encourage students to talk to each other outside class as they go through the Creed steps.

Another possibility comes to mind. With the Beyond Diversity seminar and James Ikande's presentation fresh in mind, knowing Nuri's willingness to deal with race directly in his poetry, I wonder if he had been invited as James was invited to consider race as one of the influences on his life, could Nuri have moved past his writer's block with the project? Encouraged to speak his truth on the ticklish topic of race, might Nuri have risen to the occasion in a way he would be even more likely to remember than his "On the Spot" presentation? Could this opportunity to "get real" before such an audience have left Nuri a lifelong memory of a transformative moment? Would such a memory have done anything to steer him on a path different from the one that has led him, with his unit, to a city north of Baghdad, from where PFC Lundy, doing a job in hopes of surviving his tour of duty and enjoying the benefits, has just sent me three new poems?

In the event that more teachers and their students began to create such experiences as I have tried to describe, and that such transformations—of classes, teachers, and individual students—are indeed possible amid all the other duties teachers are responsible for, then it may be possible for *satisfying learning* to become much more common than it is today. If this is to happen, we must first understand *learning* itself at a deeper level. This is the purpose of Part Two.

Part Two

A New Look Toward Learning

The real voyage of discovery consists not in seeking new
landscapes but in having new eyes.

—Marcel Proust

Part One of this book begins by pointing to the essential weakness of the con-
ventional school approach to learning, and ends by establishing that students
find the kind of learning they experience in the Creed Project *satisfying*. In
Part Two, my purpose is to shed light on *why* the Creed Project works, to
make out the principles behind this satisfaction. I want to reshape the rest of
my teaching in a way that students can find *more* of their learning satisfying.
("Satisfying" to me, by the way, does *not* mean learning should come without
struggle or frustration, which I believe are powerful, essential ingredients of
ultimately satisfying learning.)

Why, presented with an assignment most find deeply challenging, are taciturn teens suddenly itching to share things they would not ordinarily share,
and having tender feelings for classmates they would not ordinarily have?
What makes students' experiences with this project so different from the
experiences they have with other activities in my classes and possibly in
yours? And what, finally, *does* make learning satisfying? Where are the
springs of pleasure that source the waters of learning? By the end of Part Two
you will have answers I have found to these questions.

My quest for these answers sent me on a journey of discovery that has
begun to crystallize only recently. But before I could come across answers I
first needed better-defined questions. I first had to think about learning in a
series of ways that were new to me. This thinking led me to continue following James Moffett's trail, to a series of other unusual thinkers' thoughts about
learning, some of which I share with you, and to a series of realizations. These
things have come together piece by seemingly random piece, and not actually
in the neat linear fashion my narrative suggests. The thinking culminates in
Chapter Eight, with the following:

- A brief collection of cardinal points that accumulates through Part
  Two and culminates in what I am calling a New Look Toward
  Learning

- A visual representation of a proposed central aim of twenty-first century learning, the secondary purposes, and goals of teaching and learning practices that support this aim and these purposes, in a Beginning Model of Twenty-First-Century Learning
- An attempt to apply the thinking of the New Look and the Beginning Model to the teaching of English, in a cross-section of Twenty-First-Century English Curriculum

Two of these representations also may be found in this book's front matter, and they are all found at universeWired.com, along with a Two-Legged (academic and personal) design for my sophomore English course (described in Part Three) in which I attempt to apply all these realizations.

 CHAPTER FIVE

The Core Evolutionary Process

No one can get me interested in English.
—Stephanie Hill, December 1999

To find what works, we often start with what doesn't. Coming to understand more fully what doesn't satisfy learners, I hoped, would help me understand what does. Spotlighting education's main problem, James Moffett uses the phrase "depersonalization of schooling." Does he refer to a process of gradual dilution, errant decades or centuries that sapped school of what once made learning satisfying and ennobling? Perhaps. American college education during the seventeenth and into the eighteenth centuries was delivered by tutors serving no more than ten or twelve students, tutors who were also responsible for "overseeing the students' moral and spiritual development" (Halloran 192). Fostering students' overall development was a primary goal, probably dating back to Plato's notions of well-rounded education in *The Republic*. But it was also true that all of these students in both ancient Greece and early American colleges were males, white, and most from only the wealthiest families. How much from such a system could be transplanted in today's world? And so I could see that Moffett wasn't using "depersonalization" to suggest that our task is to recharge a great tradition with lost personal juices.

I believe he intends "depersonalization" to describe the *effect* of current schooling, not on educational traditions, but on the lives of today's students and their societies. Today's processes of schooling, he is saying, drain from us the essence of what it is to be persons. Do schools and educators *intend* to perpetrate this drain on the persons of innocent students? Hardly. The problem Moffett sees is that we have reached the juncture in human evolution when it has become necessary to *re-envision*, not just the *practices* of teaching and the *experiences* of

43

learning, but, as he very nearly says here, the very *nature of learning itself:*

> Public education will have to be totally reconceived—what it's for and how it's to work.
>
> —James Moffett (xii)

When most of us think of change, we think of *doing* things differently. But Moffett believes we must begin our change *before* the "doing" stage. He calls for something deeper:

> The time has come to situate education in a perspective that comprises far more than management of schooling and that thus redirects thinking to intrinsic issues of human development.
>
> —Moffett (xiii)

To change what students experience all day in school so that it actually begins to *matter* to most of them most of the time, to *mean* something *personally*, Moffett asks us to direct our thinking to "intrinsic issues of human development." That sounded right to me. But I still needed a clearer idea of the essential place of *learning* in the largest scheme of things and beings. Those of us who work for school change cannot make an arbitrary decision to junk the assembly line model of education and move on to remodel our schools and teaching practices so that students automatically learn with joy. Reconfiguring our classrooms and our schools—creative scheduling of time, flexible use of space, individualizing instruction—to create a more homey learning environment, as many of us try to do, is great; but it won't magically culminate in personally meaningful transcripts.

We first need time to stop and think. If the problem begins with the limitations in our current thinking about the central aim of learning, the solution begins with understanding those limitations:

> I have come to regard not only school but school reform as suffering from systemic thinking that is too limited because the system on which it is based is *partial*.
>
> —Moffett (my emphasis, xiii)

I steer away from using the terms "education" or "school" for this very reason—they have become hopelessly "partial." Because of their associations with traditions, with institutions and systems, both terms connote experiences that are often hugely impersonal and therefore powerfully depersonalizing. When people want to put a comfortable distance between themselves and schools or teachers, they often dispense with the simple word "teacher," in favor of the subtly dismissive term "schoolteacher." The term calls up an image of a lonely soul with a hair bun devoted to a regimented institution of educational force-feeding. Perhaps the most disturbing use of the term appears in *Beloved*, where Toni Morrison gives the name "Schoolteacher" to the slavemaster who represents the theory that separates blacks altogether from the category of persons. Indeed, the words "school" and "education" carry so much impersonal and depersonalizing freight that the meanings they convey, and the thinking they inspire, can no longer be anything but "partial."

A far more useful term for me is *learning*. Aside from the vernacular usage that equates it to knowledge (larnin'), *learning* suggests a process of self-creation and self-development; and it encourages thinking that is much less partial. Moffett calls for a framework for learning that is all-encompassing:

> The only solution consists of making the most inclusive system of all the framework for education.
>
> —Moffett (xiii)

I am finding it helpful, in fact, to go all the way—to see learning as a process inside a larger process, a process very far from partial. Because it encompasses just about everything in earthly experience, this far-from-partial larger process indeed fits what Moffett means by "the most inclusive system of all." Yes, I mean evolution. And yes, I am about to bring up Charles Darwin (who had little to do with most of the ideas for which he is villified). How, then, according to Darwin, is learning important to human evolution?

(If you prefer to bypass a short sortie into evolutionary theory, just skip the next six paragraphs and resume with the paragraph just before statement number one on page 47, beginning with the sentence "What, then, has this little detour. . . .")

In *Darwin's Lost Theory of Love*, psychologist and futurist David Loye makes an exhaustive study of Darwin's final book, *The Descent of Man*. According to Loye, for a series of interrelated reasons the crucial message of *Descent* has been lost on the vast majority of his audience. Even today, when we think of Darwin we think mainly of *The Origin of Species*. This to Loye is no surprise. Darwin's followers, the Darwinians who gave us most of our ideas about Darwin, based their understanding of Darwin's insights into the biological evolution of species, the combination of processes he called "natural selection," on the ideas he laid out in *The Origin of Species*. What the Darwinians didn't understand in the later *Descent of Man*, Loye contends, is that Darwin perceived the processes of natural selection—random variation, adaptation, survival of the fittest—as most active in the *biological* evolution of species, yet not so immediately important in the processes that shaped and continue to shape *human* evolution.

Human evolution, he believed, is a considerably more complex set of processes. It entails both *additional* processes to those of biological evolution, and processes of different *kinds*. Intellectual, moral, and spiritual advancement, in particular, are part of human but not of biological evolution. The more elemental *biological* processes of natural selection, Darwin appears to have believed, can be overridden by these intertwined processes in the *human* portion of evolution. For instance, Darwin comments in *The Descent of Man* on the process of moral advancement:

> For moral qualities are advanced . . . much more through the effects
> of habit, by our reasoning powers, by instruction, by religion, etc.,
> than through natural selection. . . . (my emphasis, 359)
> —Charles Darwin, quoted in Loye (192)

This sentence, for all its murkiness, locates learning quite clearly in a central position in evolution. Let's take this a step at a time.

"Habit," "reasoning powers," "instruction," and "religion," Darwin concluded, have a greater effect on the advancement of moral qualities than does natural selection. Yet, of these four processes, isn't *one* primary? One of them provides us the basic building blocks to make the others possible—to form and refine our habits, acquire and sharpen our reasoning powers, give and receive instruction, and process information to make thoughtful choices about religion.

Perhaps where I'm going is obvious: Could any of the processes Darwin links to moral advancement above perpetuate themselves without what he calls "instruction"—without what I choose to call *teaching* and *learning*? The habits, reasoning powers, and religion Darwin believed enable us to advance *morally*, then, depend for their existence and quality on *how we are taught* and *how we learn*. We can distill this to an even more essential level. Of the two components of what Darwin calls "instruction"—teaching and learning—*learning* is the most fundamental process, because learning can occur without a teacher, while teaching is not possible without a learner.

Learning, then, is basic to *moral* advancement. Isn't it reasonable to suppose that learning is also primary in other key sets of processes that comprise human evolution: *intellectual* and *spiritual* advancement? In a talk at the 2000 Conference of NCTE's Assembly for Expanded Perspectives on Learning (AEPL), David Loye clarifed this line of thought for me when he declared categorically: "What Darwin believed is that *learning and education are the core drive of evolution.*"

A thought-provoking notion to a teacher—learning as the central process of evolution. But do plants and animals really *learn*? Yes, because even biological adaptation is a rudimentary form of learning. Consider this famous example. Ninety-nine percent of the peppered moths observed by naturalists near Manchester in England two centuries ago were grey, allowing them to spread their wings on the trunks of local trees the same mottled grey color and blend in, safe from predator birds. About 1 percent of the moths were observed to be a much darker color. By the early twentieth century, the situation had reversed itself. The darker moths now comprised 99 percent of the population, the lighter grey ones the rare 1 percent. Manchester had become industrialized, and smoke from burning coal had coated the trees. The dark moths now had the camouflage advantage, and the genes for the darker color came to dominate the population through natural selection. In order to survive, the species had "learned" to change its appearance. So even at the biological level, this example suggests, learning could indeed be as Loye said: the "core drive of evolution."

How does all this relate to the Creed Project? I wanted to understand students' enthusiasm for the project, so that I might discover how to bring more satisfying learning into my classes. Moffett seemed to tell me that if I wanted more satisfied learners, I needed first to understand the central problem of schooling. If, understanding the problem—depersonalization—I wanted to help correct it in my classes, Moffett told me I needed to understand learning in a different way.

What, then, has this little detour into Darwin helped me understand about learning that I didn't before? Something powerful and useful. Darwin, through Loye, tells me that learning is nothing less than *the core drive of evolution.* This is an answer that, if not yet *fully* satisfying, does provoke thought. To make it more particular to human beings, I've slightly revised Loye's statement. My version goes like this:

---

1. Learning is the core drive of human advancement.

Here, I decided, we have something essential enough to call the first "cardinal point" in a New Look Toward Learning.

This premise—that learning is at the center of the numerous processes of human evolution—is a good first step toward more satisfying learning, beginning at the societal level. Up front, this view of learning takes education out of the hinterlands. High-profile policies to mandate high stakes testing command vast sums of money, commandeer enormous shares of time, energy, and material resources, and create a needlessly anxious national learning environment. And for what? To measure and track numbers (test scores) that educator Linda McNeil identifies as likely "the least significant results of learning." This hardly heralds a deep societal commitment to the core human activity: learning. Quite the opposite. The high stakes spotlight may be trained on test scores; but *learning* remains in shadow in the American hinterlands. If we are to achieve a genuine commitment to learning—

at district, state, and national levels—it will be necessary to recapture teaching and learning from the forces who have stepped in and for what many believe are highly questionable purposes built walls of "measurement" between teachers and learners. This first cardinal point will help in this.

If we plan, say, to ask for commitments from policy makers and voters to a deeper, more personally involving kind of learning than can be assessed by mere test scores (a proposition probably even more expensive than high stakes testing), we might be wise to first make a convincing case for an elevated importance of learning itself. A vision of learning at the heart of evolutionary processes—put forward in a manner so as not to needlessly alienate those who misunderstand evolution as a concept opposed to a spiritual view of the universe—could very well inspire the beginnings of such a commitment. Coming into the public mind in the right way, such a vision would increase the value our society places on learning, allowing an enhanced dignity to be associated with the acts of teaching and learning, and offering real long-term hopes, as we'll see, for solving intractable societal problems. What is needed now is a federally supported national study of *learning*.

Why, the public might ask, should our society commit more thought, caring, and resources to the study of learning than ever before? Because it is time to acknowledge that learning is the most essential technology of survival that has ever been, is now, and will ever be at the disposal of the human species. If we are to discover a way beyond the crisis in the Middle East, it will be discovered as a result of a deeper learning than we have yet ventured to undertake. If we are to discover a way to pool and distribute the resources of the world so that the majority of its citizens have basic human necessities and ultimately the chance to determine the quality of their own lives and destinies, it will come as a result of learning. If the United States is to reach its potential to stand before the world as a model of a high civilization—demonstrating privilege without abuse, liberty without license, and the steadfast refusal to use superior power for self-aggrandizement—we will have had to learn a few things. Deep, comprehensive, balanced learning, and not looking smart or sexy or feeling powerful, is the key to survival and to happiness.

With a new sense of learning's place in the big picture and a more accurate notion of its essential *value*, I could now return to Moffett and others and consider what should be the *central aim* of satisfying learning.

 # CHAPTER SIX

The Person Missing

Everybody has some special road of thought along which
they travel when they are alone to themselves.

—Zora Neale Hurston

Perhaps I am growing forgetful. But, with the exception of the workshops I have begun offering, in my fifteen years of teaching, a year of
education courses and six years of undergraduate and graduate school
courses, I do not recall one assigned reading, education class conversation, workshop or seminar discussion on the central aim of learning.
Pulling out the cardboard box containing my education textbooks, I
began exploring this suprising absence.

"Learning theory is primarily *descriptive*," I read, having checked
the index of my educational psychology text under "learning."
Descriptive of what? I read on. "Learning theory studies conditions,
processes, and dynamics which influence learning and which control
behavior" (Davis 124). In a nearly 700-page education text, the near-
est thing I can find to a statement on the purpose of learning appears to
give *learning* a status equivalent to the *controlling of behavior*? This is
as revealing as it is disturbing. It's a teaching version of Stephen
Covey's image of corporate executives who master the art of "climbing the ladder of success, only to discover it's leaning against the
wrong wall." No matter how cleverly we climb, "every step we take
just gets us to the wrong place faster" (98). Nothing on the central purpose of learning there.

Surely a book titled *Writing to Learn* pauses to contemplate the
purpose of learning. Hmm. Not that I can find. In another called
Teaching as a Subversive Activity I find that the purpose of schools is
to counteract the dominant shallow conception of learning, to "subvert
attitudes, beliefs, and assumptions that foster chaos and uselessness"

49

(Postman 15). Since we each make our own reality, authors Postman and Weingartner argue, "we have no common world," and each learner ought always to "be the content" of the lesson; the lesson is about helping him or her create *meanings* (96–97). Now this got me closer, I thought, to a statement about a central purpose of learning. But I wasn't there yet.

Putting the textbooks back in the box, I decided to let myself become a human bulletin board for quotes from points anywhere and everywhere, from anyone and everyone. Great souls think alike, if often unconventionally, and scrutinizing these thoughts I found much agreement from unusual minds on the essential purpose of learning. James Moffett offers not only a central aim of learning but a rationale for it:

> I argue that personal development must be central, because all solutions to public problems, no matter how collective the action, depend on mature, enlightened individuals to call for and indeed insist on these solutions. (xvi)

Moffet draws his rationale from an inference that is as lucid as it is unusual: Personal development should be the central aim of learning. Why? Because a democracy requires "mature, enlightened individuals" to make it work and to preserve it. When have we heard widespread calls for personal learning to preserve democracy? Not in my lifetime. Moffett predicts that, ultimately

> . . . as unresolved societal problems threaten catastrophe, the realization will take hold that only personal development will save the situation. (6)

Perhaps we only discover the hard way that learning is *inherently personal*, and that it should always aim to *nourish* learners, more than merely inform them with facts and equip them with skills. The Roman philosopher Seneca put it this way:

> To educate the mind without the heart is no education at all.
>
> —Seneca

David Xu, a particularly insightful student friend whose thoughts often fit right in among those of "unusual thinkers," reflects in his sophomore portfolio that an inherent aim of learning is to explore what makes each of us unique:

> The true purpose of education is to unlock one's individuality.
>
> —David Xu, June 2001

David's choice of verb—*unlock*—I happen to know, is no accident. Fuming that school as it exists today imprisons individuality, David recommends we put aside pretense and simply issue all students prison uniforms. Actually, the Latin root of the word "education," *edu-care*, means "to nourish, to cause to grow." Expanding on this definition, anthropologist Ashley Montagu enlarges upon David Xu's idea of unlocking individuality:

> The continuing traditional methods of "education" have really noth-ing whatever to do with the functions and purposes of a genuine edu-cation, namely, to nourish and to cause the individual's uniqueness and creativity to grow.
>
> —Ashley Montagu

If part of the purpose of learning is to nourish the growth of a unique and creative person, then what *kind* of growth should we aim for? This question occupied Albert Einstein:

> The school should always have as its aim that the young [person] leave it as a harmonious personality, not as a specialist.
>
> —Albert Einstein (71)

Einstein's goal of assisting a learner to achieve a harmonious balance in learning led me with increasing clarity toward a complete statement of the central aim of learning. Einstein is also famous for saying:

> The significant problems we face can never be solved at the level of thinking that created them.
>
> —Einstein

I have no reluctance to climbing on the escalator to shop on the upper floors of my favorite discount department store. Nor do I have qualms about taking thought escalators to find solutions to problems on levels of thought higher than where a problem began. In a purportedly reve-latory text called *The Urantia Book,* I find a statement that might rep-resent a different level of thinking about learning:

> The purpose of all education should be to foster and further the supreme purpose of life, the development of a majestic and well-balanced personality.
>
> —*The Urantia Book* (2086)

While not ideal, the statement strikes me as a remarkably good synthe-sis of the sampling of thoughts we have just considered. First, the phrase "to foster and further" approximates the meanings "nourish" and "grow" in the Latin root *educare*. The royal overtones in the word "majestic" seem a little over the top. But "majestic" has other, less royal meanings. It is also defined as having "greatness or splendor of quality or character," a meaning that rings with some of the "unique-ness" and possibly the "creativity" in Montagu's formulation, as well as the "individuality" in David Xu's. "Majestic" does directly modify "personality" in the sentence, seeming to emphasize the second, non-royal meaning. Finally, the phrase "well-balanced personality" in the statement fits remarkably well with Seneca's combined education of heart and mind, and Einstein's urging that schooling leave a learner with a "harmonious personality."

With a little tailoring (for me, "majestic" is still a bit much), until something better comes along, this sentence has my nomination for central aim of twenty-first-century education. James Moffett, Albert Einstein, and many more great souls and unusual minds than I've had space to quote here concur—learning is first and foremost a matter of personal unfolding. This seemed a good place to launch a second cardinal point in the unfolding of this New Look Toward Learning:

---

1. Learning is the core drive of human advancement.
2. The central aim of learning is the growth and development of a fully realized, well-balanced personality.

With this thinking coming together, we can begin visually representing the model (see Figure 6–1).

Central Aim of Twenty-First-Century Learning

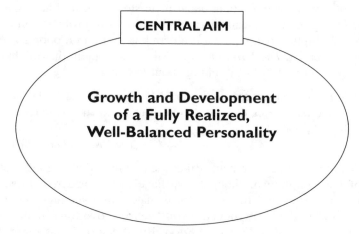

CENTRAL AIM

**Growth and Development
of a Fully Realized,
Well-Balanced Personality**

Figure 6–1 Central Aim of Twenty-First-Century Learning

▼ CHAPTER SEVEN

The Learning Continuum

Education that consists in learning things and not the meaning of them is feeding upon the husks and not the corn.
                                                    —Mark Twain

If that aim seems a far cry from where we are now, it is. Our current de facto purpose of education—to inform students with facts and equip them with skills for productive, responsible, and rewarding roles in society—fails to guide us to achieve *even these things*. This aim, again, will never be sufficient because it is too partial, because it fails to take into account enough of human experience. However, while gaining knowledge and acquiring skills are not the stuff of a *central* aim of learning, they do have a place in an updated, more universal and comprehensive model of learning. They belong more properly in a continuum of secondary aims that, for clarity, I refer to from now on as a *Continuum of Learning Purposes,* or simply the *Learning Continuum.*

In the introduction, you read that the Creed Project asks students to "reflect on how the facts, meanings, and values of their lives can become interrelated, interdependent phases of their learning." I also said that such reflections may lead to "exciting" learning and growth. Why exciting?

Aside from the depersonalizing effects of school, perhaps the thing that most frustrates all of us is that school as we know it is not completely in touch with reality. I mean this quite literally. With the old purpose of education—inform and equip them with facts and skills—students are effectively cut off from whole regions of thought and experience, locked in prison as David Xu might say, caged away from essential parts of reality. It is no accident that a proverbial student response to much of what happens in the classroom is "Get real!"

Centering our understanding of learning on the most broadly encompassing possible aim of learning, on *several* other hands, gives us permission to think of learning in relation to a fuller view of reality. Learning is nothing less than the core drive of human advancement (Chapter Five). The central aim of learning is to help us unfold the full and balanced potentials of our personalities (Chapter Six). Must not learning experiences, then, help us intimately engage considerably more of life than the testable parts of reality selected by a corporation for ease of measurement and profitability?

In thinking through all this, I am excited by the very same realization that excites students and teachers as the Creed Project unfolds: At last, learning begins to more fully engage reality. Where is this going? To a discourse on reality, this one in only four short and uncomplicated paragraphs.

To understand learning in a more satisfying way, it can be useful to consider that we apprehend reality by means of three interdependent and connected elements—facts, meanings, and values. Whether I've thought in quite this fashion about it or not, *experience* has taught me that these three elements depend on each other for their mutual existence. I must face the *facts* of the material world; there's no escaping them. Yet if I revel only in the factual rewards of my status and possessions, sooner or later I will tire of my Maseratis and my gourmet hot dogs; sooner or later my life will become meaningless. When I decide to find someone to talk to, for I've realized I am not made for fine food and fast cars alone, I have taken the *facts* of my life and constructed a judgement, a type of *meaning*. When eventually I tire altogether of my dissipated life in the fast lane, and realize I need to slow down and find something beyond sleek cars and gourmet dogs to live for, I am reaching for *values*, something in my life to stand for. The facts of my life become blocks I use to build meanings, and meanings become the road to discovering my values. By "values," I do not mean a predetermined set of mores one simply adopts because they are approved by the traditions of a particular group. I mean the principles, beliefs, and attitudes one has embraced because one's experience in life has taught that these things ring true and bear fruit that is good.

But this is not a simple progression or a hierarchy that hits a ceiling; it is a *continuum*. Once I have found something to stand for in life—have discovered some values based on the facts of my life and my contemplation of those facts—I am drawn to do something factual about it: Values instigate action in the material world, and I want to act upon mine. Action in the factual world leads me to reflect on the meaning of this action. Enough reflection, and I might be led to reassess my values, which in turn may lead me to create new facts of my life, and so forth. Leah Johnson suggests this learning continuum is more accu-

Continuum of Twenty-First-Century Learning Purposes

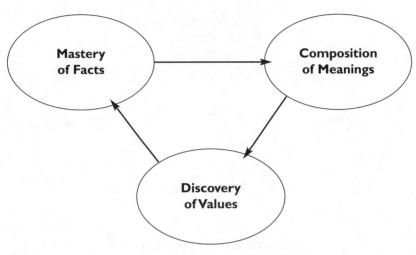

Figure 7–1 Continuum of Twenty-First-Century Learning Purposes

rately a spiral, and we revisit certain issues again and again—family, love, integrity, and so on—but on ascending levels.

Our best learning occurs in the very same way we best engage reality—in a continuum, through the intertwined processes of *mastering facts, composing meanings*, and *discovering values*. Learning that is satisfying simply offers learning experiences that allow the learner to *engage all parts of the continuum*. It is remarkably uncomplicated.

And this perception is not foreign to us. *Any* experience that leaves a deep impression has probably engaged all three of these elements in us. A moving musical performance is a collection of material *facts*: The performers, the audience, the musical notes played, the architectural features of the performance space—these are factual ingredients of the performance. As the factual elements interact, the performance inspires the audience to create countless *meanings* on numerous levels in the mind and emotions: harmonies, feelings, thoughts about the period and history of the music, fantasies, personal realizations about life prompted by the music. When the harmonies or lyrics stir something so deep in me that I resonate with it because it touches a part of who I am, what I am about, what I am here in this world to experience spiritually, the performance is engaging my *values*. The performance moves me deeply because it engages me fully—materially (facts), mentally (meanings), spiritually (values). The experience is total, not

Central Aim and Purposes of
Twenty-First-Century Learning

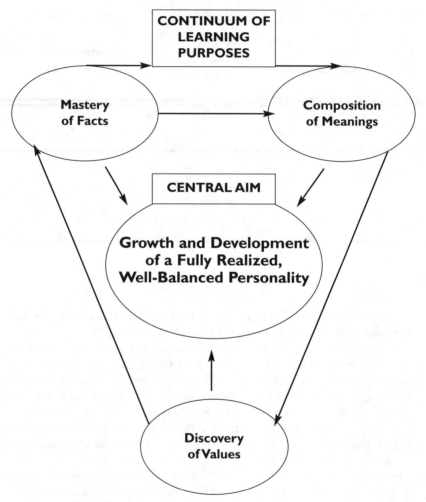

Figure 7–2 Central Aim and Purposes of Twenty-First-Century Learning

partial. And here's perhaps the main point of this book: Learning that does this for us is *exciting*. By design of reality, it is *satisfying*. Figure 7-1 gives you the beginnings of a multi-dimensional picture.

This leads us to a third cardinal point in this New Look Toward Learning:

1. Learning is the core drive of human advancement.

2. The central aim of learning is the growth and development of a fully realized, well-balanced personality.

3. The personality develops best, is most satisfied, when learning is balanced among the mastery of facts, the composing of meaning, and the discovery of values.

Putting cardinal points two and three together, we can visualize the interrelationships among the central aim of learning and continuum of learning purposes and begin to see the essential outlines of a new vision of learning for the twenty-first century (see Figure 7–2):

It is easy to see where on the model to find most of what we now do in school. Mastering facts and skills, traditionally called "acquiring knowledge," consumes the overwhelming majority of students' time and energy. Occasional relief from the memorizing comes when we ask them to interpret facts, but we teachers are usually looking for interpretations (meanings) specific to the facts of our disciplines or of larger societal questions. Only willy-nilly in their educations, to my knowledge, have students ever been asked to create meanings with the facts of their own lives.

Even more rarely do we ask students to consider how their life experiences (facts) are helping build their opinions and viewpoints and understandings of life (meanings), and how these understandings are contributing to their acquirement of enduring wisdom (values). And this is what I want to learn how to design into the rest of the learning students experience in my classes. Chapter Fourteen outlines some ways I am finding to begin doing this.

In this chapter we have begun to explore the secret behind what I am calling satisfying learning. In Chapter Nine you'll see how I stumbled in my thinking (literally in the desert) into an understanding of how precisely the Creed Project validates this model, asking students to interrelate and correlate the facts, meanings, and values of their lives.

But before we do, with a clear sense of the essential aim and purposes of a new kind of learning, in the final chapter in Part Two we will look briefly at an overview of the means to carry out this new kind of learning—teaching and learning practices that best support this central aim and these supporting purposes.

▼ CHAPTER EIGHT

Goals for Twenty-First-Century Teaching and Learning Practices

> Perhaps as the universe evolves, one day the truth will be revealed. Because it's not water that flows in the River Styx; it's us.
>
> —David Xu, January 2001

One of the challenges in making the transition to this kind of learning—a transition that is already under way in many classrooms and schools—is that the role of teacher must shift from subject expert and authority figure to one who establishes favorable conditions for growth. For the past fifteen or twenty years, progressive teachers have tried to play a role as different from the traditional teacher as a "guide on the side" from a "sage on the stage." Many excellent books are available on this kind of teaching, notably those by Harvey Daniels and friends on Best Practices and methods. I am not referring here to a later co-opting of this term by forces attempting to enforce a predetermined political agenda upon students and educators. (Remember, we are not here, as James Moffett reminds us, "to be molded by the state" or by the forces of commerce.) *Best Practice*, the title of Steven Zemmelman, Daniels, and Arthur Hyde's 1993 book, and their 1998 revision, is a term these progressive teacher-authors borrowed from law and medicine to denote the drawing together of ideas, a consensus from practicing teachers around the country of what constitutes the best teaching and learning methods. These practices, further amplified in Daniels and Marilyn Bizar's 1998 *Methods That Matter*, are excellent starting places for what I am calling satisfying learning, first of all because they are authentic syntheses of the most effective teaching from around the country. Jim Burke's books are another example of collections of practices that have been created and tested by enlightened teachers in classrooms for students rather than for an ideology. It does not matter what we call a given method or orientation to teaching; truly satisfied learners are being guided through the continuum of learning whether or not anyone realizes it.

While the constellation of teaching methods and approaches called Best Practices may not delineate the discovery of values per se, reflection is a major Best Practice emphasis, as it is of all teaching capable of deeply engaging students. Perhaps what is new in what I call *satisfying learning* is a sharpened focus on the ongoing discovery of values as part of a curriculum centered on personal learning. Leah Johnson in an email wrote that these assignments centering on personal learning seemed to her to "grow from a deeper curriculum than the one presented by the educational system." This is an insight we will explore in Part Three.

Another new feature of the ideas and practices in this book is that the teacher learns to play an expanded role—as one who not only coaches students in absorbing *facts*, not only guides them in interpreting facts *meaningfully*, but provides carefully designed learning experiences that ask students to reflect on how the facts of their own lives and the meanings they create from those facts relate to what they stand for, to their *values*. To consider thoroughly teaching and learning practices that best support the aim and purposes I have set out here is beyond the scope of this book. But we can set some general goals.

Growth-Centered Practices

First, practices that support growth-centered learning must themselves be growth-centered. Skills, then, cannot be considered ends in themselves but means to the end of learners fully developing their personalities. On the ground, some degree of standardization will be necessary as our learning system reorients increasingly toward personal learning. During the interim, however, when faced with choices as to whether to create or support programs and policies, we should whenever possible favor the development of the individual over the tendency to standardize learning. Toward this end, in what I am calling Two-Legged Design, teachers and schools plan for personal learning alongside academic learning at every stage of course and program design.

Learning Through Interaction and Service with Diverse Others

The aim of personal learning and growth is best supported by practices that engage learners in interaction with others. Learners should interact with other learners in the classroom and in service activities, in school and in the community. While "diversity" is one of those ideas that has been bandied about so much by both its supporters and those who fear it that its meaning is freighted with fuzziness, I believe it is an essential element of learning. Coming to terms with those different from ourselves has much to do, by design, with how we become fully ourselves. Learning in diverse teams—diverse by race, gender, culture, class, or any other means—is a main method, I think, of ultimately satisfying learning. In virtually all cultures, unequal conditions and opportunities for people of "different" races or genders or cultures or classes add the powerful moral and spiritual challenge of injustice to the process of learning in diverse teams. It is this challenge that provides the opportunity for the powerful influence of *conscience* in learning. Grappling healthily with this challenge can engage the team in the full learning continuum: ascertaining a base of facts about the differences in conditions and opportunities; interpreting them in a way that leads to the team's deepened understanding not only of historical and current events but of team members for one another; and contemplating how these understandings connect to learners' values. The Beyond Diversity seminar I mentioned in Chapter Four is an especially successful example of learning and serving in diverse teams. Inevitable friction in interactions among diverse teammates can be reduced when teammates have the common task of serving a higher purpose, such as feeding the hungry, or bringing equity to learning. Service, then, should be part of the design.

Learners Teach / Teachers Learn

Interactions among teachers and learners should be frequent, reciprocal and dynamic, with teachers often assuming the various roles of learners, not merely to model the skills of learning but to share actual learning they are experiencing in connection with students' learning. Learners should often be given the opportunity to teach others, age-peers and younger peers, and should not be strangers to the experience of teaching their teachers.

Integration of School, Home, Community

Methods and practices that support twenty-first-century learning should seek to incorporate and integrate the various composite parts of students' makeup and life experience. For example, we should begin much more seriously allowing students to integrate their learning experiences among school, home, and their community. What James Moffett in *The Universal Schoolhouse* calls "community learning systems" deserves the most serious study, as do internship programs such as that at Best Practice High School in Chicago, described in *Rethinking High School*. It is unwise, even dangerous, to emphasize learning only at school. With the kind of community learning system Moffett describes, and Chicago's Best Practice High School implements, students less often question the time they do spend in desks and doing homework. What better way to take back the schools from the business and government forces of occupation than to take learning and learners to the streets? The more learning is found to be going on in the community, the less students will dismiss it as that annoying and too often abusive regimen forced on them in schools. The case can then be made to parents and children that home, too, is a learning environment, and that time we spend before the screen and between earphones should be limited to make space for minds and hearts to develop healthily.

Integration of Body, Mind, Heart, Spirit

Another essential support of person-centered learning is to break the twentieth-century philosophical paralysis that continues to work against the healthy integration of physical, intellectual, emotional, and spiritual learning. As serious as the debates may seem at times, in reality they are rooted in silliness. The rightful separation of church and state was never intended to be misinterpreted and misapplied in the unnatural separation of spirit from learning. It should come as no surprise that education for spiritually vital students like Duron, Huda, and so many of us amounts to going through minimally meaningful motions for even less meaningful certificates of completion. In isolation from the growth of the deepest parts of ourselves that hunger for the deepest connections to life and to others, students' motivation to learn can never be fully operative. It is entirely possible, in fact essential, to allow students to bring the spiritual part of their awarenesses to their studies. This can happen as long as the learning situation is set up in such a way that no one religious viewpoint predominates, that sharing and not preaching becomes the mode of discussion, and that those with different religious viewpoints, including atheism and agnosticism, are made to feel included and honored in discussions.

One appropriate way to begin establishing such a climate is to create a study of wisdom. Our literature anthology has a sizable and diverse collection of short pieces from most major world cultures on wisdom, including selections from the Bible, the Qur'an, and several eastern texts regarded as sacred. Our purpose, however, is not to study religion but to study wisdom, a beginning-of-year pursuit with societal and personal applications that set up very nicely for the Personal Creed Project at the end. Satisfying learning should involve teachers and learners, body, mind, heart, and spirit. See Chapter Fourteen, Appendix II, and the website for more on the Wisdom Project.

Learning Through Multiple Perspectives

Several related tripartite realities also make highly involving ongoing studies as they arise in learning. The relationships among beauty, truth, and goodness make a fascinating inquiry across all disciplines, along with—particularly in the arts and humanities—their connections to love. These connections can be brought out in the study of poetry, for example. The varied perspectives of science, philosophy, and spirituality are natural training for the different modes of thinking needed for different purposes, as past, present, and future are differing lenses through which to perceive time. Finally, experience (fact), philosophy (meaning), and wisdom (value) can be seen as building blocks of character, as my sophomore classes have the chance to discover in the introductory Wisdom Project.

Learning Through Experience and Following Natural Urges

In all this, it is important to remember that satisfying learning as explored here is not about direct teaching of values. The goal is to equip students to create meanings from facts, and follow those meanings as they genuinely discover values for themselves. This is not "character education." The teaching (and, even more, parenting) art lies in setting up the learning situation so that learners can create meanings that, in turn, lead them to positive values they come to own because they were allowed the experience of discovering them for themselves. The alternative is mere obedience, and we don't genuinely learn values by obeying orders. It certainly may develop, however, that we are led to rediscover values for ourselves that we have been taught directly. All the better. There is an implied faith in the goodness of the universe in trusting that learners in conducive, hopefully inspiring conditions will discover positive values. Rather than direct teaching, the teacher's role—and, as and where necessary, society's role—is to set up those conditions. This is part of what the Creed process seems to accomplish.

A final quality of practices and methods worthy of a new-century vision of learning is naturalness. Learning fuels itself when learners follow natural urges. Learning by doing is probably the main idea here, and this is why internships such as those at Best Practice High School make so much sense. This is especially true if students choose internships based on natural talents and curiosities identified by the influx of counselors Moffett calls for in *The Universal Schoolhouse* to begin paying attention to students in upper elementary grades. Once natural interests and abilities are identified, it's important to allow learners to use natural means to explore them. Creating and following the leads of Big Questions is a powerful approach that can be worked into any existing course or program. Searching, researching, exploring, and discovering are natural urges engaged when we follow Big Questions. (See Chapters Ten and Fourteen.) Finally, creating original works of all kinds satisfies natural urges—in art, music, literature, architecture, horticulture. Moffett believed that an arts-centered curriculum is about as ideal an approach as is possible.

This collection of general recommendations for teaching and learning practices to support satisfying, person-centered learning is purposefully nonspecific. It is intended to be a starting point for further development, and not an exhaustive, definitive grouping. These general goals for satisfying practices complete this draft of a beginning model of learning for the new century (see Figure 8–1).

Updating our developing set of cardinal points, we can add a fourth:

A New Look Toward Learning

1. Learning is the core drive of human advancement.

2. The central aim of learning is the growth and development of a fully realized, well-balanced personality.

3. The personality develops best, is most satisfied, when learning is balanced among the mastery of facts, the composing of meaning, and the discovery of values.

4. Twenty-first-century teaching and learning practices should be growth-centered rather than skills-centered, integrative rather than isolative, should harness natural curiosities and urges rather than artificial motivation to learn, employ service as a means of harmonizing learning among learners from diverse backgrounds, acknowledge that the wise separation of church and state was never intended to result in the unnatural separation of learning from spirit, and should allow frequent opportunities for learners to teach and teachers to learn.

A Beginning Model of Twenty-First-Century Learning
in 2025? 2050? 2100?

GOALS FOR TEACHING AND LEARNING PRACTICES

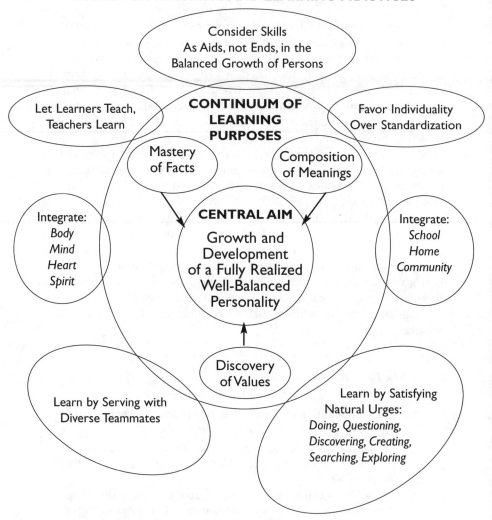

Consider Skills
As Aids, not Ends, in the
Balanced Growth of Persons

Let Learners Teach,
Teachers Learn

**CONTINUUM OF
LEARNING
PURPOSES**

Favor Individuality
Over Standardization

Mastery
of Facts

Composition
of Meanings

Integrate:
*Body
Mind
Heart
Spirit*

CENTRAL AIM
Growth and
Development
of a Fully Realized
Well-Balanced
Personality

Integrate:
*School
Home
Community*

Discovery
of Values

Learn by Serving with
Diverse Teammates

Learn by Satisfying
Natural Urges:
*Doing, Questioning,
Discovering, Creating,
Searching, Exploring*

Figure 8–1 A Beginning Model of Twenty-First-Century Learning

One more practice deserves to be added to this collection of cardinal points. Strictly speaking, this is more of a planning practice than a teaching practice. The idea sprang into my mind one day in the car within a week after Brett Nelson shared his medicine wheel with my sophomore classes and was refined with help from David Xu. It is a simple concept:

Each branch of study should have personal learning at its center.

What does this mean? I can only answer this question in general terms, for while it may make some sense for *academic* learning goals to be standardized to some degree by states and nations, *personal* learning goals can be determined democratically by each school community. Chapters Ten and Fourteen, introducing Two-Legged Design, will develop this idea more fully. (Also, my article in the February 2002 issue of *California English* lays out some examples. See website.) In the meantime, here are visual representations of how a given English department could conceive a curriculum for the twenty-

Cross Section of Twenty-First-Century English Curriculum

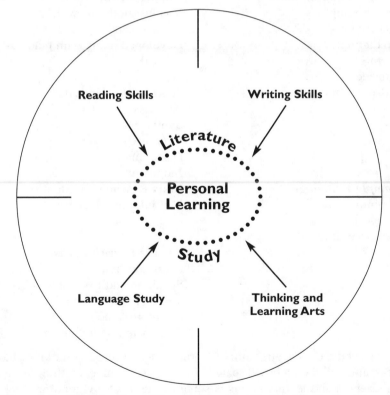

Figure 8–2 Cross Section of Twenty-First-Century English Curriculum. *Special thanks to David Xu for conversation leading to the ideas represented here.*

first century. The personal learning goals in English, at the center of the cross-section, as for all other departments, would derive from the personal learning goals the school community has developed. Personal learning, then, becomes the curricular core that integrates and brings meaning to the academic parts (see Figure 8–2).

In the breakdown below, English teachers will notice the absence of the traditional category of Speaking and Listening Skills, which are included under a newer category: Learning Arts. Another new category is Thinking Arts. These two additions are inspired by the work of Gordon Dryden and Jeanette Vos in their groundbreaking *The Learning Revolution*. Dryden and Voss make a strong case for a new emphasis on teaching students to think and to learn, critical areas to which we give more lip service than legwork. This breakdown is still in the brainstorm phase and needs more perspectives and experimentation from more teachers:

Sample Reading Skills
Questioning
Clarifying
Predicting
Picturing
Connecting
Adapting approach to text

Sample Writing Skills
Various modes as widely
    accepted
Developed along with reading
    skill

Sample Thinking Arts
Analysis
Synthesis
Inference
Discernment
Judgment
Brain Research on Memory
Multiple Intelligences

Sample Language Study
Grammar
Usage
Sentence Study

Sample Learning Arts
Learning Styles
Speaking and Listening Skills
Memory Access and
    Improvement
Suspension of Judgment

To settle on a central aim of learning, something I don't know has been attempted on a broad scale before, is to rethink everything we do as teachers and learners. This is some of the most invigorating thinking I've ever had the opportunity to do, some of the most personally rewarding and, I hope, widely useful. Here is the New Look Toward Learning for now. I look forward to many invigorating conversations to test its soundness and learn its applicability. In many respects, Part Three is intended to stimulate a conversation about applying and implementing these ideas. Here, then, is the completed New Look.

A New Look Toward Learning

1. Learning is the core drive of human advancement.

2. The central aim of learning is the growth and development of a fully realized, well-balanced personality.

3. The personality develops best, is most satisfied, when learning is balanced among the mastery of facts, the composing of meaning, and the discovery of values.

4. Twenty-first-century teaching and learning practices should be growth-centered rather than skills-centered, integrative rather than isolative, should harness natural curiosities and urges rather than artificial motivation to learn, employ service as a means of harmonizing learning among learners from diverse backgrounds, acknowledge that the wise separation of church and state was never intended to result in the unnatural separation of learning from spirit, and should allow frequent opportunities for learners to teach and teachers to learn.

5. Each branch of study should have personal learning at its center, so that personal learning becomes the curricular core that integrates and brings meaning to the academic parts.

Part Three

Guiding the Personal Creed Project: The Nuts and Reflective Bolts

> Everything that can be counted isn't worth counting, and everything that is worth counting isn't always countable.
> Albert Einstein

You have weathered the testimonials and theories of Parts One and Two; baptized with fresh insights, you arrive here ready, I hope, to dip your students' reflective feet in shimmering water. Or, ducking my windy windup, you've skipped to Part Three for the nuts and bolts. Or you could be hybridizing, flipping back and forth in your own approach. However you arrive, welcome to the how-to part! Here I pledge to offer student samples only when I believe illustrations will help you in guiding *your* students—and not when another great insight from one of mine (however much it illuminates *my* soul) just *had* to be put in. So if you have braved the weather or flipped around, congratulations—along the way you may already have picked up some of the nuts and bolts you're about to read in the following overview. If, on the other hand, this is your starting place, I'll keep you in mind and try to refer you to earlier parts when you are likely to be getting mystified. Part One showed you *what* the Creed Project is; Part Two explored *why* it works. In Part Three, you find out *how* it works. Onward!

⚜ CHAPTER NINE

Overview and Planning

> The Creed Project taught me that students you would never
> expect could have life hard do.
>
> Calvin Crunk, June 2003

Project Overlook

If the rudiments of the Creed Project are not generally fresh in your
mind, you may want to skim back over the project overview you read
in the Introduction. The two quadrants on the following pages will give
you a good visual overlook at the entire process and begin to acquaint
you with the particulars of each step. (Thanks once more to Brett
Nelson for the quadrant idea, and for the Native American connection
to the Creed process. See Chapter Three.) Perusing the quadrants, you
can survey the contents of the Step I–IV reflections (Figure 9–1) and
the Step V presentation (Figure 9–2). An approximate project timeline,
geared to my sophomores, is included; you'll need to cut and paste a
schedule to fit your own teaching situation. More later on this.

In Figure 9-1, a rough breakdown of Creed reflections Steps I
through IV, you see that in Step I students explore the factors that have
influenced or inspired them. To stretch the project out over the semester, this past year we lengthened this step substantially. (Step I took
most of third quarter, with students moving through a reflection per
week.) Step II asks a student to consider the influences complied in
Step I and make a judgment about them: Which of these influences
does he or she most value or admire, and which least? Drawing on
these reflections and judgments concerning the people and events, the
circumstances, questions and qualities that have influenced him, for
Step III he goes on to reflect on what most matters to him, what in life
he most cares about, what principles, ideals, or values are most impor-

71

Contents of Personal Creed Reflections, Steps I–IV

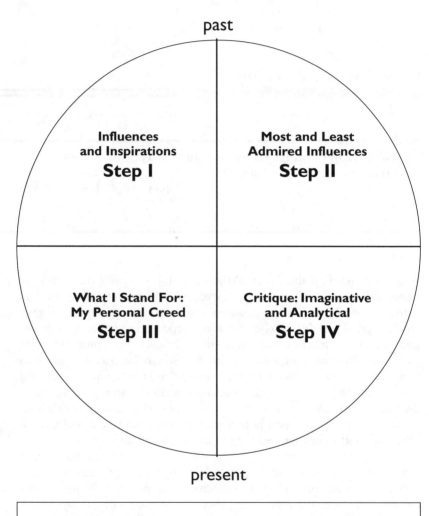

past

Influences and Inspirations
Step I

Most and Least Admired Influences
Step II

What I Stand For: My Personal Creed
Step III

Critique: Imaginative and Analytical
Step IV

present

Rough Project Timeline
  Step I—7 to 8 weeks
  Step II—2 weeks
  Step III—3 weeks
  Step IV—2 weeks

Figure 9–1 Contents of Personal Creed Reflections, Steps I–IV

Contents of Personal Creed Presentations, Step V

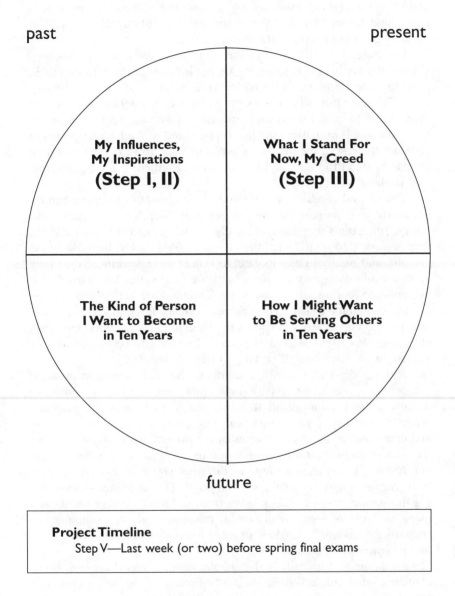

past   present

My Influences,
My Inspirations
(Step I, II)

What I Stand For
Now, My Creed
(Step III)

The Kind of Person
I Want to Become
in Ten Years

How I Might Want
to Be Serving Others
in Ten Years

future

Project Timeline
Step V—Last week (or two) before spring final exams

Figure 9–2 Contents of Personal Creed Presentations, Step V

tant to him and might inspire his commitment. This is when he articulates a tentative statement of his personal creed. To explore the depth of this stated commitment, in Step IV students undertake both imaginative and analytical exercises to *critique* the values they have said they stand for in Step III. You'll see more details unfold in each of these steps in the chapters ahead.

For roughly the first half of the semester, then, a student has considered mainly his *past,* reflecting on his influences (Step I), and then, moving *toward* the present, making an evaluation of these influences (Step II). In the following weeks, Steps III and IV ask him to move *into* the present, to think clearly and critically about what his reflections on his past can tell him about the person he is today. And, as he begins to consider the rest of his life, he is asked to think toward what he might choose to stand for, now and in the future. So there is a time progression in these reflections.

The second quadrant, Figure 9–2, shows how this thinking continues as students prepare for the presentation (Step V). After reexamining the reflections they have made about their *pasts* (in Steps I and II), they are asked to revisit what they have decided they value now, in the *present*, and finally to extrapolate, to reflect more specifically on how all this thinking might take shape in the *future*. On the day of her Creed presentation before the class, a student airs her reflections on the influences that have shaped her, shares what she has realized as a result about her own values, and shows the thinking she has done ten years ahead into her life: the kind of person she wants to be then, and how she might envision herself serving or helping others.

A quick departure from the content, and a comment on process: Notice in the previous two paragraphs that there is a kind of *spiraling* in how I am presenting all this for you. I went over the project's reflections and its presentation from the perspective of their content and then covered these two phases of the project again, this time from the standpoint of their time association in the student's life (past, present, future). I also used a range of different words and phrases, carefully varying them to explain a given point. This approach—introducing the various steps of this project from different vantage points and using an array of terms with similar meanings—seems to help more students get aboard, as it does in most learning situations. More later on this spiraling approach.

As the project unfolds in the chapters ahead, you'll see how these elements break down further. At the beginning of the section on each Creed step, you'll find a graphic "overlook" of the contents of that step. Chapters include the instructions my students actually receive, accompanied by annotations I hope give you just enough help, but not too much, to create your adaptation of the project with your students.

Whenever possible, annotations appear on pages facing a given piece of instruction for students. Essentially, in this portion of the book I share the project as I've developed it with my students and invite you to make your own version, whether you decide to model closely or more loosely on what I've done.

Scheduling

To create time for the presentations, I plan spring semester so most classroom work finishes the week *before* Dead Week (for us, Dead Week is the week just before finals week). It is a week when we're "supposed" to ease up on assigning homework. So, beyond adding final touches to their Creed presentations and finishing up our last novel in time to prepare for their final exam, my sophomores have little homework during spring Dead Week. Well, I wish that were entirely true. The truth is that I am still wrestling with how best to fit portfolios into all this—how to collect some portfolios late enough so that students who want to write up the experience of their Creed presentations (Step V) for their portfolio piece called A Moment That Mattered can do so, yet not so late that I am buried alive in portfolios the weekend before a strenuous week of reading final exam essays and figuring semester grades.

My goal is to schedule things so that while in other classes students and teachers are busily cramming the content that hasn't found its way yet into students' brains, Dead Week in English comes alive—Alive Week would not be an entirely silly name for it—with something refreshingly different and refreshingly personal. This contrast between the Creed presentations in English and what is going on in the rest of their classes tends to boost students' enthusiasm even more for an activity that has by this time begun to appeal to most. Every year at about this point I see a number of persistently lukewarm students, however come-lately, finally warming up to English.

Over the years I have developed three different versions of the Creed Project. They range from the abbreviated version for teacher workshops, which I don't recommend for teenage students, who need much more time to reorganize their brains for a new kind of thinking, to the new semester-long version, which stretches out over most of spring semester. Until this past year, we had used a mid-length, end-of-semester version, shoehorning the entire project into the last four or five weeks of spring semester. By the way, even if you have dutifully read Part One, you may still be wondering why we wait until the end of spring semester to run this project. If it creates such positive results, why not do it earlier? Students, colleagues, and workshop participants have often asked this question, as I have. Perhaps now you can see, with students confiding in their classmates and teacher the people, events, and circumstances that have molded their lives—often some pretty eye-opening and heart-wrenching tales as you saw in Part One and will again in Chapters Eleven through Thirteen—that the Creed presentations depend on an especially high level of trust. With the just over four hours we have together each week on a secondary schedule, I find such trust takes us a year to build. But I've slowly realized that while the presentations themselves seem clearly to belong at the end of the year, this doesn't mean the entire project needs to be done at the end in a hurry. In fact, in recent years students have urged, no, begged, no, prodded me to allow more time for the project. For a number of reasons, extending the project makes excellent sense.

The best of these reasons is simply this: When we ask most sophomores to do the kind of reflection the project asks for, we are asking them to break new thinking ground. This past year, teaching my first honors classes since long before the 2001 presentations convinced me to pay closer attention to the project's effects on students, I was surprised to discover that this kind of thinking is unfamiliar even to accomplished, highly motivated students. Even serious writers like Elyse, who naturally enjoys thinking deeply about things, found that the project asked her and her honors classmates for thinking that was "much more than we bargained for":

> The Creed Project introduced to me a new style of learning where I went deeper and studied myself. I had never really considered who I was or what I stood for before in my life, and so some parts of this project were hard for me because the questions were ones I have never really given any thought to, and ones I felt had no definite answer. . . .
>
> —Elyse Kirker, June 2003

From a different part of the academic spectrum, though he is certainly rich in intelligence and experiences to learn from, David, an Asian American gang member who narrowly escaped expulsion the previous year after an aborted gang fight in the parking lot of another high school in town, wrote in his final exam essay about the kind of thinking the project elicits:

> This project gave students new avenues of thought which would help them to ascribe a better future to themselves. One can compare the Creed Project to a light emerging forth from one's head, and awakening a person from a coma.
>
> —David Luong, June 2002

While few are provoked to such dramatic imagery as David's, these responses join a unanimous wave of student opinion on both coasts (see pages 16–18) in favor of lengthening the amount of time students have to learn this new kind of mental operation and practice it effectively in their Creed reflections.

Stretching out the project this past year had a number of advantages. Best of all, it allowed what Elyse called the "new style of learning" time to gestate. I handed out the first packet of instructions (with an auspicious sweetness, I must say) on Valentine's Day. This allowed students the entire third quarter to undertake these reflections at the comfortable rate of one manageable portion per week, due Mondays so they'd have weekends to reflect. (More on Monday due dates coming.) This lengthened gestation time may partly explain the especially high levels of engagement and enjoyment in this year's written responses to the project, and the amazing depth of some of the 2003 presentations (see Chapter Thirteen for examples).

Another reason I prefer the semester-long version is that the end-of-semester approach put unnecessary time pressure on other end-of-year coursework like final novels and essay projects—and most of all portfolios—which in the last few weeks can get suddenly displaced. This plan gave students the option to complete their portfolios well before Creed presentations. The semester-long plan also spreads out the impact on students' reading schedules and allows them time weeknights to concentrate on non-Creed-related writing assignments. But even *with* the lengthened schedule, students found themselves left on their own to finish the last half of our final novel, Zora Neale Hurston's *Their Eyes Were Watching God,* without the benefit of class discussion. Given the richness of Hurston's ending, this was a high price to pay. To avoid paying it again next year, I plan to extend the presentations themselves over two weeks. Not only will this allow us to spend part of each day discussing the final novel and preparing for the final exam, but the added week will give more students the option to write up their Creed presentations for their portfolio Moment That Mattered, and me the chance to collect more portfolios earlier, easing some of my pressure during finals week.

A good general scheduling lesson I take from all this is to stretch out personal learning over time, *weaving* this kind of reflection *alongside* academic activities over the length of a semester or year, rather than fitting the personal pieces into small spaces in the schedule, as pressure from the present depersonalizing obsession with test scores tends to dictate. As we will develop in Chapters Ten and Fourteen, this weaving approach appears to be better for both academic and personal kinds of learning.

This book guides you through the semester-long version of the project. (If you'd like to experiment with the mid-length version in your classroom or use the abbreviated workshop version for training purposes, you can find instructions for both on the website.) Since second semester for us is nicely out of the starting blocks by February 14, I plan to adopt Valentine's Day as our annual Creed Project kick-off day. It makes both practical and sentimental sense.

Management

Each Creed step is broken into a number of ministeps, or inquiries, referred to by letter: Creed Inquiry IA, IB, IC. . . . In the end-of-semester version, students often hurried through three or more Creed inquiries a week. Again, the new semester-long version allows the more leisurely pace of a single inquiry per week. At the end of this past year, the first year of the semester-long version, students complained that I had "overstuffed" Step I, breaking it down into too many seemingly repetitive ministeps. In Chapter Eleven you are guided through a newly tightened version of Step I, designed to take eight weeks. The three parts of Step II need only two weeks, with Step III needing another three weeks. Step IV, in two parts, will take two more weeks. This totals approximately fifteen weeks, leaving three weeks in our eighteen-week semester. I try to allow students at least three weekends—four is better—to prepare Step V, the Creed presentations, which you'll want to schedule for the last week or two weeks before finals week. To give them as much weekend time as possible on these presentations, I introduce Step V as soon as we've finished Step III. Once students have started thinking about and planning their presentations, Step IV can be easily finished during the first two of these four to five weeks.

Students need only the most basic gear. Each will need a Creed Inquiry Journal—a spiral notebook for students who prefer to rough out their reflections by hand, or a desktop folder for those comfortable soul-searching at the keyboard. This past year I had students handwrite Creed inquiries starting at the back of their regular journals (non-Creed spiral notebooks) and working back to front. Some students elected to type. Since the handwriters faced a sudden volume of typing when it came time to turn in the Step I–IV packets, this year I'll suggest that students with computers at home try to get comfortable reflecting onscreen from the beginning. This will also make it easy to add material after an initial writing, a real advantage. I ask students to aim for at least a page and a half for each Creed inquiry. Though some will moan at the outset, I've found page length in this project tends to accumulate. More coming on this.

A typical week, starting with Friday, unfolds along the following lines. At the top of our Friday agenda, I'll read aloud the instructions for the Creed inquiry that will be due Monday. (In the coming chapters, you'll see annotated versions of these instructions; you can find

complete unannotated versions on my website, www.universeWired
.com.) Inviting discussion, I field questions, checking for understanding as seems comfortable. If, early in the project, few questions are
raised, I just ask students to make a note of any that come up over the
weekend; we'll discuss them Monday. For many reasons (some of
them good), in my garden variety college prep classes I rarely set
Monday due dates; it's often a pretty skimpy pile that comes in. Yet
one of my clues that something is different about the Creed Project is
that week by week more and more students come to school Mondays
with Creed inquiries ready for me to spotcheck. (For a vignette depicting such a case, see Zarlasht's at the end of Chapter Eleven.) This time
of year I'm typically carrying more sets of unread essays than I can
count, much less imagine finding time to read. So rather than add more
to my pile, Mondays I just walk the room spotchecking (stamping)
these steps. Unless a student has obviously just scribbled a few lines
hoping to get the stamp, sitting there with ink still glistening, I give her
a stamp whether or not she has written a page and a half. Many students, you'll see shortly, tend to add more material later. After I stamp,
we talk about how this weekend's Creed inquiry went, and I'll field
more questions. Probably the most important thing I do during all our
conversations about the Creed Project is listen. Students see that I am
sincerely interested in what they are experiencing and in how I can
help them during the weeks of their reflections. During the week, when
hands go up with Creed-related questions, no matter what else is vying
for our time I'm *always* willing to keep this conversation going. And,
as the project goes on, students insist on it.

After a few years of June presentations, whether inadvertently or
otherwise, students will have left behind a few visual aids from their
own presentations. Don't throw these out, especially ones you think
will give next year's students a good idea where all this is going! More
and more, as the project becomes a tradition at American High School,
students actually present me with their visual aids for the benefit of
classes in coming years. My oldest sample from the early years is a
surrealistic paper mache sculpture from Jeremy (a creative child, if a
bit strange by his own admission) depicting a swelling extraterrestrial
landscape studded with action figurines. Last year Jason Ichimaru
donated his beautiful Japanese garden scene made of wood, gravel, and
greenery. And I now have a portfolio containing Creed presentation
posters by students from cultures around the country and world. Once
students have done a Creed inquiry or two, I'll set up my sample visual
aids around the room and take them on a tour. This is a great way to
help them get a feel for the many possibilities the project can allow.

Toward the end of third quarter, I collect Steps I through IV in a
packet with a cover and rubric (see the end of Chapter Twelve). If you

find yourself itching to know how their reflections are progressing, it would make equally good sense to divide up the rubric and collect Steps I and II in one chunk, and III and IV in another. Or, if your curiosity is too much, you could collect Step I when complete. However you do it, you'll need to remember to have students print out an extra copy for themselves (and of course save and back up all these files), because the project is cumulative and they'll need to refer to previous steps to write the next ones.

A crucial factor in all this is trust. As you discovered in Part One, some students are going to be writing about things they may never have put on paper before, and will likely feel squeamish sharing these things with you. As part of the trust we need to build for the presentations, before I collect their written reflections I announce that if students have parts they'd rather keep private they may either delete them from my copy, or put self-adhesive notes over sensitive places, or write notes telling me what not to read. I honor their requests, and only partly because it reduces my reading load. You can bet that most students, at some point during the reflections, will find themselves in a serious mode of self-discovery, a new experience for many if not most. Issues possibly not thought about before may tumble out unexpectedly. So it's important for them to feel this whole process of personal reflection is something that is theirs and that they have control over. This becomes especially true when we come to the presentations (Chapter Thirteen).

I mentioned in the previous section that more students can get aboard the project when we introduce its steps from different perspectives and use varying language in our explanations. This spiraling approach is also important because hearing the same words over and over again is *boring*, and therefore mind-numbing. So when responding to their questions I tend to give them several terms in a string. In explaining Step IIIA, for example, I might say:

> So in Step IG you wrote about what you think the people who influenced you *stand for*, what they *value*, *what's important* to them. Remember? Here in Step IIIA you'll be taking that same thinking operation, asking that same question—*what does someone care about? what matters most to them? what do they stand for?*—but this time you'll be turning the question toward yourself. [terms are italicized]

I try to vary the *order* in which I give these terms, and I'm always looking for new ones to flavor the soup. We want the message to be consistent without being predictable. There's a certain quality of mystery to keep alive in all this, and language has its part to play. This mystery is not something that needs to be manufactured, just kept alive. We already are the most serious mysteries we encounter; it's just that we don't take the opportunity to think about our mysteries much. But it's also true that mysteries can be better understood with sincere and consistent effort. This may be a good moment to reread the Rumi poem at the beginning of Chapter One.

As students learn to become comfortable with this "new style of learning," they tend, I mentioned earlier, to have more to say. Knowing this now, I invite them to go back and add material at any point during the fifteen weeks or so of reflections to any Step I through IV inquiry they've started. This very often happens even without my invitation. Students who have not been sighted all year with a question about homework look up apologetically as I walk the room stamping papers and ask if it's okay if they add more to a given Creed inquiry—days or even weeks after I've stamped it.

Joe is bright and yet almost on principle has severe allergies to schoolwork. Toward the end of the semester the only actual entry in his otherwise blank row in my gradebook was a decent score for his Creed Project. This is Joe's most committed and genuine writing of the year:

> The creed project has helped me find out things about myself that I would have never known before. At first I thought that this project was going to be the same stupid work that had to do with learning and school, but after I started getting into it I was so infatuated with this creed project. This project allowed me to experience deeper thoughts and explorations of my mind and soul. I found out things about my family and friends that all of a sudden appeared in my head. . . . This project was tough at times to understand but paid off in the end. . . . It was a good experience for my mind because the farther I got the more the project meant to me.
>
> —Joe Deanda, June 2003

This is another of those statements whose sincerity is pretty much beyond suspicion. Even had I been gripped by an unwarranted (in Joe's case) outpouring of mercy, Joe's chances of passing the class were an iceberg's in Iraq in July. Yet Joe's comment shows how students' ability or inclination to engage in personal reflection seems to increase as the process becomes more familiar. And Joe goes on to capture the essence of the enthusiastic thirst for self-discovery that I see increasingly each June, the same enthusiasm that fuels me in writing this book during my summer vacation. And Joe leads me to something I want you to see.

Why by all indications did the Creed experience excite every one of my sophomores this past year—from Joe, who earned one of the lowest Fs in my most squirrelly (if sweetest) class, to Elyse, who earned an A+ in one of the brightest, most hardworking honors contingents I have ever encountered? There is, I think I have discovered, a *specific* reason for this.

The *Aha!* Beneath Invisible Water

When I first realized it, we had recently crossed over into Nevada from southwestern Utah, driving home from Mesa Verde National Park. I was sitting in the passenger seat, legs outstretched on the dash during my wife's stint at the wheel, our two daughters in the back of the van, napping or reading. Most people, I'm slowly realizing, aren't like this, but there's almost no place I'd rather *think* than in Nevada. It's the expanse and the deceptive subtlety of the landscape. My daughters think it's flat and boring. But to me it's endlessly fascinating, with the succession of ranges and basins and the always present sense that you're driving at the bottom of what was once an inland sea, hundreds, sometimes thousands of feet of prehistoric water towering up there overhead.

I was thinking back on the workshop I had offered a few days before at a conference in Estes Park, Colorado. Just before this workshop was to begin, I got the idea that workshop participants might want to actually *experience* the Creed Project, rather than simply read a summary or listen to me tell about it. Writing quickly on transparencies in the minutes before participants arrived, I had developed the first workshop-length Personal Creed process. (This one took us all of twenty-five minutes.) What I was thinking about as the Nevada landscape stretched out my thinking space was the look on the face of one teacher-participant. In the opening parts of the workshop he had seemed only mildly interested. But once my instructions for the Creed Project simulation went onscreen and participants began their reflections, his appearance seemed to change. He bent intently over his writing. Looking up suddenly, he interrupted the writing silence to ask if the instructions onscreen were in the workshop handout. It was the look on his face when he learned that they were not: That was the look I was thinking about now. He looked *bereft*!

I had already developed the continuum-of-learning idea you read about in Chapter Seven, the understanding that learning is inherently satisfying when it involves us in the coordinated processes of mastering facts, composing meanings, and discovering values. What crashed suddenly into my mind is that my teacher-friend looked bereft because he was having an experience he found *satisfying*, so satisfying in that moment that, being a teacher, he wanted to be able pass it right along to his students. His learning was in flow—he was *in the continuum*! And when he learned that these scribbled onscreen instructions for what he later told me was the most valuable experience in this workshop for him—and potentially for his students—when he heard that these instructions were not even in the handout, he was dumbfounded. *Why in the world,* his expression had asked me, *would you leave the main item in your workshop out of your handout?* Only crossing into Nevada did I suddenly realize more specifically what was happening to my teacher-friend Rick Brunson, an art teacher in Detroit.

All this had come from my urge to understand the increasingly enthusiastic response year by year to the Creed Project I had stumbled into developing with my students. This urge had led me to a series of readings in James Moffett, in *The Urantia Book,* and elsewhere on topics such as the importance of interrelating facts, meanings, and values in how we make sense of the universe (see Chapters Five, Six, and Seven). Ruminating on all this, still trying to understand my students' enthusiasm, I had extrapolated the Continuum of Learning Purposes (Figure 7–1), which forms the core of what I call the Central Aim and Purposes of Twenty-First-Century Learning (Figure 7–2). Adding in goals for practice, I finally went on to synthesize the Model of Twenty-First-Century Learning (Figure 8–1). I thought these graphics looked impressive in my workshop handouts. But what I had not realized in these heady ruminations, and what Rick's face helped me understand, is that *the first three steps of the Creed Project themselves comprise a sequence of learning experiences accurately described by the continuum.* I'll show you what I mean.

Creed Step I, in asking us to take an inventory of the people, events, and circumstances that have most influenced our lives, is asking us *to master certain important facts of our lives.* When in Creed Step II we are asked to evaluate these influences, to make a judgment about which influence we value most and which least, we are being asked *to consider the facts of our lives and create a meaning* from them. And now that we have formed some judgments about our influences, Step III asks us to reflect on *what about us,* at a deeper level, is inducing us to make this particular evaluation, to choose this influence as most admirable and that as least admirable? *What values,* Step III asks, *drove that judgment?* This whole thought is represented in Figure 9–3.

Extrapolating and synthesizing in trying to understand the enthusiasm, I had gone everywhere but to the very learning experience that had generated it. *This* is why the Creed Project works! On Rick's face was a validation of the reality of the learning continuum. Right in front of me, the Creed Project simulation had enabled Rick to experience a "continuum learning experience," the very source of the excitement. But these particular reflections in the Creed Project must be only one example of this kind of multilevel learning experience. Will all such learning experiences, then, generate this kind of excitement?

This particular continuum learning experience appears remarkable beyond the fact that it is a continuum learning experience. By definition, all such multilevel learning experiences allow us to con-

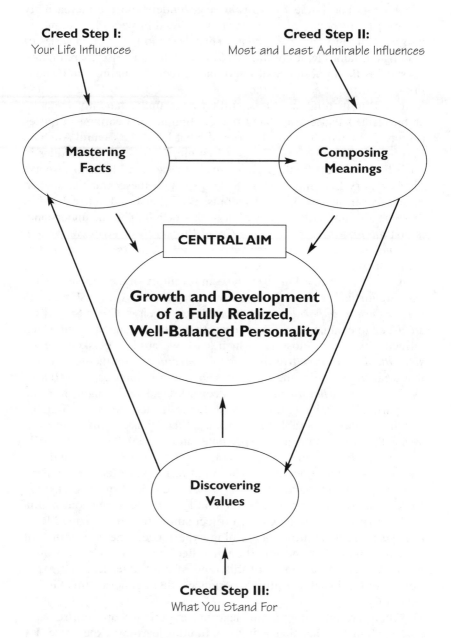

Figure 9–3 Creed Project Connections to the Learning Continuum

nect facts and meanings with the process of finding our *values* (see Chapter Seven). In any such learning experience, this values region of the continuum can bring what we are learning closer to what matters to us. But not all such multilevel learning experiences have the same potential to do that.

In a continuum learning experience on, say, mitosis, the *facts* are confined to what is scientifically observable; any *meanings* one draws from these facts, through processes like inference and analysis, usually have more relevance to science than to one's personal life. The topic of mitosis may become more personally meaningful when one's system of *values* is challenged to take a position on a congressional bill, say, on using our tax revenues to pay a corporation to research a technique that uses the process of mitosis to produce biological weapons. But it is really the moral issue, and not the process of mitosis itself that engages us personally. Still, creating a values connection to introduce a lesson on mitosis would seem a promising way to initially engage students in the lesson.

The example of attending a musical performance (p. 55) is inherently more personal, and therefore has more potential to engage, than a lesson on mitosis. True, the facts—number of performers, musical score, instruments played, physical features of the performance space— while potentially more personally relevant than the scientific facts concerning mitosis, are simply facts, not *necessarily* relevant personally to the listener. But the meanings the performance can call from a listener are more likely to become quite personal. They could range from a matter-of-fact analysis of the quality of the performance's musicianship to a vibrant painting erupting out of an artist's emotional response to the experience. And the values one might be moved to contemplate or affirm as a result of the performance, the third hub of a continuum learning experience, again, are all inherently personal. Why is this musical experience more potentially engaging than the mitosis lesson? *Because two of the three continuum hubs in this experience are more likely to induce connections that are inherently personal.* And so different experiences—depending on the facts, meanings, and values associated with them—have differing potentials to matter to us personally.

An experience such as the Creed Project, compared to the two previous examples, is a different echelon of continuum learning, one that has an almost exponentially greater potential to engage learners. Again, in the mitosis example only the values connection is inherently personal, and the connection probably does not arise directly from the process of cell division; the facts and meanings derive mainly from observation and analysis. The musical performance can call up two hubs of the continuum—meanings and values—that are fundamentally personal; the facts are only personal to listeners in specific cases, such as if one were a musician, or the mother of the architect who designed the performance hall. In the Creed Project, however, not only the *values* connection but the very *facts* and *meanings* also come *directly from our lives*. Indeed, the values connection in this learning experience is *our values themselves*. The entire interconnected, interdependent, multilevel learning experience revolves around what is personal to ourselves! So the *type* of learning experience (continuum) overlaps with the *subject* of the learning experience (ourselves), and we see the kind of enthusiasm for the Creed Project that I have been trying to understand these past three years. My teacher-friend Rick's face—and nearly an entire workshop of similarly disgruntled teachers' faces several weeks later, when I failed to allow time for them to *present* their Creed reflections—showed me that, like my sophomores, we are all hungry for learning experiences that make rich connections around the learning continuum. But there is another factor involved in this hunger, I think, and other reasons why the Creed Project, or any continuum learning experience that is personally meaningful enough, can satisfy it.

Multiple Satisfactions

American culture has always admired the can-do spirit, the belief that if you strike while the iron is hot, opportunity will knock. The second President Bush described civilian administrator in charge of reconstructing Iraq L. Paul Bremer as a "can-do" kind of guy. But is the simple optimism that is so intertwined with what we have called the American dream really equal to the tasks confronting twenty-first-century American power in bringing stability and peace to a region as un-American in can-do values as the Middle East? Or will these challenges demonstrate to us that the simple American optimism of our adolescence is running out of gas (and oil) as we move toward adulthood as a culture? Can the can-do spirit alone continue to satisfy (if it ever did) our hunger for deeper connections to life and reality?

I believe we Americans are hungry for a more deeply founded reason to carry on, a deeper force that will help us rise to a challenge like those facing us in the Middle East and the necessity to reckon with the forces and causes of terror. With such daunting tasks as now face our culture in what we must recognize as a new historical period, mere optimism, a grand force when a wide-open continent is waiting to be tamed and settled, is suddenly more akin to a blind confidence in the favor of the gods. Optimism does not require reflective thought about one's life and larger purpose.

Hope, by contrast, has roots in more cosmic soil. It is not possible to engage in hope without having undertaken a consideration of who one is and what one values. Hope, as Kantor's spectrum defines it (see

Chapter One), is activated by *ideals*. Until we re-engage our own ideals at this deeper level, we will create more problems in the world, given the enormity of U.S. military power, than we'll ever solve. Learning experiences like the Creed Project have their part to play in this.

This project, in essence, is a conversation about what we stand for. The conversation begins with individual reflections, expands into wider circles as students share their reflections with classmates (as you saw in Chapters Two and Four and will see more in coming chapters), and culminates most powerfully in the Creed presentations. And the conversation, hopefully, does not end with the presentations, but goes on to include others as it continues over the course of the onetime sophomores' lives. Being a powerful conversation about what we stand for, the Creed Project is a conversation about our *ideals*. Such a conversation, according to Kantor's spectrum, has the capacity to generate large quantities of *hope*. I have often observed the immediate effect of this conversation on students. Josh is one example. Having written in his Creed reflections of difficulties during the previous year in retaining his faith in humanity, essentially of *doubts* to use Kantor's term, Josh wrote in his portfolio after witnessing several days of Creed presentations:

> After watching the presentations, my view was no longer negative of the people around me. This shows a great deal of transition in the way I view people. I am glad that this project has assisted me in becoming a more optimistic person.
>
> —Josh Hollister, June 2003

Though he uses the term "optimistic," Josh is referring to mere can-do optimism, which often seems to spring from the assumption that our lifestyle is a sign that God is smiling on America. Josh is referring to something deeper. To use Kantor's language, the culmination in the Creed presentations of our semester-long conversation about our influences and what we might stand for strengthened Josh's *ideals* enough to shift his attitude about life from *doubt* to *hope*, perhaps even somewhat rekindling his *faith* in humanity. His new view, he wrote, "shows a great deal of transition in the way I view people." Can-do optimism tells us that if we just believe in ourselves, use our heads, and stick to it, we can find a way to prosper and pass on our hard-earned prosperity to our children. Hope in the American tradition is a deeper thing. It is founded on the democratic ideals that originally grew not from pursuit of a mere lifestyle, but from *reflections* about life and purpose in the universe, reflections that made it possible for American ideals to appear in the world. Before the Founding Fathers founded, those fathers engaged in some serious reflections about their colonial pasts, what those influences gave them to believe about what was true, good, and beautiful, and what they therefore should now stand for and put their legs under. It is no wonder, then, that Josh and so many others are moved toward a more hopeful view of life as a result of the Creed presentations and the conversation about ideals they culminate. American culture has been a hopeful culture because American democracy itself is founded on a conversation about ideals. American democracy is doomed to extinction, however, if in pursuit and defense of our mere lifestyle, those of us who call ourselves Americans continue in our willingness to abandon the continuing cultivation of reflective thought that keeps democratic ideals alive and relevant to our lives today. The present administration has allowed this conversation to lapse. The Creed Project, and other experiences like it, stand to help renew the conversation.

As you prepare to set the stage to lead your students through this experience, then, it may help to keep these few points we've established in Chapter Nine not too far in the back of your mind:

- Students' and teachers' responses to the project strongly suggest that to learn by gathering facts, creating meanings from those facts, and ascertaining how these facts and meanings pertain to what one stands for is to learn in a way that is inherently satisfying.

- Such continuum learning experiences can come in various kinds with varying potentials to lead to satisfying learning. The personal nature of experiences like the Creed Project, we've seen, makes possible an even deeper level of satisfaction in learning than even other kinds of continuum learning experiences allow.

- And perhaps the Creed Project, by bringing us a personally founded conversation about ideals, also lights a pilot light that can kindle a deeper level of hope in us. If America is to rise to the challenges it faces today, and if American democracy is going to continue to keep the pilot lit on the world stage, this is an essential process.

CHAPTER TEN

Introducing the Project

Professor Johnson,
The Creed Project has been an amazing experience—it has been the one college project I have really put my heart and soul into. The most important thing I've learned, though, is taking a step back. To look at my life, to understand where I have been, to see where I may be heading.
　　　　　　　　　　—Mackenzie Ryan, American University,
　　　　　　　　　　　　　　Washington, D.C., April 2001

A search for happiness often becomes a recipe for misery. A search for meaning often produces happiness as a by-product.
　　　　　　　　　　　　　　　　　—Betty Stone

Setting the Stage Through the Year: Three Activities

In Chapter Nine you saw how I learned that for a number of reasons it makes more sense to *intertwine* the *personal learning* of the Personal Creed reflections with the ongoing *academic learning* of novels and essays (not to mention vocabulary and language study and all the other morsels on the standards-heaped plates of English classes), than it does to separate the two kinds of learning in discrete curricular chunks. This, you may recall, is one reason why I lengthened the project through an entire semester. But even before we stretched out the Creed Project this past year, I'd been experimenting with ways to honor students' calls for more of this kind of personal learning *throughout* the year. This has developed into the approach I've begun to call Two-Legged Curriculum, which you can read about in Chapter Fourteen. I think students are warming to the Creed Project more readily during the second semester in recent years, now that throughout the year they've been regularly exploring in a variety of ways and in a variety of activities the kind of learning that helps them explore themselves and consider their relationships to others and the world and universe. (I suspect that this kind of learning, carefully intertwined with academic learning, has great potential to help disengaged students engage in school.) So I try to *weave into* our schedule of academic learning a number of approaches and activities that help students do this personal learning. I think of the curriculum, then, as having two legs, academic and personal, and we talk about it this way in the classroom. Chapter Fourteen will more fully introduce the Two-Legged designing I have done, and hopefully inspire and tool you up to do some of your own. For now, I'll call your attention to the sections in Chapter Fourteen on the Wisdom Project, Big Questions, and the Thought Log. You may want to peruse what these sections say about these three activities after reading of them here. Here I'll touch only briefly on how they help set the stage for the Creed Project.

At the beginning of the year, we are not ready for the kind of deep personal reflection students will encounter second semester. The *Wisdom Project* introduces the notion of wisdom on a more general, cultural level, and opens the door to many of the themes we'll explore through the year in our study of literature. In addition to the many academic standards the Wisdom Project helps students address (see Appendix II), it introduces the notion that wisdom is something universal, something common to all cultures yet unique to each in flavor. With this scaffolding, it may be easier for students to later begin considering and approaching the more personal wisdom they attempt to find in the Creed Project. I think activating the "personal leg" of our curriculum with such a project helps seed the classroom ground for the personal learning I want to weave across the course through the year.

On the academic leg, I take "entry" diagnostic reading and writing assessments from students in the fall, and "exit" assessments, including their portfolios, in the spring. This entry-exit planning concept also works on the personal leg. If the Wisdom Project is the "entry" to the personal leg of our course, the Creed Project is the "exit." Unlike arguably measurable academic skills, personal learning, given healthy conditions to develop, lends itself to assessment more by demonstration than by measurement.

Now that we have beginning and end points, how do we carry strands of personal learning between entry and exit experiences on the personal leg? *Big Questions* are one of the ways my students weave personal learning through the year. For Inquiry 1 (see Chapter Fourteen), the first personal writing of the fall, students list all the "Big Questions" about life, reality, the world, the universe, their boyfriends, and all the other cosmic queries they can squeeze from their brains.

Choosing the top three, and later the *one* that most holds their interest, they write their first night's journal entry explaining why this one question holds their interest more than others. This is homework for Day One. (Not strangely, as you'll see in Chapter Fourteen, students' Big Questions tend to have direct connections to our course themes.)

On Day Two, I ask them to bring in an object that somehow reflects either this question or something important about themselves, and they meet their classmates in an activity called the Big Question Meet. Forming two facing lines down the center of the classroom, the new sophomores shake hands across the divide, greet one another, share their brought objects, and have a one- to two-minute conversation about their Big Questions before moving to the next person across the divide. In not much more than twenty minutes, each student has met and had a meaningful conversation with fully half her classmates.

As the year goes on, I encourage students to find ways to tailor essay assignments and even final exam essays to address their Big Questions. I also try to remind myself through the year to ask students to make Big Question connections in their journals with our literature and course activities. The activity comes to fruition during the second semester in the personal leg's "exit" project, the Creed Project. Taking the Big Question approach to a more personal level now, students reflect in both earlier and later Creed steps about how Big Questions may have influenced them, may be forming part of what they believe they stand for, or be important in their visions of their futures.

"Meaning," writes literary scholar David Patterson, "is a response to a question" (1). This particular quote, while it lends some pretty strong credence to the use of Big Questions, may be a bit abstract for some students to reflect upon. But it's a good example of the provocative quotes my students encounter in a popular activity we call the *Thought Log*. Roughly twice a week, while I'm taking roll, students will be copying such a quote from the screen into their Thought Logs, and reflecting on its meaning in a number of ways you can explore in Chapter Fourteen. When they're done writing, they share their responses to the quote in pairs or with their local teams. We'll then have a whole-class discussion. Because I often choose quotes to fit themes or literary works or current events, these discussions are often lively, and they connect well to the rest of the class activities for the day and week. Through the Thought Log, students gain a degree of practice over the year in deciphering and interpreting complex ideas and participating in team and class discussions, giving students a good deal of practice meeting a good number of reading standards and speaking and listening standards.

As I see it, though, the Thought Log most of all gives students practice in learning to think. This thinking takes shape not only as they engage new topics but also as they use new operations of thought, operations such as inferring and discerning, that assist students in making sound judgments. These are essential skills in learning to reflect. As you might suspect, all these Thought Log–related skills help students work toward the Creed Project, when each student will choose a Thought Log–style quote to represent his or her creed. In Appendix II you'll find sample Thought Log quotes from my ever-growing collection of Thought Log quotes.

These are just three examples of how personal learning can be woven through the year between personal entry and exit projects, and help set the stage for a culminating experience such as the Creed Project; Chapter Fourteen introduces a number of additional methods I use to this end. As I introduce the Wisdom Project in the fall, I make a point of mentioning the spring-semester Creed Project, and how this first project will help students prepare both academically and personally for the two final projects of the year: their portfolio and the Creed Project. I may even show them an overhead of how I visualize the course as Two-Legged (see Figure 14–2 on page 165). I want them to begin becoming conscious of their personal learning early in the year. As I see it, the personal learning component should be subtle, not overly overt, not too demystified. I want to be careful not to beat them over the head with the personal leg. That's what the academic leg is for!

Customizing the Project

If you experiment successfully with the project, perhaps you will feel led to develop your own customized version. You may even prefer to put your own stamp on the project from the beginning and rewrite the instructions to your taste. But the quickest, easiest way to get started would be to simply use the instructions you find annotated in this and coming chapters, and can download complete from my website (www.universeWired.com). Let these instructions and my annotations work in the way that is best for you and your students. Read the instructions and the annotations. Once you've got a good sense of how the project's pieces work as a whole, be creative and make your own adaptations!

If you work with students younger than high school sophomores, or with college students or adults, I suggest tailoring your own version of these instructions up front. Working with my daughter Rebecca in the year before her thirteenth birthday to create a coming-of-age project for her based on the Creed Project, I learned that, however bright they may be, twelve- and thirteen-year-olds simply do not warm up to personal reflection like fifteen- and sixteen-year-olds. Though Rebecca is quite reflective by nature, her hunger and developmental readiness

to reflect on meaning and purpose in her life may need the three inter-
vening years to mature and develop. College freshmen, however, judging by the comments from Leah Johnson and her students at American
University in Washington, D.C., take to the reflective thought the project elicits even more readily than high school sophomores. Adults,
unlike the other three groups I've mentioned, have the asset of life
experience, which may increase the hunger for reflection, yet we also
carry the potential liability of difficult-to-overcome attitudes and
habits. So you'll need to ensure a match between the written instructions you give your students and the realities of their lives. The making of such connections is part of the artistry of teaching.

If you decide to customize a version for your students, here is one
approach you might take. Put yourself as much as possible in the mental and emotional mind-set of the people you'll be taking through the
project, using meditation or whatever technique works best for you to
clear and focus your mind. Download the entire instruction packet,
print out a hard copy, and read carefully through the instructions from
beginning to end. Get out a pen and go to work, revising language and
content as you think will communicate these instructions to your students in the most natural and effective manner, noting questions you
have as you go but not turning yet to my annotations in the book. Use
your judgment. Trust your inklings. Then—once you're *invested* in the
project from inside your students' minds—read through the instructions and annotations in the book, asking yourself further questions
and making more notes.

Preparing Handout Packets

This past year, I started students out with an eight-page packet that
included the following:

- A simple cover (you can see mine on the website)
- A graphic overlook and schedule of the Creed reflections you can
  find on page 95
- Two pages of orientation and introduction (beginning on p. 96)
- Complete step-by-step instructions for Steps I and II (download-
  able from the website)

As we completed Step II, they received a second packet, this one four
pages and containing:

- Complete instructions for Steps III and IV (website)
- An overview of Step V, the presentations

Breaking the handouts into two packets has some advantages. On the practical level, you'd rather students lose an eight-page handout than the whole twelve. On the strategic level, by holding off on the last two steps, you can customize them based on up-to-the-minute developments with your students on the classroom ground. Based on questions that came up in our conversations during the first two steps of reflections this past year, I made a number of adjustments to the last two. Finally, on the learning level, doling instructions out may help some students stay focussed on the tasks at hand, and not soar prematurely off into the Creed stratosphere before they've got their reflective wings.

Let's get started then. Remember, both the instructions and the annotations are written from my perspective working with sophomores, but you should read (and revise) them with an eye to your own clientele. We begin on the next page with the Project Overlook and Schedule (Figure 10–1). Annotations begin below.

Annotations for Project Overlook and Schedule

On the reverse of a simple packet cover, I begin my instructions with a one-page preview of the project. The quadrant—you'll recognize Figure 9–1—gives students the same at-a-glance overlook you had last chapter, except that the quadrant for the presentation is absent. I save this for later because I don't want to overload them all at once and because I want them to open up as fully as possible to the first tasks at hand. In general, in the earlier phases of the project I try not to overemphasize the presentations. Many will be overly concerned about being "required" to stand and deliver their private lives. When these concerns come up, and they will, I aim for quiet reassurance. As I mentioned earlier, one way to allay such concerns is to display visual aids from students who survived the experience in the year before. At some point, you will be able to find some samples at my website. In the meantime, you might find reading aloud some of the student testimonials in various places in this book a useful method of putting your students at ease by helping them see where they are going with this project. (For more on facilitating the presentations, see the section on Coaching in Chapter Thirteen.)

If you are better at scheduling than I am, you can lay out your due dates ahead of time. But I prefer to leave the dates blank, just fixing an overall end date, and then setting due dates for intermediate steps depending on our actual progress. Remember, the thinking this project entails is new to most fifteen- and sixteen-year-olds, and the pacing of the project depends to some degree on you as well. So keep your eye on the need to finish the reflections (Steps I–IV) with enough

Creed Project Overlook and Approximate Schedule

Steps I–IV Overlook

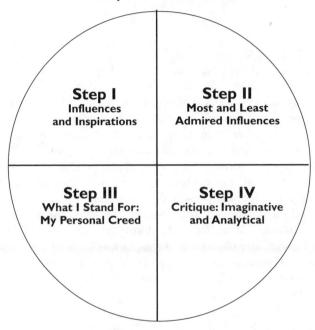

Step I
Influences
and Inspirations

Step II
Most and Least
Admired Influences

Step III
What I Stand For:
My Personal Creed

Step IV
Critique: Imaginative
and Analytical

Approximate Schedule

Steps I–IV: Creed Reflections			Points
Step I (A–G)	(7 Creed Inquiries)	Due: _____	70
Step II (A–C)	(3 Creed Inquiries)	Due: _____	30
Step III (A–D)	(4 Creed Inquiries)	Due: _____	40
Step IV (A–C)	(3 Creed Inquiries)	Due: _____	30
Writing Quality/Correctness			20
Steps I–IV Packet (w/cover sheet and rubric)		Due: _____	
		I–IV subtotal ...	**190**

Step V: Creed Presentation / Application			
Presentation Option **A** (w/Visual or other)		Due: _____	50
OR Presentation Option **B** (w/Reflective Essay)		Due: _____	or 50
AND Query Letter on Creed-Related Volunteering		Due: _____	and 10
Step V complete		V subtotal ...	**60**

Project Total ... /250

Figure 10–1 Creed Project Overlook and Approximate Schedule

time to fit in at least a week of presentations at the end of the term, but be flexible *within* that framework. If you prefer a more specific week-by-week timeline, see Figure 9–1 (p. 73) and the section on Management in Chapter Nine.

Grading

For specific suggestions on grading Creed inquiries, see the section on Management in Chapter Nine. As for overall grading, I use a point system only by default, since I haven't yet found a better way. Spring semester seems to total around 2,000 points, so the entire Creed Project comprises little more than 10 percent of students' spring semester grades, the presentation itself only around 2 percent. You'll need to adjust this scale according to your grading system, the age level of your students, and the weight you want to assign the project. Increasingly, as I feel the personal leg of the course is solid and defensible, I weight personal learning more. Most of the other personal learning activities aside from the Creed Project at this point—the Wisdom Project, Big Questions, Thought Log, and others—serve both academic and personal purposes, and so I do not yet think of separate weighting. Below, you find the opening portion of the student instructions for the Creed Project.

Student Instructions: Opening Portion

ENGLISH 10cp   WORLD LITERATURE
Envisioning a Life
The Personal Creed Project
Spring 20___

"You can know a lot,
and understand very little."
—Toni Morrison

Dear Sophomore,

With this quote, we kick off the major project on the personal leg of our course: your Personal Creed Project. One of my main hopes is that this course helps you realize the surprising way your experiences in life flow directly from your vision of life. Your personal vision is like the headwaters of your life. Not far downstream from your vision of life your values form, further along your viewpoints, then your attitudes and—only then, sometimes bobbing along far from their upstream source—your actions. Mine too.

I hope you can see how important it is for each of us to devote some care and thought to building a personal vision of life. (Remember the title of this course? Hint: check the fine print at the top center of this page.) To serve us well, a vision of life must help us harmonize the inner realities of our hearts, minds, and spirits with the often conflicting outer realities of our world. I hope this course—and particularly this project—will spark, or renew, your own search for a personal vision.

Annotations: Heading and Course Title

I'm not certain when I decided I would start giving each course I teach a name, but it was probably when I returned to American High School after two years of midcareer graduate courses in the English Department at San Francisco State University. I had taken courses that had been created and named by teachers—some wonderful teachers—rather than by the district committees that had thus far made such decisions for me, with intriguing creations like "English 9" and "English 10." After two or three years of experimenting, I settled on "Envisioning a Life" for my sophomore course. The choice stems from the thinking I continue to do on developing a schoolwide thematic curriculum using developmentally tuned grade-level themes (see Chapter Fourteen). The sophomore theme that makes most sense to me is Expanding Horizons, because sophomores are able to see further and more widely than they could as freshmen, yet are not obliged to narrow their focus on post–high school plans to the degree they will as juniors. "Envisioning a Life" also works especially well with the Creed Project. As you can see, I avoid raising district fur by also including the official course title. I've used different quotes to "kick off" the project. This one from *Song of Solomon* is my current favorite. You may find others you like in the sample Thought Log quotes in Appendix III.

Annotations: Creed Reflections Kickoff Paragraphs

The two introductory paragraphs for students that begin on page 96 have worked strangely well to introduce my sophomores to the project. Whether this is because these opening paragraphs have been developed and refined over a decade or more, or because some Dumbledorian spell has somehow worked its magic into them, I can't be sure. But neither can I recall a time when reading them aloud in class failed to produce at least the semblance of interest from students. Again, if you work with a different age group than sophomores, you may be wise to tailor up your own version of these introductory paragraphs. Just find a way to keep a little magic in them.

The two paragraphs that follow them (not reproduced here; download complete instructions at website) are self-explanatory, and again I invite you to use them verbatim or customize as you see fit. The rest of the project overview for students gives them a taste of what's coming and how it may be important for them. You are now ready to help them take Step I, in which they reflect on the influences and inspirations that have shaped them.

 CHAPTER ELEVEN

Steps I and II

The best intuition is founded on a base of knowledge.
—Sonia Choquette

Between the first two Creed steps described in this chapter, students undertake ten inquiries. In Step I they inquire mainly into their pasts; when they complete Step II, they will have begun reflecting on the present. Most Creed inquiries consist of

- a list, which generates the possibilities for
- any number of reflective paragraphs.

You'll find guidelines and tips for coaching students in writing the Creed inquiries in the Management section of Chapter Nine.

Step I—Influences and Inspirations

This is the longest step in the project. You'll need roughly eight weeks, a week each for Creed Inquiries IA through IG, with a week or so of cushion time for kicking off the project and inevitable unforseens. Remember that the reason for allotting a week per inquiry is to build in gestating time, and that this gestating time allows the project's weekly time commitment to be minimal, both in class and at home, and that these reflections should create little impact on other coursework. Step I at this point consists of seven inquiries. Figure 11–1 gives you an overlook.

Contents of Creed Step I Inquiries: Influences and Inspirations

Figure 11-1 Creed Step I Inquiries: Influences and Inspirations

Student Instructions: Creed Inquiry IA— Circumstances

- Make a list of 5 to 10 *general circumstances* that have influenced and/or inspired you. (Include at least one that may have been less than positive.) Some possibilities:
  - The place(s) I have lived
  - Nature: how connected I feel to it
  - My environment: the state of my local environment
  - The personality I have been born with
  - My gender
  - The color of my skin
  - The heritage or culture (or blend of cultures) that comes down to me:
    - History

- • Customs
- • Religion
- • Food
- • Art, music, etc.
- • Cultural attitudes/values/beliefs
- • Language
- • Others?
- • Others?

- Of these circumstances, choose 3 to 5 you feel have been most influential in shaping the person you are today.

- For each of the 3–5 most influential circumstances, write a reflective paragraph on how it has affected, influenced, inspired, or changed you.

Annotations: Creed Inquiry IA—Circumstances

Here the emphasis is on the general background facts of one's life rather than its specific events, which is the topic of the next inquiry. To make the distinction clear, it may help your students to have them compare the list of possibilities in the Step IA instructions with the Step IB list. (At any point during the project when your own level of comfort allows, you may find your students benefit from examples you can model from your own life.) Is it really essential, you may ask, that each student clearly understand the differences between the two groups of influences? I'd say it's helpful but not worth making into an enormous issue. It's more important that students wet their feet and gain practice reflecting on who and what have influenced their lives than that they make utterly clear distinctions among types of influences, though it is valuable to realize that we can reflect in different ways, from different perspectives, and for different purposes. It *is* crucial, however, that students include at least one less-than-positive influence. This is because they'll need a *range* of choices when, in Step II, they come to *evaluate* their influences.

The list of possibilities you see above in the Creed Inquiry IA section in the student instructions is not the be-all end-all list, and probably reflects my own teaching goals more than it does any ideal set of standards for reflection. For one thing, you'll notice an emphasis on race and heritage as influences, a legacy of teaching in the culturally complex San Francisco Bay Area, and especially in Fremont where I work. The item about skin color, which may seem out of place in some parts of the country, I include because one of my teaching goals is to cultivate a rich class conversation about race, which I believe can help my students of all racial backgrounds whose daily experience, and therefore approach to learning, is particularly affected by race (see Chapter Four). Of course, it is not only students of color whose daily lives are affected by race.

Because religion, the lack thereof, or the reaction thereagainst significantly shape most of us, and can likewise powerfully shape our attitudes toward learning, I also include an invitation to reflect on the influence of religion or spirituality. Again, I am careful when this topic comes up to model tolerance and understanding, and to make it clear that our emphasis in the Creed Project is personal rather than doctrinal, on sharing rather than on preaching, and that it is important that no one in the room, including atheists and agnostics, feel excluded during this process. Rarely have we had difficulties in this area.

Even when one parent took the opportunity of having been included in his child's Creed presentation video to expound at some length onscreen on the student's Christian faith, and I felt a fairly strong hint of preaching, I chose not to overreact. Over the past decade and a half in Fremont, students of such different racial, cultural, and religious backgrounds have grown up in the same neighborhoods and schools that, as strange as this may sound in many places, intolerance is generally no longer a great problem. In this global suburb, many students are actually interested in learning about one another's religions, and I felt no strong indications of discomfort among students over this presentation. I simply joined in the applause when the presentation ended and the next day found a good moment to put out a gentle, general reminder that as much as possible we try to keep the particulars of specific religions to a minimum and, if we choose to share our religion, we focus more on its effects in our lives than on the beliefs themselves. To underscore the free wills of all, I think it is also important to regularly remind students that the items on the list are only sample possibilities for reflection, and that students should decide which list items to emphasize and which to leave out. If you are ready to invite this issue into the mix, you'll need to attune yourself to the religious realities in the community where you teach. A very solid resource on dealing with religion appropriately in the classroom is *Taking Religion Seriously Across the Curriculum*, by Warren A. Nord and Charles C. Haynes. To whatever degree you can, I suggest tailoring your lists as I have done to reflect your own teaching interests and especially the real lives of your students.

When he later picked out the most influential facts of his life from among his Step IA reflections, Erik chose only two: that his family had lived in nine different houses and apartments from the West Coast to the Midwest, and the color of his skin. Reflecting on having moved so often, Erik wrote:

I have lost many friendships to people I had been really close to . . .
That makes friendships even harder for me to sustain today, since
there's always the chance that I could move away again. Now I've
become afraid of getting too close with my friends, because I'm
scared that the same thing could happen to me all over again.

—Erik Ellingsen, June 2003

Many teenage males, myself included at one time, have a special
difficulty putting such fears into words at all. Being able to realize, put
in writing, and then share such things in a presentation can't have done
Erik any harm.

Erik, who is white, also chose race as a most significant influence.
Outnumbered in his honors classes by classmates from various Asian
backgrounds, he wrote:

I know that it's not true that your appearance determines the type of person you are, but I do think that it can affect how you feel about it. I'm
proud of my heritage and all, but sometimes I feel like I'm an outcast,
someone who sticks out among the crowd. I'm alright if my friends joke
about it a little, but I still get that feeling that I don't belong with them,
and the color of my skin makes me unwanted. It's not a great feeling,
especially when people judge you by the color of your skin. Now, I'm
not saying that I view people differently because of their ethnicity, but it
really is hard to suppress sometimes the feeling like you don't belong.

Having lived in East Palo Alto, a black community where mine was
one of the only white faces on our street, I know a little of how Erik
feels. I can also say that having had this experience I am a little more
aware of how those who are treated as racial minorities feel. This
awareness helps me to understand more people more deeply, which I
think helps me get along better in my life and my work with teens of
all colors. For Erik's sake, I'm pleased he had the chance to think and
write about, and later share these feelings in his presentation. The race
conversation may certainly grow ticklish at times, but when an opportunity comes along to speak one's truth in a trusting room, it is a conversation that can lead to learning and healing for all of us.

Megan chose her beliefs, her personal environment, her goals, and
her gender as her four most influential life circumstances. While not
religious in the traditional sense, she wrote in her Creed IA reflection:

My beliefs have influenced me to think that I am always watched over
by spirit guides. . . . Knowing that something is always taking care of
me and everyone around me is an influence . . . lets me know that
everything happens for a reason. So altogether my beliefs give me a
reason to see everything positively.

—Megan Wood, June 2003

Megan went on to share an example of how her spiritual life informs the rest of her life. When younger, she had lived with a stepparent whose verbal and physical abuse of her younger stepsister became intolerable for her. Drawing on her inner sense of what was right, Megan had eventually found the conviction and strength to speak out against the abuse and went on to report the stepparent to the authorities. This has made her especially grateful now to be living with her mother. Her goal of working to support herself well so she can afford to have fun with friends and family, Megan realized, also shapes her life. These goals "inspire me to work, to do all my schoolwork, and to get good grades in more challenging classes than the average person may take. If I can accomplish all these things this will change me into the ideal person I want to become." An important aspect of this person Megan envisions herself becoming is her gender:

> My gender motivates me continually to not be a stay-at-home mom, who knits stockings and socks all day, but to work towards my goals to prevent the life [forced upon] many women in the world's history. I want to make a difference as female, and be inspirational to girls all over the world. I feel that my athleticism, wit, intelligence, and personal drive have already contributed to wanting to be an individual woman and a leader as a woman for women.

These are two examples that may give you and your students some ideas on how we can reflect on the circumstances of our lives. The next Creed Inquiry deals with more specific experiences.

Student Instructions: Creed Inquiry IB— Experiences/Events/Activities

- Make a list of 5 to 10 specific events, experiences, or activities that have affected the growth of your character, positively or negatively. (Include at least one that may have been less than positive.) Some possibilities:
  - Important events that have affected my character
  - Turning points in my life
  - Illness or loss I've dealt with
  - The things I enjoy learning—in school or out of school
  - The way(s) that help me learn best
  - The things I like to think and/or learn about
  - The kinds of books I am drawn to read
  - My feelings about reading
  - The films, art, or music I have been attracted to
  - Imagination: my own creative efforts in art, music, etc.
  - Physical or athletic activities
  - Spiritual experiences
  - Others?

- Of these experiences, choose 3 to 5 you feel have been most influential in shaping the person you are today.

- For each of the 3–5 specific experiences that have most influenced you, write a reflective paragraph on how it has affected, influenced, changed, or inspired you.

Annotations: Creed Inquiry IB—Experiences, Events, Activities

The process in Step IB is the same as in IA, except that students are listing and reflecting on *specific* events or activities rather than general facts of their lives. Again, it's important that students include at least one less-than-positive influence. Erik made full use of this opportunity:

> . . . one major event that changed me was when my family went through separation and divorce. It was really hard on me, because there was nothing I could do about it, and it made me feel like I was the one to blame. This is something I have been reflecting on ever since it happened; I just can't get it out of my head, because everything I do today is because of the divorce. I still don't know how to feel about what happened. My life was completely changed by it, and forever will be. As of now, I view it as a negative influence, because I can see no good that came out of it, and it's not really something I can learn from. It definitely changed my view of "my perfect world," that I was going to grow up into the perfect family.

Erik may not have needed the Creed Project to inspire him to begin reflecting on this situation in his life. The project, however, provided him the opportunity to gain perspective and strength by bringing this challenge into the open among trusted friends and classmates. Like Erik, Megan chose her parents' divorce as a negative influence, and looked as he did directly and honestly at some painful and uncomfortable effects of the separation in her life. She shared how she is also moving ahead, and goes on to cite a positive influence—her boyfriend—that has risen from the ashes of the experience:

> Having a boyfriend gives me a person that I can confide in because he has an almost identical dilemma with his parents as I do, except his problem lies with his mother. Talking to him and having him be able to give me experienced advice and comments helps me out so much and makes every day I feel down easier because once I let it all out I automatically feel better.

Having a boyfriend to confide in, Megan goes on to say, also helps her overcome her previous tendency to avoid school. Since now she knows he is waiting for her there mornings, available to listen, she rarely misses school. This example suggests that opportunities for students to unburden themselves emotionally, whether in a supportive relationship or in the context of a carefully structured forum like the Creed Project, may indeed lead to greater academic commitment and performance.

Before moving to Step IC and contemplating the *people* in their lives, this past year my students had the option to chart the main circumstances and experiences that have influenced their lives in a Life Chart, a practice from Allen L. Roland's book *Radical Therapy*. Roland's chart gives students added perspective by asking them to evaluate these experiences by placing each on the chart in an appropriate position with respect to the timeline, which serves also to separate positive from negative experiences. The Life Chart asks students not only to evaluate each influential circumstance or event in terms of its positive or negative effect on them, but to place it in relation to other influences. This first year using these charts I didn't collect them, and only asked my classes about it in passing, and don't yet have an accurate sense of how they worked for students in general. However, Brittany Carlson's chart, I think, shows that this activity has good potential to help students start seeing their lives with some perspective (Figure 11–2).

In Appendix I, you can see a blank sample Life Chart and one I've done for my own life. And it's on to the influence of people.

Student Instructions: Creed Inquiry IC—People

- Make a list of 5 to 10 people who have influenced or inspired you. (Include one or two who may have been less-than-positive influences.)
  - The family I've been born into
  - The friends I've found
  - Neighbors I've come to know
  - Teachers I've had
  - Characters in books I've read
  - Authors of books that have influenced me (*please do include at least one character or author. Hey, it's English!*)
  - Characters in films, shows, or cartoons who have influenced me
  - Community members I've talked with
  - Public figures—actors, sports figures, singers, dancers, etc.—that have inspired or influenced me
- Choose 3 to 5 people who have influenced or inspired you most.
- Write a reflective paragraph on each of the 3–5 people explaining how he or she has influenced, inspired, or affected you.
- Which of these people have experienced changes of the kind that force us to rethink what we are about? Comment, adding material to each of your 3–5 paragraphs as appropriate.

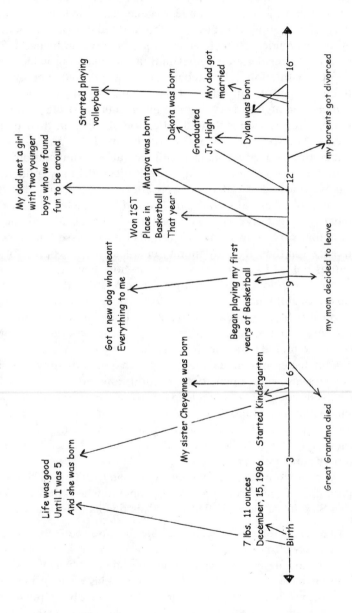

Figure 11-2 Brittany's Life Chart

Annotations: Creed Inquiry IC—People

Since people tend to influence us more directly and certainly more personally than events or circumstances, this is one of the most rewarding steps in the project. Again students generate a long list, and go on to reflect on the people who have most influenced or inspired them. Again they are reminded to include less-than-positive influences. But this time a new consideration comes into play—changing values. The last Step IC instruction asks students to consider whether any of the influential people in their lives have passed through changes significant enough to lead them to reconsider what they value in life. Later, in Step III, students will reflect on changes in their own value systems. And so I want them first to have tried this probably unfamiliar operation at a safe distance, with the value systems of others.

In the early versions of the Creed Project, the only influences students were asked to reflect on were literary characters—a minimum of seven, to tell all. Slowly the realities of life as a teacher—by which I mean the real lives of my students—have disabused me of the notion that very many of them, even in honors classes, are powerfully influenced in their lives by literary characters. (I was probably in my twenties before I had the perspective to honestly say that a character in a book had done more than inspire me, and had actually gone on to exert an influence on my life.) You can see that of nine possibilities on my list, only two vestiges of those early days of teaching innocence remain. Now, with the realism of experience, I only ask students to include *one* literary character *or* author in their list of people who have influenced them most. In general, however, I think teenagers are wide open to suggestion, and my list is just a start. Perhaps it would be less of a leap for my students to consider whether a character like Hugo's Jean Valjean or Hurston's Janie Crawford could shape their lives if I wove in a strand asking them to reflect periodically through the year on the influence of friends, family, and public figures on their lives.

As I mention back in Chapter Two, many students take the opportunity of the Creed Project to honor people to whom they feel grateful. In his Step IC reflections, Erik offers his thanks to his mother:

> She has the biggest effect on my life, because she is the one who made my life possible. My mom is a single working mom, who works ten hours a day just to support me and my brother. My mom has really inspired me to be as great of a parent to my kids when I get married, as she was to me. She has also inspired me to be a better person, and to put others' needs before my own. I could choose anything I own right now, and use that as a symbolic representation of her influence

on my life, because everything I have now is because of her.

Erik's last sentence, which he added later, is one of his responses to the request (coming in Step IG) that he create a symbolic representation of the influences he most values. Megan also takes this opportunity to express her gratitude to her mother:

> My mom is the most influential person in my life. Whenever I'm out at the mall or a restaurant or any other place, I constantly see teenagers with their parents and very few . . . seem to have the relationship my mom and I have. We get along extremely well and she has been able to raise me in a way that she totally trusts me and in a way that I never disobey her so therefore I never get into trouble. She inspires me to be a good person and to not do anything that would be upsetting. Of course she gave birth to me, has housed me, fed me, and cared and loved me my entire life, but she does everything she can to go a step further. Everyday I see the person that she really is and I long to be a person just like her.

Reading them out of context, some less articulate such statements may perhaps sound pat or even maudlin. This may be worth pausing to address. Even in the presentations, coming from less confident students than Megan, remarks like these may even *sound* perfunctory in the moment. During the week of presentations, however, we tend to realize that how something may sound in the moment may not really tell us much about the person saying it. In her portfolio Moment That Mattered, Elyse observed:

> The project also taught me a lot about being careful about judging other people. Some of my classmates who presented were people I thought I knew, but after listening to them talk about themselves and what they stand for, I've found that there is so much more to them than I could have ever imagined.
>
> —Elyse Kirker, June 2003

As you may recall from several of the student testimonials in Chapters Two and Four, in a room full of similar realizations during an entire week of presentations, the cumulative effect can be breathtaking. After a series of particularly full presentations this past year in which friends used the opportunity to acknowledge and appreciate one another with some of the most touching public tenderness I have ever witnessed, Marisa reflected in her own Moment That Mattered:

> Then the bell rang, but everyone stayed a while and talked and wiped away tears. I sat in my seat and watched my classmates be the most honest, the most kind, and the most supportive of each other that they had been all year. That day I realized how wonderful and how beautiful my classmates' spirits are. . . . This was the most love I have ever

experienced at school. At that moment I fell in love with every person in that room.

It may be fruitless to invent theories explaining why students periodically write of the power of these presentations to elicit love for one's classmates. But Marisa goes on to offer some insight:

> I adored each of them for the shining qualities they showed each other for that few minutes. . . . I won't ever forget that day. That was the most content I have ever been at school. I just simply love all of them.
> —Marisa Weiler, June 2003

Perhaps in a semester-long reflection about what to us is most important, many of us learn that what we thought we stood for differs in some respects from what we actually discover matters most to us. Perhaps this inner contrast between appearance and reality can tend to open us up to similar contrasts in others, and makes it possible for us to become more open to them. This is a refreshing, somewhat different twist from how we normally treat the theme of appearance versus reality in the classroom. On now to two other unusual categories of influence.

Student Instructions: Creed Inquiry ID—Questions

- Make a list of 3 to 7 Big Questions about life, the world, reality, the universe that have claimed your attention enough to call them an influence. If you haven't brainstormed Big Questions before, you might need to stay with this a while. If questions don't come, try some breathing exercises, or take a short break, and come back to it later. Big Questions should be deep issues about life you have wondered about more than once. Here are some examples students have come up with:
  - Is there life on other planets?
  - Why was I put on the earth?
  - Is there life after death?
  - How can adults expect us to resolve problems peacefully when they provide such a poor example?

  Get the idea? Please ask for help if you need it.

- Choose 1 to 3 Big Questions that influence you the most. Write a reflective paragraph on how each of your most influential Big Questions influences, inspires, or affects you.

Student Instructions: Creed Inquiry IE—Qualities

- Create a Catalogue of your own qualities that may have helped you become the person you are today and might assist you to become the person you wish to be.
  - Capabilities I have shown?

- examples of my Creativity?
- instances of my Courage?
- an example of my Compassion?
- an instance of my Resolution/Determination?
- Gifts or Talents I have shown?
- other Strengths I possess?
- the source of my Energy
- other qualities?

For each of three or more of the qualities on your list, write a paragraph describing a situation when this quality came out in you. End each paragraph by (or add another paragraph) commenting on how this quality is significant in your life.

Annotations: Creed Inquiries ID and IE— Questions and Qualities

In Creed Steps IA through IC, students have looked at external influences, from the background circumstances of their lives to the more pointed influence of other people. The next two steps guide their thinking on a more internal level. If your students have used Big Questions before to guide their learning (as suggested in Chapter Ten and enlarged on in Chapter Fourteen), this Creed step can serve as a culmination of Big Question contemplations during the year, taking their reflections to a more personal level. If they have not, this step can introduce them to the practice of following their own questions in learning and life. Either way, it is a powerful notion—an empowering one for students to consider— that the questions we ask can mold the people we are and are becoming. And indeed, our own questions can be particularly potent forces. The circumstances, events, and people in our lives can shape us either passively or actively, with or without our intention. But as we allow our own questions to guide us we become more dynamic participants in shaping ourselves. Many of us may have questions we follow without being fully conscious we are doing so. This step encourages my students to attempt to become aware of such currents in their subconscious lives, and to consider bringing these forces to a more conscious level.

Step IE asks students to contemplate their own natures, not through attempting to plumb the depths of an amorphous whole, but by considering specific qualities that in part comprise their makeup. This is a new step I am adding in hopes of helping students to deepen their more interior reflections. These eight qualities come from my conversation with writer and teacher Nan Phifer about her guidebook on writing spiritual memoirs, *Memoir of the Soul: Writing Your Spiritual Autobiography* (Writer's Digest Books 2002). While I have yet to test this step with live students, judging by Marisa's comment above that it was the specific qualities of her classmates that most moved her, it seems to be a good fit here, and I'm excited to see how it works for students next year. I invite you to let me know how it works for your students, by leaving a comment at universeWired.com. Time now for these reflections to consolidate.

Student Instructions: Creed Inquiry IF— Short List of Your Most Significant Influences

*   Looking over your Creed Inquiries A–D, create your Short List of influences—your 3–5 most important influences. (Again, be sure to include one or two less-than-positive influences. You'll see why I'm asking in Creed Step II.)

*   For each influence on your Short List, reread the Creed inquiry in which you first wrote about it, and let your mind reflect some more. What else comes to mind about how this person, event, circumstance, question or quality has affected, influenced, changed, or inspired you? Add these reflections to your previous ones.

Annotations: Creed Inquiry IF—Short List

At this point the expansive movement of students' reflections makes a transition to consolidation. Rereading all their reflections in the five sets from Steps IA through IE, students narrow them down to the four to seven influences from across these lists that have had the most significant effects on their lives. These are their Short Lists. This past year I asked students in this step to write separate paragraphs on why they chose each influence on their short lists, but their feedback was that this made for unnecessary repetition. So this year, on a student suggestion, after creating their Short Lists in this step I will only ask them to add to their previous reflections any new material that comes to mind for these four to seven most significant influences.

Student Instructions: Creed Inquiry IG— Values Represented

*   For each influence on your Short List, write a paragraph addressing this question: What in life does this person seem to stand for—to most value or most care about? What value(s) or principles or beliefs does the event, circumstance, question, or quality stand for in your mind? Respond to your choice of the questions in the box below and in the Overview.

What in life is most important, or most matters, to him or her? Family? Career? Hobbies? Lifestyle? Personal Development? Relationships? Race or ethnicity? Religious or spiritual things? Looking through his or her eyes—or through what you have learned from an experience, or from asking a Big Question—what kind of place does the universe appear to be? Does the person see—or does the experience or quality suggest—that life is a place where might makes right, where only the best fighters or the smoothest operators survive? Or does this person see the world as a place in which we each must stand for something beyond ourselves? Does he or she see life as a struggle to "get yours" before someone else gets it, or as a place where you get what you need in life by serving others? Does this person believe—or does the event seem to demonstrate—that "life is hell and then you die"? Or does she or he see this life as a first taste of an endless life in a loving universe? These are only some of the possibilities.

- For each influence on your Short List, find a way of creatively representing the influence of this particular circumstance, event, or person on your life. Some possibilities:
  - A visual symbol
  - A picture
  - A question
  - A quotation
  - A poem or song
  - A melody
  - Others?

Annotations: Creed Inquiry IG—
Values Represented

Your students are now reaching a turning point in the Creed process. For the first time, they are asked to contemplate not the *effect* of a particular influence on their lives but what that influence—that person, event, circumstance, quality, or question—*stands for*. If the influence is a person, what does that person appear to care about, or value; what is most important to that person? If the influence is an event or circumstance, question or quality, what value(s) or principle(s) or belief(s) does the influence stand for in your mind?

This step begins a new operation in the process of reflective thought: extrapolating from your observations of how a thing or person affects you—primarily *facts* and *meanings* in the learning continuum to this point—to what values (in the case of a person) motivate that person at a deep level, or what values (in the case of an impersonal influence) that influence signifies in your own mind. In either case, the focus of thought shifts along the learning continuum—from facts and meanings to *values*. Because I have found it is often difficult for sophomores (or anyone for that matter) to discern what another person stands for, I offer them a boxed array of questions, and refer them to a second box from the project overview earlier in their packets. (See website.) I hope the prompts in these boxes give them a jump start in learning to discern the values of those who have influenced them, or to represent in their own minds the values the impersonal forces that shape them.

In Chapter Nine, I explained how I realized that Steps I through III of the Creed Project correspond to the three hubs of a continuum learning experience: compiling facts, discerning meanings, and discovering values. Soon, in Step II, you may remember, students will evaluate, or make a judgment about, the people and forces that have molded them. In so doing they construct meanings from those facts of their lives. In the picture I presented for you, in moving from Step I to Step II the project takes a grand leap from fact to meaning. But the appearance is not the reality.

The truth is that students have been evaluating these influences at nearly every point in Step I. They have done so each time they have narrowed down their initial lists, choosing the most significant several influences, and finally chosen the *most* significant influences of their Short Lists. In making these *judgments,* even before making the grand leap to Step II they were creating meanings from the facts of their lives. Now they are ready for Step II, when they will perform a somewhat different kind of judgment.

But first, for the last piece in Step I, they are asked to strengthen their understanding of the most significant shapers of their lives by looking at them from a metaphorical perspective. In creating or finding a visual symbol, picture, question, quotation, a poem or song, a melody or any other kind of metaphor, they gain an imaginative perspective on this influence, a refreshing balance for the factual or analytical. And in creating a symbol, they take a step toward interpreting meanings.

Whether or not one understands all these interrelationships I attempt to describe, the Step I reflections are a rich experience. One morning a year or more before I had suspected all these connections and cross-connections, I saw a strong indication of this richness. Here is an entry from a journal I began keeping that year:

Creed Journal 15 May 2002: Day 3

Today was the first Creed Project due date this year. Before I even picked up the roll binder, Zarlasht Zemarialai had walked past me on the way to her seat. Not sure at first whether we had a new class member, I did a double take when I realized it was Zarlasht. She was on time, for one thing. Normally taciturn and a little slovenly, today she was in dark slacks with a white blouse. Was that a *wave* in her hair? Probably the new look has some other explanation. But a moment after sitting down at her desk she reached into her backpack. Several times this year Zarlasht has had to look for her papers in the red "Anonymous" tray, to where they had been relegated because she had turned in work without bothering to write her name. Few students I've seen in fifteen years of teaching are quite as adept as Zarlasht at emanating a "this is dogshit" attitude about schoolwork without being truly offensive. But now as I stood up behind my desk I saw she held several sheets of typed paper between her thumbs and middlefingers, her index fingers elevated with a certain subtle import. This was something she cared about; the way she held them told me so. She was ready. My eyes scanned to her side of the room taking roll. "Look, Mr. Creger," she said, a new cherubic look on her round Afghan face. "I finished Step I. Hey, and I did it the old way. You know, before you changed it. I wrote about what the people stood for first. Mr. Creger, I like this project." Releasing the neatly typed sheets now that I'd seen them, she let them fall to her desk. "I like essays," she concluded, her eyes leaving mine for pathos.

While it's entirely possible that Zarlasht had other reasons for the change in her appearance and comportment (which did not end up magically permanent), and while the hope of impressing me into a favorable state of mind concerning her currently failing grade may have been among those reasons, this was the one occasion all year that I saw this kind of engagement in her. Spring semester she passed with a C– (a full grade above her fall semester grade).

In the seven or eight weeks of Step I, students have catalogued, reflected on, and finally consolidated the most significant people and forces that have shaped their lives. Along the way, in listing influences and choosing the most significant among them, they have been regularly cycling back and forth in the learning continuum between cataloguing facts and creating meanings. In Step II they will create further meanings from the facts of their lives, this time in evaluating the influences they selected for their Short List. But this time, they will do so in a way that creates meanings further along the continuum toward the values hub.

Step II—Most and Least Admired Influences

Instead of asking the more general question as in Step I, of which influence has had the greatest impact, in Step II students explore more

Contents of Creed Step II Inquiries:
Most and Least Admired Influences

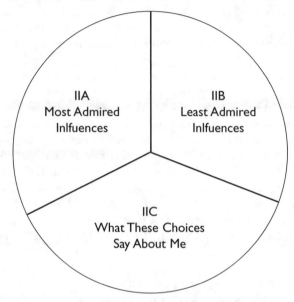

Figure 11-3 Contents of Creed Step II Inquiries: Most and Least Admired Influences

specifically which influence they most *admire,* and then consider why. This is a judgment that asks us to go beyond assessing the *effect* of an influence, to reflecting on what in this influence we particularly *value.* In Step IG, when they attempted to represent values in their minds, whether of people or forces, students practiced this probably new kind of thinking. In Figure 11–3 above, then, you see an overlook at the thinking they will do in Step II.

Student Instructions: Creed Inquiry IIA—
Most Admired

Look over your Short List of influences from Step I. Which of these real people or characters, experiences, circumstances, or questions do you *most admire* for the vision or values he or she or it represents to you? Why? Write a reflective paragraph giving one or two specific examples showing why you admire this influence most of all. What one or two others of your influences do you also admire? Write a second (brief) paragraph explaining why.

Student Instructions: Creed Inquiry IIB— Least Admired

Once again, look over your Short List. Which item on this list do you *least admire—or least value—*for the influence he, she, or it has had on you? In a third reflective paragraph, explain, giving specific examples. What other characters or people from your list do you *not* admire much? Why? Briefly address these two questions in a fourth reflective paragraph.

Student Instructions: Creed Inquiry IIC— What This Says

You have just made two choices. You have chosen one of your influences—a person, event, or circumstance—as the influence you most admire or value, and you have chosen another influence you admire or value least.

Write a fifth reflective paragraph in response to this question: What do my choices of most and least admirable influences say about my own values? In other words, if I most admire ___, what does this say about what I value? If I least admire ___, what does this say about what I value? Please develop this paragraph with examples.

Annotations: Creed Steps IIA, IIB, and IIC

In Step II, students must choose one influence they most admire and one they least admire. This may or may not be difficult. They must then explain *why* these are their choices. In answering this question, they may or may not yet begin to approach what they themselves stand for. Finally, they are asked to reflect on what these choices tell them about what they themselves value. Let's follow Megan's thinking in Steps IIA and IIB.

Megan most admires her mother and cites, among others, these reasons: "She is always available to talk to and get advice from and I strongly admire her for these reasons. The most significant reason that leads me to admire my mom is the fact that she is very strong emotionally, mentally, and physically." These are wonderful reasons, of course. But they haven't yet led Megan to become aware of her own values. Asked in Step IIB to choose the influence she *least* admires, Megan settles on her father's remarriage. In explaining why, she writes: "I feel this way because my dad did not consider my sister's and my well-being when he married. Most of all, this event was the greatest poor effect on my life so far. That alone makes it very hard to admire." Here again, Megan's explanation, while it tells clearly what Megan does *not* value or admire, may not yet arise from a clear perception of what she *does* stand for. Megan is right on track. These two steps help students attune to the values they see represented in other people or forces—this time just two specific people or forces: those they admire most and least. Abdullah Nezami writes: "Through writing these two Creed inquiries, I discovered that I not only admire my family and friends as people, but I also admire their vision and values that they represent and stand for."

Students' next task, then, in Step IIC, is to ask themselves what they can infer from their choices of most and least valued influences—*about their own values*. If Megan most admires her mother for her openness, willingness to be available, and her strength, what does this say about what *Megan* values? If she least admires her father's remarriage because her father failed to consider its negative consequences, what does this tell her about what *she* values? Here is Megan's response to Step IIC:

> My choices of most and least admirable influences suggest that I care strongly about honesty and good character. It also suggests I value ambitions and strong wills. Since I admire my mom because of her qualities of being a strong person, being funny, and extremely kind-hearted, it suggests that I value these characteristics. Also the way I do not admire meanness and abandonment propose that I care about joy, kindness, and togetherness with friends and family. It shows that I value being close to my family and that I strongly dislike being separated both emotionally and physically.

In a sense, the entire sequence of reflections on their influences in Steps I and II has students, few of whom have yet engaged in such contemplations, walk backwards into a consideration of what they themselves stand for: the focus of Creed Step III.

❦ CHAPTER TWELVE

Steps III and IV

> That which you value is that which you seek to impart to others.
> —T. Thomas

Preliminary Creed Statement

Step III is the center of the Creed Project. Here students begin the process of reflecting on what they stand for by again responding, as they did in Step IG, to their choice of questions in boxed arrays, the questions they feel "speak" to them. This approach seems to work well, since it honors the fact that we each are differently drawn to a differently emphasized different combination of values, yet it still provides guidance. The questions in these boxes are the same ones students considered when attempting to represent what their influences stood for in Step IG, except now they are phrased in the first person. Again, this is not an exhaustive list, and students can find suggestions for thinking beyond it at the end of the Step IIIA instructions. Figure 12–1 gives you an overlook at Step III.

Student Instructions: Creed Inquiry IIIA— The Big Picture

You have reflected on people and events who have influenced you and what they might stand for. You have begun considering what your feelings about *their* values might say about your *own* values. Now you will write a preliminary statement of your own personal creed—the vision of life or values you hold at this point in highest regard. This might come together as you ask yourself the questions that follow:

- What values or ideas, questions or principles do I feel are important enough to guide my life? What, in other words, am I willing to "stand for"?

Contents of Creed Step III Inquiries: Preliminary Creed Statement

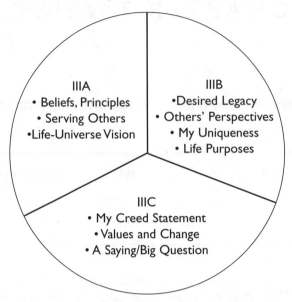

IIIA
• Beliefs, Principles
• Serving Others
•Life-Universe Vision

IIIB
•Desired Legacy
• Others' Perspectives
• My Uniqueness
• Life Purposes

IIIC
• My Creed Statement
• Values and Change
• A Saying/Big Question

Figure 12–1 Contents of Creed Step III Inquiries: Preliminary Creed Statement

You responded in Step IG to your choice of the questions in the boxes in Step I and the Overview of this project. This time, ask yourself the questions in the boxes below. Write a first page in which you respond to whichever questions below *speak* to you.

- What ideas or principles, beliefs or questions, people or things do I *care about* most?
- What brings *meaning* to my life?
- In what way do I enjoy *serving others*?
- What *vision of life*, what *values*, do I most *stand for*?
- What in life is most important, or most matters, to me? Family? Career? Hobbies? Lifestyle? Personal Development? Relationships? Race or ethnicity? Religious or spiritual things?
- What kind of place does the universe appear to me to be? Is life a place where might makes right, where only the best fighters or the smoothest operators survive? Or is the world a place in which we each must stand for something beyond ourselves?

- Do I see life as a struggle to "get yours" before someone else gets it, or as a place where you get what you need in life by serving others? Do I believe that "life is hell and then you die"? Or do I see this life as a first taste of an endless life in a loving universe?

These are only some of the possibilities. Be sure to respond to at least three of these questions—and/or any other questions that come to you about what you might stand for. Feel free to include values (or questions) you have learned from your family, religion (if you profess one), your race, ethnicity, culture, school, peers, personal experience, music, films, or any other source—including books you have read.

Student Instructions: Creed Inquiry IIIB— You in the Big Picture

- After you have responded to the questions you have chosen, consider the following additional questions. Let your responses to the questions below that *speak* to you compose your second page.

- What legacy of influences do I want to pass on to my children? What values would I like them to have when they become adults? What kind of people do I wish them to be? What do I want *them* to stand for? What, then, do my hopes for my children suggest *I myself stand for*?
- When I ask one or more of the people who have influenced me what they think *I* stand for, how do they respond? How do their answers to this question compare with my own? Are there differences between my perceptions and theirs?
- What makes me *unique* among all the people I know?
- What *question* do I have to give to the world that comes uniquely from me? What would a person who gives this question to the world stand for?
- Do I see myself as having a purpose here on earth? If so, how would I express it? Am I here to get what I can grab before I die? Or am I here to learn about myself and learn to understand and love one more person every day? Am I here to accumulate wealth and security? Or am I here to learn what it means to serve others? Am I here primarily to survive as comfortably as possible and make a good life for my family? Or am I here to find some way to leave the world a better place for my having lived here?

Annotations: Creed Inquiry IIIA and IIIB— Building Toward a Creed Statement

The difference between the questions in Steps IIIA and IIIB is not especially important, except that the ones in IIIA are more general, more cosmic in scope. In IIIB they focus more specifically on the student's life. The first four questions in the IIIB box have been added in the past couple of years, mainly as a result of conversations with students. I have David Xu to thank for his help in formulating the first one, about hopes for one's children's values. This is a powerful stimulus to think clearly, even at sixteen, about one's own values. A class conversation arising after I shared the story of Nuri Lundy's "On the Spot" presentation (see Chapter Four) led to my including the second question in the instruction packet. This past year, as a result, students could enjoy some of the consultative benefits of Nuri's approach without the considerable public risks. The third question comes from the extraordinary uniqueness of a number of people who walked into my own life and later became influences. These amazing folks provoked me to begin asking questions that have now borne fruit, helping me understand the importance of the uniquely personal in the largest scheme of things. My daughter Hana's gymnastic coach, Luis T. Nava, an exceptional teacher who goes by the name Nacho Ice, once told me that he wants his students' experience in gymnastics to give them insight into how they are unique, and to show forth this uniqueness. To him, our uniqueness is the source of our deepest questions. And so I have Nacho to thank for the fourth question. The final question in the IIIB box asks students to begin considering whether they may have a purpose in life, a link back to the more cosmic questioning they did in Step IIIA. Again, distinctions between these categories are less important than that students are discovering things about themselves they may not have known, or expressed, before.

Student Instructions: Creed Inquiry IIIC— Draft Creed Statement

- Reread your response to Step IIC, and everything you've written so far in Step III. Bringing it all together, write a draft statement of your personal creed, what you stand for at this point in your life. This could be a paragraph, a list, a map, or anything that helps you take in all your reflections so far in Step III and respond to the question: At this point in my life what I stand for (or value, or any other way you prefer to put it) is . . .

- Or, you could try this approach: At this point in my life, my ideals are beginning to take shape.... Stay tuned in class for further help on this.

- Which of my own values do I feel are probably constant (unchanging)? Which do I predict may change in time? In a paragraph, please explain.

- Find or create a *saying* or a *Big Question* that reflects your personal creed. For one good example, see the saying from Toni Morrison at the beginning of these instructions. For other possibilities, try your Thought Log or a book of quotations. Record this saying or Big Question here so you can use it on the cover of the write-up you will be creating and turning in for Steps I–IV of this project. In case you're stuck, here are two sayings that may help:
  - Fight for your own ideals, not for the ideals of others. (Silvia Vazquez)
  - Seek the inner life and its ideals, so that when the realistic outer life falls apart, you will not be in a blizzard but in a gentle rain shower that quickly passes. (T. Daniel)

Annotations: Creed Inquiry IIIC— Draft Creed Statement

It is now time for students to synthesize all their reflections—especially Steps IIC and IIIA and B—and draft a statement that embodies what they stand for as they approach the midpoint of their high school careers and move past the midpoint of their second decade of life. This is an opportunity to express the personal wisdom they have accumulated to this point, and if they have engaged in a more general study of wisdom at the beginning of the year, this is a good time for them to reflect on whether any fruits of that study might be brought forward for this present, more personal purpose.

One way to help students get started is to provide some sentence starters. Here are some rather obvious ones:

- At this point in my life, what I stand for is . . .
- What matters most to me at this point in my life is . . .
- What I most value at this point in my life is . . .
- At this point in my life, the ideals I embrace are . . .

You may find it helpful to use these to initiate a class brainstorm for further sentence-starter possibilities. If students prefer, you might provide them with two or three simple graphic organizers to help collect thoughts before writing this statement. Jim Burke's *Tools for Thought* is an excellent source of graphic options.

Indeed, my goal here is to provide options. I prefer not to be too prescriptive about the form these statements should take. After all, these may be the most personal pieces of writing many students have done to date. The very difficulty is part of the value in this step. Lauren wrote:

> The most challenging problem I had was forming my creed. What I thought and believed in had never been questioned. I felt myself asking, "What do I stand for?" and "What values do I believe in?" without knowing how to respond. It took a while but after analyzing my influences my creed began to emerge and take shape in my mind.
>
> —Lauren Kaapcke, June 2003

Tina's written Creed statement is especially moving when considered in connection with her presentation, described in the next chapter. She wrote:

> At this point in my life, what I stand for is the idea that even though the world is a cruel and cold place where might makes right, [a place] that can hypothetically survive without people-to-people relationships, the most golden unchanging values are still friendship, trust and loyalty. I stand for the belief that although life may seem like misery, living for one's friend[s] and promoting their laughter should be everyone's purpose here on Earth. I may sound like someone who is a depressed teenager, but I can't help it if I feel this way. I feel that laughter truly is and always will be the best medicine. Laughing relieves stress, it makes you happy and it's also contagious. I value friendship, trust and loyalty. Since friends are the reason that I'm living, it's a no-brainer that I would value friendship. But loyalty and trust are also two things that I greatly value. Those two things are what friendship is built out of. That's the reason why I object to divorces and people that lie. I make a big deal out of something that is small because you have to walk a step before you can walk a thousand miles. I want to instill in people values that will follow throughout their lives and I want them to learn it when I'm still around to teach it.
>
> —Tina Chung, June 2003

Tina's was one of a number of powerfully moving statements from her class.

Back in Step IC, students considered whether any of the people who have influenced them have undergone changes in what they value. Here in the second part of Step IIIC, they take up the topic of change again, but this time in the first person. The task is to predict which of the values they have included in their own Creed statements will remain constant and which may change with time. Not all our values, of course, are etched in stone or permanent marker.

For the last part of Step III, students find or create a saying or Big Question that reflects their personal creed. Having averaged two Thought Logs most weeks, my students have up to fifty quotes in the Thought Log sections of their binders to consider using, along with their lists of Big Questions from early in the year or their more recent ones from Step ID. They can find hundreds more possible quotes on the Internet. This saying or question will go on the cover of the Steps I–IV packet. The Step III instructions end with a quote from gymnastics coach Nacho Ice's mother. Nacho tells the story behind it.

When he emerged as a top student in high school in Mexico, his political science teacher began trying to convince him to attend meetings and become a student leader in a political party opposed to the government. The teacher was so persistent that Nacho felt himself becoming committed to the cause and was preparing to attend a demonstration. Under the repressive PRI government, this was dangerous activity. After a visit with his mother during this period, they were saying goodbye at the airport when she gave him this piece of advice:

Fight for your own ideals, not for the ideals of others.

Based on his mother's advice, Nacho decided to pursue his studies and athletic interests rather than become associated with the political group. Many years later, studying at San Jose University in California, he discovered that had he joined the political group he would have been inducted into a large group of young idealists who later went on to become *carne de cañon,* cannon flesh. His teacher, probably knowingly, would have sent him to his death. Nacho credits this one saying (and his mother) with saving his life.

This, along with another quote on the role of ideas I pass along from one of my favorite teachers, is the kind of saying or question I want my students to find if they can, a suitable capstone in the process of discovering what in the universe matters to them. Erik, whose creed among other things emphasized the special importance of friends, chose this one: "If all my friends were to jump off a bridge, I wouldn't jump with them, I'd be at the bottom to catch them."

In Step IV, they will test the truth of what they say they have discovered.

Step IV—A Hard Look

This test comes from two directions, the imagination and the analytical mind. In Figure 12–2, once again, you have an overlook.

The idea for Step IV came from a conversation with a lawyer at the

Contents of Creed Step IV Inquiries: A Hard Look

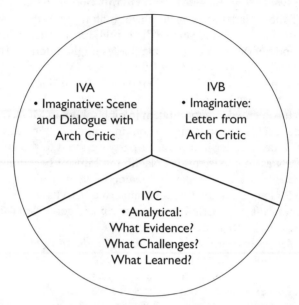

Figure 12–2 Contents of Creed Step IV Inquiries: A Hard Look

local pool in Berkeley where I swim. It's easy to say you stand for this or that, but a little harder to stand apart and examine your commitment to what you say you value. This is what the lawyer suggested I add to the project. And this is the purpose of Step IV.

Student Instructions: Creed Step IVA— Your Arch Critic—A Scene

The purpose here is to stand aside and examine from a critical point of view what you have said you stand for. First you'll use your imagination in two brief creative pieces.

* Imagine someone whose values are opposite, nearly opposite, or very different from your own, someone who would have a hard time listening to what you wrote in Step IIIC—someone whose Big Questions would be very different from yours. In your imagination, introduce yourself to your Arch Critic. In a brainstorm, imagine your Arch Critic's *specific*

complaints about what you stand for, problems he or she would have with what you wrote in your draft creed statement (Step IIIC).

- In a paragraph, describe as clearly as possible your imagined meeting with this person. What clothes is she or he wearing? What facial expression? What signals are you getting from the body language? What does he or she say? How does his or her voice sound? Write a detailed physical description of how you imagine this Arch Critic, your nemesis. Now, write the opening few sentences of a *description* of what you imagine unfolds as you meet and begin your conversation with your Arch Critic. Be sure to provide sensory details, *showing* rather than explaining the interaction.

- Then, continue, letting your description conclude with a *dialogue* between you. In this closing dialogue, your Arch Critic delivers these complaints loud and clear—complaints to which you must respond.

Student Instructions: Creed Step IVB— Your Arch Critic—A Letter

- Your Arch Critic is about to write a letter to a friend you share in common. In this letter, behind your back, he or she will complain to this friend about you, attacking the very principles or beliefs you stand for, the values or questions you care about. Now, imagine you *are* your Arch Critic. Writing as if you actually were this person, write this letter.

- In other words, through the imagined eyes of your Arch Critic, someone very different from yourself, you are creating a critique of your own vision or values. Or, if this works better for you, imagine your Arch Critic as a part of yourself—that nagging, critical voice that often intrudes on your thoughts—and write what it says about you.

Annotations: Creed Steps IVA and IVB— An Imaginative Test

These two steps are essentially a creative writing assignment, so you may want to draw on any fiction writing techniques you have worked on or studied with your students over the year. Step IVA begins inside students' imaginations, where they create their Arch Critics—their nemeses, their opposing numbers in everything that really matters. They let their minds lend forms to their arch-creations. Here's a chance to render physical details to match character traits, and any show-not-tell or other descriptive exercises you have done with them can be applied here. Once the Arch Critic has bone, breath, and britches, then, a student brainstorms all the problems this alter-self would have with what truly matters to the student himself. He then goes on to describe his imagined meeting with this countercreedal counterpart. In the last part of Step IVA, this meeting evolves into a dialogue. This is a perfect time to practice (or, depending how full your plate is, to introduce) any techniques of dialogue you may have studied. Handing out a model or two may help students enjoy the activity and feel more proud of the result. Given a lightened standardized testing load, I may even try this myself sometime!

In Step IVB, the student actually goes over to the dark side and *becomes* her Arch Critic. If the religious climate in your community allows for levity, you could ham this up in class with a mass anointing the Friday before they go off to write the letter. In this letter, written to a mutual friend, the Arch Critic takes aim at everything the student holds most precious. Students who have a hard time giving free reign to their imaginations may find it helpful to let the nitpicking, always hammering, never-satisfied compulsive voice inside themselves be the inspiration for the Arch Critic. Teens have no trouble getting the back-stabbing intent of this letter. The hard part is to have the Arch Critic actually zero in believably and attack not just themselves but the *values* that most matter to them, so as to create an effective *critique* of those values. But our job as teachers here is less to critique our students' critiques than it is to facilitate the constructively self-critical process going on in our students' minds. It's not so much what's going on the page, but what's going on in students' heads that matters here. In her letter, Tina managed to both have fun and say some deep things about the challenges we all face:

Dear Chari,

I'm glad you finally see my point of view. Welcome to the dark side, muhahaha. Honestly, I wonder what took you so long. Things like making your parents happy and doing well in school takes so much energy, and is no way to have fun. You and me are gonna be chilling a whole lot more now that you are going to study less and just hang more. Your friend, Tina, just hasn't got the message from the real world. It just doesn't matter! For real, it doesn't. Why try? Mankind is inherently evil, anyway. At least now you won't be crushed by your own naivete. You're hella smart for agreeing with me. Why be motivated, so you can be sucked in by corporate businesses and left alone and "successful" but unhappy? Don't give in! You don't need anything but time to relax and fun to have.

Sincerely,
Arch Critic

Student Instructions: Creed Step IVC—Where's the Beef? (one paragraph each)

* What evidence in my life can I point to that suggests I actually do stand for the things I wrote in Step IIIC. What have I done, or thought, or wondered about, that points me in the directions my Creed statement articulates?

* What changes have I experienced that challenged the vision of life I said I value in Step III? How did I respond to the challenge?

* What did I learn about myself and what I stand for from going through Steps IVA and IVB? From Steps I–IV as a whole? Respond in a third paragraph.

Annotations: Creed Step IVC—An Analytical Test

Here students look for hard evidence that they are doing more than mouthing platitudes. They look for their own deeds, thoughts, or questions that show their commitment to the values they have claimed. I emphasize that thinking and wondering can qualify here, since these things do precede action. Once in a very great while, an actual usable quote pops into my mind, as happened in connection with this step. We even used this quote for a Thought Log: "Actions may indeed speak louder than words. Sometimes you know what you stand for, what you truly value, only when you look back on what you've done." Feel free to "borrow" it. Some students have seemed to light up to this. Sarah wrote:

> The evidence in my life I can point to that suggests I actually do stand for the things I wrote in step 3C is: I gave up on the guy that I liked a lot to a friend because she liked him and it would make her happy to go out with him so I put my feelings aside even though it hurt me a lot. I value trust, honesty, and respect but I realized that, that is what I also look for in a friend or in a relationship.
>
> —Sarah Danielli, June 2003

In his Step IV letter, Erik allowed his Arch Critic to make some fairly hurtful criticisms of the value he places on family and friends: "Look at his family, they're practically torn apart. They don't even talk to each other. I don't see why he even goes home after school, if you can even call it a home." In the analytical part of Step IV, he wrote:

> The only real evidence of my value of friendship is the return of friendship I get when I try my best to help them out, or make them feel better. That's not really something you can show proof of, but rather express it. Actually, there isn't much evidence of my value of family either. But for me, I don't need any evidence that I value my family, that's just one of the principles I have to live by.

Continuing on the project's change-exploring strand (Steps IC and IIIC), here in IVC students look for changes they have undergone that have challenged what they stand for. And they describe how they responded—withstood or caved in, as the case may be—to this challenge. This will be a new addition this year (inspired by a suggestion from Elyse Kirker).

For the final step in the reflective portion of the project, students reflect on what they've learned, first from Step IV, and then from the entire project so far. As simple as it seems to ask students what they've learned, this may be the single most important question teachers can ask students. Only this past year did I add this step (and only the part about Step IV). Now, if my time is short when I look through students' Creed reflections, this is the one place I can stop to find answers to this most important question. Let's look at a few.

Sarah, who has come a long way since some difficult years when she regularly cut her flesh seeking to restore her deadened emotions, wrote:

> I have learned that I really don't care about myself but I care about other people a lot more. I have learned that friendships are way more important than most things in my life. When I asked my friends what they thought I stood for, I realized that I do more for others and that I am a very honest person. I realized that there might be a lot more to me than I thought. I might start to care more about my life now that I have realized that I have never cared about it.

If my intuition is correct, Erik may have been a little shaken by the severity of his Arch Critic's attacks on what he stands for. But his final reflections are revealing:

> After writing this Step IV, the first thing I would think I have learned is just some reasons to give up my beliefs and values. But as I think about it, I've only given myself more reason to uphold my values, to overcome my Arch-Critic. It's easy to give up after you see what's wrong in things, but that's not what life is about. It's about looking past doubt and uncertainty, and not taking the easy way out. From this project, I have come to realize what I truly value in my life, and that those values will never change, no matter what happens in my life.

Tina's closing reflections show that she too made good use of the Arch Critic exercise:

> I have learned that I have many views on life and that I have lived behind many masks. This project has made me realize that I have good values in life and that [though] sometimes I may wander off the course, I always return to it because my friends encourage me to. My

Personal Creed Project Steps I–IV Reflections: Scoring Rubric

	Missing:	Needs work:	
I—Influences and Inspirations			/70
• Reflections on three to five of each kind of influences/inspirations:	—	—	
A. circumstances	—	—	
B. events	—	—	
C. people	—	—	
• addresses issue of changing values	—	—	
• *at least* one is a character from a book (could also be an author)	—	—	
D. big questions	—	—	
E. qualities	—	—	
F. Short List of three to five Most Significant Influences:	—	—	
• material added to previous reflections	—	—	
G. a paragraph on what each influence on Short List stands for	—	—	
• a symbolic representation of the influence	—	—	
• Other Requirements:			
• Most steps include at least one negative influence (could be hypothetical)	—	—	
• addresses **at least three questions** from the paragraphs of "your choice" questions (Instructions, p. 2 or 6)	—	—	
• *Length*: **four** typed pages *minimum* (**single**-spaced)	—	—	
II - Most and Least Admired Influences			/30
A. Two paragraphs on the one influence you admire *most*, and why	—	—	
B. Two paragraphs on the one influence you admire *least*, and why	—	—	
C. Paragraph on what these choices might say about you and your own vision of life and/or values	—	—	
• *Length*: **at least 5 paragraphs, 3/4 typed page** *minimum* (**single**-spaced)	—	—	
III - Preliminary Creed Statement			/40
• half page responding to your choice of **at least three** IIIA questions	—	—	
• half page responding to your choice of **at least three** IIIB questions	—	—	
• draft statement of your personal creed, what you stand for, value	—	—	
• includes an attempt to describe your vision of life, reality, the world, the universe, or your purpose on earth	—	—	
• addresses the possibility of *changes* in your values	—	—	
• includes a *saying* or *question* that reflects your personal creed	—	—	
• center this saying on your attractive cover sheet	—	—	
• *Length*: **at least one and a half** typed pages *minimum* (**single**-spaced)	—	—	
IV - A Hard Look (two *critiques* of your creed— imaginative and analytic)			/30
A. your Arch-Critic, a scene with brainstorm, description, dialogue	—	—	
B. **Arch Critic's letter** to a mutual friend attacking what *you* stand for	—	—	
C. three paragraphs: evidence, challenges, what you learned	—	—	
• *Length*: **full typed page** *minimum* (**single**-spaced)	—	—	

Correctness / Effectiveness /20

Spelling   Capitalization   Punctuation Fragments   Run-on sentences Subject-verb errors
Typed Neatly   1 inch margins sides and bottom   Paragraphing   Attractive Cover Sheet

Comments: **Total:** ___ /190

Figure 12–3 Personal Creed Project Steps I–IV Reflections: Scoring Rubric

values have been my guide in life and without them I would become corrupted by society. This last step of my creed project has shown me what I would be without what I believe in and I pray that I'll never turn into "Arch Critic." From this project, I have learned so much about myself. Thank you, for letting me have time to reflect on my life and beliefs.

Assessing the Creed Reflections

You may be thinking that I use a fairly detailed rubric. To be honest, the detail is more to give students a clear set of expectations than for me to grade with laser accuracy. In fact, it's designed so I only need to make a mark when I see something missing or needing work. This newly revised rubric corresponds pretty closely to the instructions, in terms of both content and sequence, so it should move fairly quickly. You can have students staple the rubric just under their cover sheets or, as I prefer, on the bottom of the stack. You can use the rubric strictly if your time and energy allow or loosely if you're strapped. My only caution has to do with the Correctness/ Effectiveness category.

Piled especially high with papers this past year, I whipped through the projects as fast as I could, giving little thought to corrections. During most of the year I'm pretty faithful when it comes to error correction. When major essays come back to them, my college prep students are responsible for tallying and graphing their errors, *all* of which I have marked. In their portfolios they reflect on what they learn from studying these graphs, with an eye to which errors they'll need to continue reducing next year. I think it's a comprehensive, long-term approach to error correction. For good reasons, then, including brute survival, in the last two or three weeks of the year error correction is not at the top of my list. And so, with portfolios about to wrap up the correctness strand for the year, I felt little guilt in flying through the Creed Projects without marking errors, and giving full credit in the correctness part of the rubric without much scrutiny. Until, that is, shortly after returning the projects to students I received my first disgruntled email from a parent. Though I was at first a bit miffed that she could not look past her son's many errors and appreciate what he had learned about himself in his Creed reflections, I can see her side too. I'll try to circle repeating error categories on the rubric next time around. Or, if I'm under especially egregious enemy fire from stacks of angry unread essays as I so often am at the end of the year, and my wife and children are advertising for a new husband and father, I'll just white-out that part and change the total before copying the rubric!

Given the fascinating nature of these particular papers, it's indeed a shame to fly through them. But it beats getting paved over by student papers. As my longtime colleague Dan Toft is wont to say: first the teacher survives; then the students learn.

I don't obsess over the form of the reflections. After all, much of what is fascinating in the reflections will soon come out in the presentations, the focus of the next chapter.

❦ CHAPTER THIRTEEN

Step V: The Presentations

> I wasn't really sure what to expect when we began our pre-
> sentations, but after nearly a week of listening to the stories
> my classmates have to share, I've learned that [this is an
> experience in which] you can learn about yourself and those
> you thought you knew. Each day we learn more about more
> students, and each day I grow more and more impressed with
> the people this world has to offer.
>
> —Elyse Kirker, June 2003

If Step III is the center of the Creed Project, Step V is its pinnacle. In Chapters Two, Three, and Four of this book you became acquainted with the project by reading accounts of the Step V presentations. If these and the various other previews scattered through this book have not yet made clear why in the Introduction I call the Creed presentations "the most powerfully affecting classroom experiences I have witnessed in the decade and a half since I became a teacher," this chapter will. My primary aim in this chapter is to help you guide your students into and through this Creed presentation experience. In most cases, except when I think you might find an illustration helpful, I fight off my urge to pause and share a few more of the moving moments I have witnessed in these presentations. Instead, you'll find a crescendo of these experiences to reward you for reaching the end of the chapter.

Because more student instructions come with Step V than with all the rest combined, I have a strong incentive to reign in my reflections and remain matter-of-fact in my explaining and annotating. For veteran teachers, some of my coaching in this chapter may seem overly specific. But I prefer to leave as little mystery as possible when it comes to the logistics. Not having to reinvent the instructional wheel with your own students, perhaps you will be free to take in some of the real personal magic these presentations will bring you. Let's return to the last page of the Steps I–IV packet, then, where you'll find a preview of Step V.

Step V Preview: Put It All Together (Do Option A or Options B and C)

Option A

Make a presentation that expresses your personal creed. In any feasible visual format—poster, mobile, collage, PowerPoint, or video project—express and explain your personal creed (further options to follow). You could do this with great fanfare, in a meditative silence, or anywhere in between. The visual project you may do individually or in a group of three, maximum. If group presentations become an option this year, each participant must make a separate contribution clearly differentiating her or his own personal creed from those of other group members. Please, no "creed dittos"! Feel free to incorporate your Big Question(s). OR . . .

Option B

Write a reflective essay expressing your personal creed (specific instructions to follow). Incorporate objections another might raise to your values. Then show why you persist in holding your values or beliefs despite others' objections. Refer in your essay to your influences described in Step I. AND . . .

Option C: Put Legs Under What You Stand For

Make a phone call or write an email to a local agency (list of possibilities to follow) inquiring about volunteering this summer. Feel free to explore a volunteer position that connects in some way to your Personal Creed or one of your Big Questions. Although you are encouraged, you are not required to actually volunteer, only to request information, and write a paragraph explaining what you did and what you learned.

- Creative visual projects will be presented to the class.
- Essays will be summarized aloud in class.
- Conclude your presentation—or reading of your essay—by describing one thing you have done, now do, or could do to put your creed into action.

Background on the Step V Options

In the early years of the project, Step V for *all* my sophomores consisted of both a Personal Creed reflective essay as preparation *and* a visual aid to use in the actual presentation. This was before I learned much about multiple intelligences, and realized that writing is not the best way for all students to learn all things. It was before I became a parent and began to doubt the wisdom of spending most of my earth life scrawling red trails through stacks of student essays in what my eldest daughter calls my burrow. Once I blithely collected major essays a week before final exams, took in portfolios the day of the final, read them while students wrote exam essays, which I then took to my burrow that night into the wee hours, turning in 150 grades with a weak smile later that morning. No more! Not only because surviving my career is a good thing, but because giving students choices is also a good thing, the reflective essay is now Option B. Option A embodies a range of presentation choices, described on pages 193–194.

This way works much better for all of us. Those few who will *choose* to write essays this late in the year tend to be serious writers, and I enjoy reading what they come up with. These writers are pleased to be excused from making a visual aid for their presentations and to be expected only to briefly summarize whatever parts of their essay they wish to share; this works nicely for shy students. The majority of students, who choose from the Option A list, get a well-earned break from writing the week before they write final exam essays. And my plate is not insanely full, merely impossibly so.

The Group Presentation Option

Before we look over the Option A possibilities, a word about group Creed presentations. That word (three actually) has become: "rarely if ever." Though I leave vestiges of the possibility in various instructions, for several years now I've discouraged the group option. Why? Three more words: "too much fun." I'm all for group projects, and can't imagine real learning without a generous helping of fun. Occasional voluntary sharing of progress in Creed reflections can be quite helpful. But working in teams simply hasn't seemed to mesh with this project. For one thing, the girls tend to get silly. We had a very entertaining video in June 2000, for example, called "Creed Central," with one girl in the role of anchor and several others roving around town as reporters following breaking developments on location, in the unfolding story of their various values and visions of life. Entertaining as it was, when it was all over I wasn't sure who really stood for what and why, and I doubt I was alone in this. The guys tend to go for action. We've had a number of group skateboarding video Creed presentations, and a number of groups comprised of football and basketball teammates. Such presentations could actually share some worthwhile insights about the value of qualities such as persistence, teamwork, dedication, and respect. The problem is that, presenting in groups, teenage guys tend to feel the need to invite the souls of their favorite professional athletes into their bodies. In a presentation, a little swagger goes a long way. But when more than one teenage guy is in the spotlight at the same time, there is a kind of snowballing swagger effect that magnifies things in every direction but toward helping an audience understand, again, who stands for what and why. I think it's important to keep the Creed process light, and the teacher's guidance gentle. But the beginning of the end of the group Creed presentation in my classroom came a few years ago when an especially shy student who had joined a group presentation wrote in her course evaluation:

> One project I enjoyed was the Creed Project. . . . One thing I would change if I had a chance to do the creed project next year I would probably do the presentation by myself, just so I can express some of my own thoughts and be recognized for them.

This confirmed for me that there was a real rite-of-passage value in going through these presentations on one's own. Native American vision quests are not group affairs, and there may be a reason for that.

If you choose to try the group option, be sure to emphasize that at some point each individual teammate must face the audience or "camera" alone, and share her creed, the main people and forces that have shaped it, and the kind of person and service she envisions for herself in the future. And, group presentations or no, be sure to emphasize that Creed "dittoes" won't cut it. You might say something like:

> Be sure you don't hitchhike on your teammates [or classmates] by saying, "Well, I have pretty much the same values as Vince." If you are Catholic, please don't say, "I'm a Catholic and I stand for everything the Catholics stand for." Don't cheat yourself out of the chance to make your own statement about what you stand for and explain how you arrived at these values through your personal experience.

From what I've seen, these hitchhiking tendencies crop up more often in group presentations than in individual ones. But I'll leave you the option to try the group possibility with your students; perhaps they'll work with you better than they have with us. Audrey said it best:

> I have learned that the best way to learn about life is to take your experiences and use them to guide your life.
>
> —Audrey Nakamura, June 2003

Creed-Related Volunteering

Option C, although I bill it in the instructions as a requirement rather than an option, is there in hopes that I'll find the wherewithal to activate it some year. One year students did turn in unsealed stamped letters requesting information on volunteering, which I then read, recorded, sealed, and mailed. But with the increased use of email, and increasing end-of-year tizzies, I have yet to find this piece a regular place in the mix. I recognize the apparent hypocrisy of including it here under the circumstance, and do so only because requiring students to put some legs under what they stand for by at least looking into the possibility of volunteering in a position that in some way connects to their personal creed is too good an idea to let get completely away. Perhaps you will recover what I, for now at least, have fumbled. Leah Johnson has managed better. One of her American University freshmen wrote:

> The volunteer work was a great way to execute my beliefs and try to do something useful with them. Helping others who have similar issues that I once had really means a lot to me and I think it could definitely be something I do in the near future.
> —Jackie Tane, Washington, D.C., April 2001

Two Step V Handout Packets

My sophomores all get an initial packet that contains the following sequence (see Appendix I and the website):

- Guidelines and Possibilities for Option A: Creative Visual Presentations (two sides)
- Two graphic representations of presentation contents (two sides):
  - Quadrant Graphic (Figure 9–2)
  - Tree Graphic (see Appendix I for both graphics)
- Instructions for Option B: Reflective Essay (two sides)
- Scoring Rubrics (two sides):
  - Evaluation Sheet for Option A—Visual Presentation
  - Scoring Rubric for Option B—Essay

These are basics I think would fit most classroom situations. The purpose of this packet is to give students enough information on the options to make a choice and get started. I put Option A and Option B rubrics on opposite sides of the sheet at the bottom of the packet. Before the "dog" gets it, you may want to have them tear off and save this sheet in a safe place: Option A rubrics for my students are due, with name, on the day of a student's presentation.

Essay writers will use their Option B rubric as the cover sheet for their essays, which I do my best to collect a Friday or two *before* the week of presentations. A few days after I hand out this packet—which, again, is about the time they finish Step III—I'll ask how many are seriously considering writing the essay. Taking a count, I'll make each of these potential essayists a second packet containing

- two or three sample Step V reflective essays
- a more detailed, annotated set of instructions for the reflective essay. (You can find both of these in Appendix I and on the website)
- some occasions for reflections

A few days later I'll recollect packets from those potential reflective essayists who've decided to go with the visual presentation instead, and Step V is up and running. Remember that they need *at least* three good weekends of preparation time (four is better) for their presentations or essays.

During these preparation weeks this past year, I noticed that Jenny in first period was failing. This surprised me, as she was one of the more talented (and more delightfully cantankerous) writers in all my classes. I called her up for a chat. Though she didn't have much to say about all her missing assignments, Jenny really wanted to talk about the Creed presentations. Her face lit with a mischievous glee, as her words spilled out:

> I already tell people all the time about my influences and those creed kinds of things. At least I try to: Even my friends don't have enough attention span to listen to me. But now I get to present these things to a whole class—and they have to listen!
>
> —Jenny McManamon, June 2003

Creative Visual Presentation Possibilities: Option A

Let's look over the Option A guidelines (see Appendix I). After an explanation of the presentation's purposes (purposes that also apply to the abbreviated presentations from reflective essayists), grading criteria for visual presentations, and a few surviving words on the team presentation unlikelihood, you'll see the possibilities grouped in boxed categories. Some comments on various ones.

Posters

Whether it's mainly attributable to our large contingent of Asian and Asian American students, I don't know. But there has been an explosion in recent years of talented students working in the Japanese anime tradition of cartoon art. And anime is a presence of its own in the Creed presentations, especially among girls. When I think of the most talented anime artists among my female students in the past several years,

I think of a Filipina, a European American, and several Chinese Americans; so the phenomena spreads across ethnicities. At least part of the commitment to the form seems to be the appeal of anime's female superheroes to girls whose real home lives are often filled with parental expectations for academic perfection, preferential treatment of family males, and an emotional distance that many find quite painful. Indeed, a significant portion of girls known to cut themselves come from Asian backgrounds. Invincible anime superheroes who stand up and fight against oppression can have great appeal to girls who feel these pressures.

A number of the most moving presentations this past year in my two honors sections came from talented, high-achieving, outwardly success-ful Asian girls whose inner lives, I was surprised to discover, were filled with a quiet suffering they could find few to confide in about. Anime was an evident coping mechanism for a number of these students. Jennifer Liu, a highly accomplished anime artist and fiction writer, used cartoon art in her presentation to convey a central part of her creed—that life is not mainly blacks and whites but full of grays. I wonder if Jennifer real-ized just how wonderfully this tied back to our study of that marvelous coping mechanism, Taoism, in the fall Wisdom Project.

Sometimes making a little simple sense of the tangled events of our lives can start us in fruitful reflections. For students who could use help putting significant events in perspective, the illustrated timeline is a good option. The Life Chart variation mentioned in Chapter Eleven can serve the added purpose of helping students evaluate and compare their influences, placing them above or below the timeline as positive or neg-ative. (See Brittany's example in Chapter Eleven, and a blank and my own examples in Appendix I.) For students who come from two or more distinct cultural backgrounds, or whose influences include more than one family or household, or who for some other reason would like to represent their influences or creed in an overlapping manner, the Venn diagram is a good option. Of course, Venn diagrams are not lim-ited to two circles but can include three or more, and be grouped around horizontal as well as vertical axes. See Jim Burke's *Tools for Thought* for many more graphic options to share with your students. The metaphorical representation may come easily to students who made good use of the second part of Step IG (Chapter Eleven). As hard as it is to imagine anyone being inspired by my crude artwork, students this past year actually began using the new tree motif from the Step V packet, representing their influences as the roots, their creed as the trunk, and their future as the branches (see Appendix I for illustration).

The most popular poster option is the photo gallery, which students adapt in a variety of ways. Photos are the simplest and most effective way to share and honor those who have influenced us, as I do in my own presentation in plastic sleeves I pass around the room (though next year I plan to scan them into my PowerPoint presentation). A student who uses the tree motif might display photos of his influences across the bottom "roots" of the poster. Photos also work well in an increasingly popular motif, the quadrant, also new this past year, which allots equivalent space to the four required presentation bases (see Figure 9–2). Photos can go in the Influences sector, and/or in the futures sectors, the bottom two quadrants. For other forms of art, we've had a number of paintings over the years, along with the sculpture and garden scene I mentioned earlier. Mobiles, too, pop up occasionally.

Dramatic Performances

You read toward the beginning of Chapter Four my account of Hewan's performance of her original song. From her portfolio Moment That Mattered, you can get a sense of how she prepared and what she gained from her performance:

> My creed project was primarily about school and my aspirations to be successful. I wrote a song called "Experiences." I prepared to sing the song to the class for four days straight. I would ask people to give me some help, but everyone said they couldn't because it was my creed, not theirs. I learned a lot about myself while writing this song. I sat in a dark isolated room reflecting about my life. The first thought that came into my mind was school and its importance. I feel our experiences, like school, make us who we are . . . . At the end of my presentation I was proud of myself and felt as if I [had overcome] my greatest fear. I know I have a nice voice, but my constant fear is that I will get so nervous you can hear it in my voice. . . . When some[one] sings it's as if they open up their soul to whomever is listening. My moment that mattered was the one time I was allowed to express myself in a way I had never done before in front of a class.
>
> —Hewan Abede, June 2002

Not only does singing for the first time in front of one's peers take courage—but singing about the importance of *school*? Even given the fact that coming from an immigrant family can help one appreciate the opportunities of education more than most, Hewan rose above a peer pressure that keeps most of us from singing public praises to school even without a tune! Like Brett Nelson in Chapter Three, she stood up for what she stands for. (She had no need to impress me for her A.)

Jordan McMurray is one of those talented souls for whom school as we know it is just *too* mundane. An accomplished jazz saxophonist and a consummate rapper as a sophomore, Jordan has won the "flow" competition two years running at our schoolwide Black History Month rally. Though I think he and I had a good personal connection in class and out, doing "the work" to pass was just not his thing. But then he realized that he could pull out all the creative stops in this thing called a Creed presentation. And he went for it. Jordan's presentation was my first exposure to the artistry and power of hip-hop. His masterful performance melded PowerPoint, music, lyrics, and choreography. Floating through his lyrics, some of which I believe he improvised on the spot, were images of classroom objects like the beat-up orange chair, and repeated affirmations of the value of his kind of personal reflection. "Creed," he kept rhyming, "it's a need." I only regret not having videotaped the performance to share with colleagues at workshops. It's interesting that in reflecting on the experience, Jordan chose to write not of his own presentation but of others':

> This project made my views change dramatically towards people. [During the presentations,] I got inside their heads for five minutes and it truly helped me feel them and where they are coming from. As humans, we need more humanity in our lives . . . . This project is the essentials of how to get at that point towards others.
>
> —Jordan McMurray, June 2002

Despite failing the class, Jordan later wrote:

> . . . I insisted on doing at least this one project to the extent of my abil-ity only because I knew it was an assignment that I would look back on as an adult and realize how much I have changed over the years, and how much credit I owe to myself becoming the person I am today.
>
> —Jordan McMurray, June 2002

This is a statement I think I can take at face value. Exceptionally bright and creative, Jordan runs afoul of our present education system for the same reasons he would thrive in the kind of totally individual-ized learning system James Moffett advocates—his artistic soul requires it. Perhaps the publisher should hire Jordan to write hip adver-tising copy for this book.

The possibilities in the Option A lists serve more to give students permission to find creative ways to represent and express their creeds, than as formal models. As long as students cover the four bases in the quadrant (Figure 9–2), I tell them, and keep the simple grading criteria on the Evaluation Sheet in mind, the field is open. The possibilities are there to be combined, recombined, and added to. Some of the most dra-matic presentations are simply true stories students share from their lives, usually with a poster or PowerPoint or some other visual aid. A collection of these, some of which I have been carrying in memory for a number of years, awaits you at the end of this chapter.

Interactive Presentations

Several students in the past few years have incorporated student interviews around campus into their presentations. A basic version is just to walk up to random students at lunch or brunch and ask, "So, uh, what do you stand for?" Record ten responses and report the results in your presentation. A more thoughtful and more useful version could involve carefully worked-out questions asked with follow-up questions, or a more targeted survey of different groups for a variety of creative purposes.

Sarah this past year thought to ask a sample group of freshmen if they had thought about what they valued in life, and if so what in life they felt was most important. She then asked the same questions of another sample group of juniors who had gone through the Personal Creed Project as sophomores the previous year, and compared the results. It might be interesting to see such a survey conducted across a larger sample. The most interactive of the options so far is the On the Spot approach pioneered by Nuri Lundy. Two years ago, another bright student in difficult circumstances ran aground thinking about what she stood for. Her single mother was out of town on business much of the time, and Melissa was being raised by an aunt who had eight children of her own. Because, helping her aunt with the eight cousins, she "gets distracted" at home, Melissa did little or no homework, and came to the day of her Creed presentation unprepared. I asked if she'd like some help from her classmates. "Well," she giggled, finally agreeing to give it a try, "I guess most of you are my friends." Echoing Nuri's experience from three years earlier, Melissa's classmates mirrored to her what they felt she stood for. They remarked on her kindness, her willingness to listen and "be there" for others. Though the experience was squeezed into the final moments of class before the bell, Melissa giggled with apparent pleasure at her friends' insights and attention. Given the facts of her current life, this may have been a good outcome in itself.

Again, these lists of possibilities invite additions; please let me know of other options you would recommend (www.universeWired .com).

Reflective Essay: Option B

I hand out Option B packets, as I mentioned, only to students who think they might want to write reflective essays. However, I have often given all students copies of one of the earliest and most powerful examples of a Step V reflective essay. Eddie Salazar's essay is a vivid account of his involvement in a drive-by shooting that led him to a new vision of life as he reflected on a sunbeam coming through a bullet hole in the side of the van. I've read Eddie's essay aloud in class on the first day of school as a way of giving students a beginning-of-year preview of the end-of-year Creed Project. Nine months later when presentations are coming, it's remarkable how many students recall Eddie's essay like I'd read it yesterday. You can see Eddie's essay and other sample Creed Reflective Essays at the website.

I adapted the instructions for the Reflective Essay from the excellent work done on modes of writing in the late 1980s by the California Assessment Program (CAP). You can also find the more detailed, annotated instructions, these taken directly from CAP, in Appendix I. These instructions, along with my adaptation and rubric should be all you and your essayists will need.

Scheduling Presentations

By the week before presentations, everyone knows (or should know) what theirs will entail. I project a transparency and draw up a blank week's calendar. Because I need to check out a PowerPoint projector from our library in advance, the first thing I'll do is ask who's doing PowerPoint presentations; we'll schedule all those for the same day(s). Then, hoping to get some takers for Monday and Tuesday, I might ask who wants to get their presentation over with early in the week "so you can just relax and enjoy everyone else's." (If you get stone faces to this appeal, if absolutely necessary, depending on your philosophy, a little extra credit for Monday presenters can sometimes go a long way.) In the years when I did encourage group presentations, and groups were working on video presentations, I'd let them take Thursday or Friday slots, because coordinating a group might require more preparation time. I schedule Monday through Thursday first, leaving Friday scheduled as lightly as possible to allow for the inevitable postponements and absences. A good fair-minded calendar conversation usually gets everyone scheduled more or less happily.

Coaching

Once or twice a year or so, it has happened that a student has serious concerns about making such a personal presentation in front of her classmates. Knowing what I know about the lives of many teenagers, I tend to listen sympathetically to such concerns. Most of these students over the years have ended up deciding to present, and I think most have been glad they did. When a student asks if she *has* to present (often with a little whine in the question), I try to remember that sometimes there are serious and sensitive issues behind such questions. Students with histories of family or self-abuse or any number of other personal, family, or cultural difficulties may find the thought of standing before their classmates and "telling all" truly uncomfortable. On the other hand, I also know that choosing to go through with this experience can lead to remarkable personal and even academic growth.

The first approach I tend to take with such students is to ask them to try to remain open, not to shut the door on the possibility. I tell them that most students feel at least a little uncomfortable with the thought of these presentations, but that the relief most feel after presenting comes from more than just getting it over with. "If you can, hang on until the presentations begin, and get yours ready," I suggest. "Once your classmates start presenting, you might see what I mean. And then you can decide whether or not you want to go through with it." Again, most of these students have decided to make their presentations, and often been very glad they stood up to the challenge. For those who come to me repeatedly, or who seem particularly and persistently worried about the prospect, I'll tell them confidentially that one option might be to present to a small group of friends after school. Even having said this, I'll still gently urge the student to keep open to the thought of presenting for her classmates. In very rare cases, as you'll see in an example later in this chapter, I'll let a student present just for me, though I try to find ways to include others if at all possible, since sharing is one of the key benefits of the experience.

An important support person in the Creed Project, and especially in the weeks before the presentations, has been our at-risk counselor. I suggest making contact with the best counseling resource person you have available in your situation early in the Creed process. When I read in the written reflections of a pattern of abuse, or cutting, or other sensitive issues, I'll speak to the student privately and ask if she'd be comfortable speaking with the counselor. If need be, I'll volunteer to join her for her first meeting. But I make sure she gets to the counselor. Oftentimes the whole process can serve to release students from heavy burdens they may be ready to put down or at least understand a little better. But do be sure to refer instances of possible abuse to the counselor, for your own protection as well as the student's. (If you fail to do so, you could be open to lawsuits and other legal consequences.) The Creed Project seems to serve as a catalyst for a few students every year who need help. A good at-risk counselor is worth his weight in whiteboard markers.

A word about loss. This year I plan to announce that if you have lost a key person in your life and are still in the process of recovery, please come see me to talk about whether you are ready to go through this presentation. The following part I won't announce, but this past year I misjudged one of my strongest students, whose mother had died the previous year. Because this was a star athlete and an A student who appeared to be dealing with the loss quite well, and was able to talk with me privately about it, I thought I perceived a readiness to speak openly to peers about it. We had discussed the question of readiness a number of times, and as the presentation day approached I was advising the student to make a choice either way based on feelings; if the choice was not to present, the presentation grade could easily be excused. I attempted to play a neutral role, though in retrospect I may have appeared to favor the presenting option. The student did decide to present and, breaking down in sobs when reaching the part about the mother, went down the hall crying alone. Given another opportunity, I would have consulted the counselor and perhaps other adults familiar with the student and family situation. With more of a support net, the student could have explored both sides of the choice more thoroughly. In future cases of recent loss, I think I will counsel students to wait, or to present after school to a small group of invited friends and perhaps family.

Kicking Off the Presentations

In Chapter Two you read about my habit of being the first to make a presentation, kicking off Creed season. You may also recall the first year I did this—by the seat of my pants with no preparation. Taking yourself through the Creed process, if possible *before* you take your students through, is something you just might thank yourself for, if for no other reason than not to be caught asking your students to do something you've never done, as I was caught. Surprisingly few of us have actually done this kind of reflection in our lives, let alone keep them current year by year. You'll find the short, workshop version of the project on the website, and can use the full version to expand on any portion you feel drawn to explore further. You'll also find on the site a list of good resources for personal reflection.

Students really seem to appreciate my being willing to make the first presentation. This past year they asked me to present mine not the week before their presentations but a week before *that*; this gave them more time to plan theirs. After I kick it off, they seem more relaxed about having to do it themselves. And as all students will tell you who have learned to approach all schoolwork "strategically" (with an eye to their grade before a look to their learning), if the teacher's doing a PowerPoint presentation with a little narration and some music in the background, following the same general plan will bring you in a decent grade. And so they relax about the grade part. Which brings us to the last nut, or bolt, before the closing drumroll of memorable presentations.

Assessing the Presentations

The Creed Project addresses standards that have yet to be written. It may address standards that should never be written. Though I can't off the top of my head think of a California Language Arts standard on reflection or self-discovery, the Creed presentations do address Speaking and Listening standards, some of which—eye contact, voice projection, and posture—you see incorporated in the Option A Evaluation Sheet (Appendix I). You may wish to revise this rubric to more specifically reflect standards in your state or district. Other criteria on this rubric—preparation, genuineness/sincerity, and creativity— leave room for subjective evaluation, as they should in such a project. Again, in general, personal learning should be assessed more by demonstration than by measurement. So the primary purpose of this rubric is not to measure performance but to affirm that a student has passed through this experience. Since (with the group presentation option in the past) there is almost never a question of a student not taking the assignment seriously, most students receive full credit or nearly so, though I may circle eye contact or voice projection and deduct five points just to signal room for improvement on the next presentation. (The presentation grade in my class, remember, is around 20 percent of their Creed Project grade and just 2 percent of their semester grade.) Perhaps a signed certificate would be a more fitting way to honor this demonstration of personal learning. The Creed Project is, after all, a rite of passage, something students tend to remember, as my former student in the Berkeley frame store remembered it nine years later.

Creed Memory Lane

What follows, assembled from notes in some cases and memory in others, is a series of descriptions of presentations I have witnessed over the years. They are not necessarily "typical" presentations, if there are such things. Indeed, they tend not to be typical, which is probably why they have lodged in my memory. They are not all gripping. But I think, combined with the other presentations I attempt to describe in this book, they tell us something important about teenagers, about learning, and about human beings. They come in no particular order.

In appearance, they blend in easily with other students from the Middle East and India, and tend to have friends among all cultural groups at our global school. And so it's easy to forget that Afghan students come from a culture long plagued by violence. Yama is presenting on the day my daughters, ages eight and eleven, have taken the day off from school to come witness these presentations. Noticing them in class, Yama approaches me with concern. "Part of my presentation deals with violence, Mr. Creger. Are you sure I should go today with your daughters here?" Yama and I have worked together on his writing a good deal during this year, and at meetings of the female-dominated Afghan Club, which I advise, the two of us have often been the lone male presences. We are good friends, and I know his gentle, respectful nature well.

Standing tall and constrained in front of the whiteboard, summarizing his reflective essay and what he has learned about himself from writing it, Yama periodically collects himself. One night recently, during a family visit to the home of his father's eldest brother, Yama became alarmed by his uncle's sudden and enraged outburst at his son, Yama's cousin. The outburst repeated itself and as the evening went on Yama became increasingly uncomfortable. At one point, after his uncle and cousin stepped outside for a smoke, Yama went out to the car for a CD to show another cousin. About to return to the house, he heard a scream, a scream, he says, like someone was afraid of being killed. Looking quickly out through the car window, he saw his uncle, a diabetic who having had too much to drink had lost control of his impulses in diabetic shock, screaming at his son. His cousin, refusing his father's order to get in their car, turned to run. Yama saw the father chase him, catch him, and savagely beat his own son, who lay helpless on the ground under his father's fists. Afghan notions of discipline being especially harsh on his father's side of the family, Yama had been afraid to intervene, fearing for his own safety. His own father, thankfully, did not follow in these traditions, and was more like his mother's people when it came to discipline. When his cousin got to his feet, Yama could see only blood, no skin, on his face. His uncle told his cousin to get in the car and Yama watched them drive away.

Questions, Yama wrote in his reflective essay, flooded his mind, some of which he shares standing before us. What if my dad is like him? What if my cousin goes insane? What if *I* turn out to be like my uncle? What if I turn out to beat my wife for no reason and then kill her? What if I turn out to be a killer? O God help me! Shaken, Yama went inside and told his own father they needed to leave.

Driving home, he related what he'd seen. His father, swallowing, asked him to remember forever what he was about to tell him. Had Yama noticed last week how exhausted his cousin had looked? So tired he could hardly move, right? Yes, Yama remembered. Do you know why? Yama didn't. Well, his father explained carefully, your cousin had not slept for an entire week because his father was in the hospital for his diabetes. Your cousin couldn't sleep until his dad felt better. He was going to the hospital every day just to be with him.

It was only some days later that Yama understood his father's message. Despite his uncle's traditional ideas about discipline, in the face of his violent outbursts, his cousin forgave his uncle, and continued to love him. This amazed Yama. He wasn't sure he would be able to feel this way if his father were to turn on him in violence. Still, he was deeply moved by his cousin's ability to forgive one who misused him, for the sake of love. This willingness to forgive others, Yama goes on to tell us, is now part of his own creed.

But it is more than that. What he saw could have profound effects on the kind of person he will become in ten years. Will he allow violence to control him as on his father's side of the family? Or will he live in the gentler way of his mother's people? His creed, he explains, his eyes flashing, must help him make the choices that will shape the future he wants for himself.

Tearfully, Harita almost begged me not to make her give her presentation in front of the class. As I often do with students who come to me with reservations about presenting, I encouraged her to delay her final decision until she had seen more of her classmates present theirs. She might see that others wrestled with similar issues, and feel less afraid to share her own situation.

Recently arrived from Gujarat, India, Harita impressed me all year with the full and courteous attention she gave to me and anyone addressing the class. She devoted herself completely to her work, and I saw her offer to help others with what appeared to be openhearted generosity. This was why I was surprised to read in her Creed Steps I–IV write-up of her own perception that dealing with *anger* was one of the chief challenges she faced.

As the second daughter, she explains in her presentation (which I finally agreed she could do after school today just for my daughters and me), she is less entitled to the family's support, and more expected to help her younger brother. Instead of doing the extra credit lab for chemistry, so she can succeed in school and eventually help her parents as her sister is doing, she must help him with his schoolwork. Being full of intelligence and talent and brimming with ambition, Harita is furious with having to constrain her own unfolding to accommodate her family's expectations. It is a shock to me to hear how angry Harita is, as I have always been taken in (mesmerized might be a better word) by her gentle and patient manner, and I am surprised I never saw more deeply into her.

Omar is another of my failing students I had only a small picture of until his Creed presentation. We get along well, and I have been at a loss to understand what I can do to help him succeed in class. My daughters and I watch with the rest of his class as Omar explains that his parents yell a lot, and so he leaves the house a lot. Since he has nowhere really to go, he goes to his friends' houses. Different families, seeing his troubles, take him in. Over the last few years it's been kind of a hard life. He'll probably have to think more about this creed thing.

Maybe I look for such things. But what I notice is how Omar looks up there. He looks as if he's finally got a little control. He's smiling. Yes, a little hyper, alright. But he looks a little lighter, a little happy up there finally telling something true about himself in school.

Julianna, a strong, hardworking student, gets as far into the influence part of her presentation as her parents' divorce. At that point, she breaks down completely. Tears prevent her going further, and she goes to sit by herself in the hall outside the classroom door, unable to present her creed or share her hopes for ten years from now. Judging by her smile when she sees me since then, however, the experience may not have left a bad aftermath.

Though Kunal's strong A paper on his fall final exam showed his intelligence and writing talent, because he did no homework, he failed all year. Once he explained to me how busy he was helping in the family restaurant and store, and how difficult it was to find time to do homework. But I saw how often he hung around after school relaxing with friends. My diagnosis was a simple one: lazyitis.

Through his presentation I learn that there is more to Kunal's life than this appearance. He grew up always relying on his grandfather to keep him studying and applying his especially bright mind. With his grandfather's death two years earlier, he explains in his presentation, his career as an academic nonperformer began. He begins crying, his shoulders shaking gently. I now realize that Kunal is one who may have benefited from a conversation or two concerning his readiness to present. It may take Kunal a while to sort out his creed. Again, if it's possible to judge from his special warmth toward me since then, despite the sadness it brought up the experience may have somehow helped him.

Jackie, a blonde cheerleader, stands at the front of the theater where we did Creed presentations in the early years, holding up a jar half-filled with water. A few years earlier, the jar had been full, she explains. Then her father died. Struggling to make ends meet, her mother hasn't been able to afford the kinds of clothes for Jackie that her friends wear. This drained some water out of the jar. It's hard to keep a cheerleading uniform looking good when you have to make it last longer than it should. Taking a part-time job to help her mother, Jackie has less time for homework, and has had to drop some of her honors classes. The water level dropped further. She isn't sure how much lower it can go before she is all dried out. Her creed is to keep going until things get better. By the time Jackie finishes, not an eye in the theater is dry and all of her cheerleading squadmates in the class have gone up to stand with her, tears leaving streaks on their faces.

Steven Reyes is a quiet, attentive, hardworking student. I never would have suspected the story he tells would be part of his life. His problems revolve around his older brothers dealing drugs in neighboring Union City. His parents may also be implicated. He will always be thankful to after-school sports for preventing him from going home the day the police were tearing apart his house. Had he arrived home that afternoon he could have been sent to a foster home. Success in school is Steven's ticket to a better life. A central part of his creed is to be a good father to his children.

Julie leads a double life. She was in my freshman class, and so we've had an extra year to become friends. She knows I respect her talent and intellect, and enjoy her wide-eyed, whacky sense of humor. I knew nothing of her home life, however, until she transferred into my sophomore class second semester the following year. At school, Julie's wit and smile give a happy-go-lucky impression. As time goes on, I become the teacher she confides in. Julie goes home every day right after school to nurse her mother, who is ill with cancer, and tend to the daycare that is the only family income. She is responsible for all the housework and cooking. Her younger brother needs more attention than she or her mother can provide, is on the verge of expulsion from middle school, and the family is stretched to the point that physical and verbal abuse fly in every direction. No matter how much Julie does for her mother and brother, she never hears a kind word at home. Only one friend at school knows anything about Julie's home life. Most people assume the lighthearted party-girl image is the real Julie.

In her Creed presentation, Julie stands before her classmates and for the first time tells them the truth about her life at home. Though she needs a good stack of Kleenex, and falters once or twice, she tells her story refusing my offer to invite someone up to support her. The room fills with admiration for her when she tells us that despite the misery of her daily life she does not blame her family. They don't know better. And because she has grown up in a home without role models in this area, she explains, her face by now shining with tears, neither does she. Julie's creed and vision of her life center on this question: How can I learn to be a loving person? For some time after Julie sits down, the Kleenex box quietly makes the rounds in the room.

Tina, the honors student whose Creed statement you read in the last chapter, made her presentation in the same series you read about in Chapter Eleven, the presentations that moved Marisa to her observations on the loving qualities of her classmates. Tina invites her best friend to her presentation, and asks her to sit in a front seat. As her presentation gets under way, Tina tells about her distant relations with her family, and credits her friends with giving her the strength to keep living. Toward the end of her presentation, she pulls off a central detachable portion of her poster that had covered a rectangular hole. Taking the resulting frame to her best friend's seat, Tina holds this frame lovingly around her friend's head, honoring her in front of the class by saying that she filled a hole in her life and deserved to be thanked publicly among friends. About Tina's presentation, Marisa wrote:

> Slowly her eyes filled up with tears as she talked about her home life. She struggled through, and ended her presentation with one of the most sincere thank yous I have ever witnessed. When she walked back to her seat, I glanced around. As I scanned the room I realized almost every girl in the entire class was crying.
>
> —Marisa Weiler

I can also attest to at least two moist male eyes. Again I was struck with the difference between the outward appearance of success in some students and the inner realities of loneliness and isolation. What a fine way to honor both unhappy truths about one's own inner life and the loving support from a trusted friend. Tina's friend Jennifer observed,

> Both hope and hopelessness are emotions that human beings go through in order to later achieve goodness.
>
> —Jennifer Chien, June 2003

Far from being a distraction to academic performance, opportunities to safely share such personal truths have great potential to allow high-powered and less motivated students alike to focus more freely on their studies.

Jimmy *almost* waited until it was too late to do something about failing English. Though I can't be sure to what degree the enthusiasm in his statement is influenced by Jimmy's distaste for summer school, there does seem a sincerity worth sharing:

> The Creed Project became a major inspiration in my life. Knowing my values very clearly made me realize what was wrong and why I wasn't doing so well. . . . I suggest the Creed would have to come a lot earlier in the year so I would've been on the right track a lot sooner.
>
> —Jimmy Sanchez, June 2001

Desperation factor notwithstanding, statements like Jimmy's keep me searching for ways to move some of the benefits of this experience to an earlier point in the year. But could a mini–Creed project earlier in the year, with a lesser degree of classroom trust built over a shorter period, have become a "major inspiration" for Jimmy? Would an earlier experience diminish the impact of the project as it is now sequenced? Perhaps the goal is to continue finding ways to weave satisfying personal learning into the course, while retaining the benefits of the year-end presentations.

Writing in her portfolio Moment That Mattered about her Creed presentation, honors student Megan observed:

> I never took the time to stop and think about influencing factors in my life, nor did I think about things that I valued. Ever since I have and have shared it with my classmates, I feel that I know who I am and I know what I stand for in life. Knowing myself helps me do everything a little easier. I can definitely learn easier now that I know all about the most important person in my life, me. Knowing myself is a

huge obstacle of learning out of my way, which allows me to focus on schoolwork, homework and other learning. I feel that I have more time to be educated about things that aren't related to me now, whereas before I always wanted to know more about myself rather than anything else.

As much or more than anything I've written here, Megan's unprompted statement illuminates the central message of this book: The primary task of twenty-first-century educators is to align what happens in school with what we know and can continue to discover about the nature of learning. Before we can truly care about and personally benefit from academic learning, we must engage in personal learning that leads us to begin making meaning from the facts of our lives, and aligning these facts and meanings with something universal we discover we value, something we are willing to stand for and put legs under.

Not that aligning curriculum and tests with standards aren't valid pursuits. But these efforts should grow out of—and not hamper—the more essential move to correlate school life with fresh awareness of how human beings perceive reality and therefore how we best learn. Megan certainly doesn't mean to say that she has learned all there is to learn about herself. But her evident relief in what she has discovered thus far underscores the truth of many of the insights in Chapter Six— observations from thinkers such as James Moffett, Albert Einstein, and David Xu, the sophomore who wrote "The true purpose of education is to unlock one's individuality." Megan's relief smacks of a satisfaction arising from finding herself engaged in this true purpose. Her relief, indeed, points to the deeper value of the self-discovery that can result from the reflection the Creed Project facilitates. In his own explorations, David Xu put it with a special eloquence. He wrote of discovering "a new self that is emerging from the deep pond of soul."

CHAPTER FOURTEEN

Life, Literature, and the Two-Legged Pursuit of Learning

> The purpose of education is to create in a person the ability to look at the world for himself, to make his own decisions . . . to ask questions of the universe and then learn to live with those questions. [This] is the way he achieves his own identity.
>
> —James Baldwin

At the beginning of Part Two, you read of my desire to learn to reshape my teaching so that my students can find more of their learning satisfying. This chapter will introduce the reshaping I have so far done in the sophomore English course I teach, share some plans for school-wide reshaping that are growing out of the entire Creed experience, and even set the conversation in a bit of global culture–reshaping.

The approach I share here is a collection of methods and activities I have put together over a number of years to reach the goal of spreading out across my students' year the kind of enjoyment and engagement in learning I have seen among them during the Creed Project. To create this approach, I've used the same "process" I described at the end of Chapter Three—staying open to inklings, creating and implementing activities that arise from them, paying attention to insights from class discussions and student thinking-partners on how activities are working and might work better, making changes accordingly, following more inklings, and on around the loop. My task now was to find ways to alchemize all this with our existing academic curriculum into a coherent, developmentally attuned, and *satisfying* learning sequence for a year of sophomore English. As far as I've tested it with my students, I think the developing approach you're about to explore makes good logical and intuitive sense. But it's far from the only way to reach the goal of making learning more satisfying. You may have one that works as well or better, or may dream one up next week. Ultimately, it will be the combining and recombining of what's best in all of our approaches that launches us into awarenesses of learning and practices of teaching worthy of a new century.

Overview

Put simply, as you've already read in various places in this book, Two-Legged Curriculum (or Two-Legged Design or Learning) is a way to think about and plan classroom experiences for students and teachers that sets out to honor both the *academic* and *personal* dimensions of learning. The central aim of a Two-Legged approach is to create sets of learning experiences for students that assist them as much in gaining personal wisdom and insight as it does in developing more factual knowledge and skills. The idea first came to me as I thought through one of the more powerful points I came upon as I made my fascinated way through James Moffett's *The Universal Schoolhouse*. It's worth a short walk in theory before I sketch out what I've come up with to this point in practice.

Background of the Two-Legged Idea

Moffett identifies the present foundation stones of U.S. education as *nationalism* and *economics*. Such a foundation, he argues, is incapable of supporting the approach to teaching and learning we will need to develop if we are to thrive or even survive as a society in the new century. Business and government today complain, just as they did in the 1960s after the launching of *Sputnik,* that "American students don't know enough science and math and that they lack skills in communicating, collaborating, analyzing, and creative problem solving." The space race of the sixties was part and parcel of the military, economic, and political confrontation between the superpowers; it was also the rationale for the federal government's instigation of the period's curricular reform. Moffett lays out the problem with this government-mandated approach to learning: "Both then and now what spurred school reform was fear of a decline in technology as measured by nationalistic competition. This leads to wrongheaded thinking about public education" (33).

If centering education policy on the national interest was wrongheaded in the sixties, it makes even less sense today. For one thing, as the global economy develops, nations become less important as economic forces. Today, "American and Japanese automobile companies are marketing each other's products, building factories in each other's countries, and jointly producing some cars." The labels "Made in the USA" or "Made in Taiwan" can no longer tell us "the nationality of the company, of the capital, or of the components." Not only is this result unintended but it runs *counter* to the initial intention of nations to out-perform the economies of other nations: "In this ironic sense, business is leading the way to global thinking" (34). Another problem with con-tinuing to base our system of learning on keeping the nation competi-tive is that competition itself is diminishing in global importance. It is increasingly in the interests of the global corporations whose labels and logos often wield more influence than the flags and insignia of nations to *share* technology, markets, and information. Yet, despite the increasing preeminence of networking and collaboration as modes of doing business effectively and profitably, corporate and national sys-tems continue to be organized around competition. Writing a decade ago, Moffett noted, "In today's global interdependence, competition no longer pays off, though for the moment multinational corporations still have not found all the necessary ways to replace it, just as nations still limit collaboration largely to regional alliances" (35). But ultimately, reluctance or inability to reshape and retool cannot stop the transfor-mation. Writing five years after Moffett in *Natural Capitalism* (1999), Paul Hawkens and Amory and L. Hunter Lovins compare this global situation to

> a train that is at the station about to go. The train doesn't know if your company, country, or city is safely on board, nor whether your ticket is punched or not. There is now sufficient evidence of change to sug-gest that if your corporation or institution is not paying attention to this revolution, it will lose competitive advantage. (xiii)

If it is ironic that corporations mainly interested in profit have led the way through the old systems of nationalistic competition to the "global thinking" of networking and collaboration, it's also ironic that unless we realize the limitations of the competitive mind-set and its creations we lose competitive edge. The irony is especially intense in education.

Because education is the "institution" that for better or worse guides learning, it is education, given the central influence of learning on human progress, that most needs to be "paying attention" to the rev-olution of which Hawkens and the Lovinses speak. We need to recog-nize that our education systems are based on the old notion that learn-ing is mainly a means of maintaining competitive advantage, and that today this assumption is *dangerously inadequate*. Here is the crux of the irony: Either we acknowledge the inadequacy of this assumption and move to correct it, or not merely will we continue failing to foster

the personal unfolding that should be at the core of genuine learning—
and for the want of which America is rapidly abandoning its legacy of
democracy and putting its own survival at serious risk—but we will
miss the very train to the future we intend our old-style accountability
measures to guarantee. Aren't these the true "high stakes" we should
be talking and legislating about, and beginning to design our cultures
around?

Because we continue to regard the purpose of education and learning as merely to serve the interests of business, rather than as the key
to human surviving and thriving, we put the core survival mechanism
of learning—we put our survival itself—at risk. The continuing
national emphasis on "measuring" a process as complex and individu-
alized as learning by arraying mere test scores, just as baseball stand-
ings are ranked on the sports page or stocks and bonds are compared
in the business section, shows that the increasingly outmoded systems
that drove the engines of nationalistic competition continue to drive
education policy. Moffett warns: "To base school reform on the old
nationalistic economic competition would lock education into a past
that is dying for good reasons" (36).

A central source of the problem derives from the choice to form
education policy in response to the fear of declining competitive
power, a choice that puts us in the position of basing national education policy on fear. This is a weak starting position. From Kantor's
spectrum (Chapter One), we can see that much of the reason so many
students and teachers find themselves disengaged and demoralized is
that the essential attitude that drives education policy—*fear*—naturally
generates doubt and despair. How do we find a better way?

Culture and Consciousness
and Teetering on the Brink

> The evolutionary purpose of liberty may be to force human beings,
> through the very adversities it causes, into a more spiritual conscious-
> ness.
>
> —James Moffett (70–71)

Presciently in *The Universal Schoolhouse*, Moffett argues that a transition is already under way, and that the tired industrial-age underpinnings of nationalism and economics are gradually being edged out
from beneath the edifice of education by two new foundation stones.
He calls these new underpinnings *culture* and *consciousness*. This evolutionary transition is intertwined with the one noted by cultural histo-
rian Riane Eisler in her equally important *The Chalice and the Blade*.

In Eisler's vision, world society in our period is teetering back and forth on the brink of a shift from one model of societal organization to another. In the old *dominator* model, on one hand, societies are most characterized by the *ranking* of gender, class, race, and other distinctions. In the emerging cultures based on the *partnership* model, on the other hand, one increasingly sees a more pronounced *linking* of individuals from among groups formerly separated by the old dominator hierarchies. Intentionally or not, multinational corporations have facilitated certain early phases of this linking process with the transnational collaboration discussed above, and even more the linking of individuals is made possible through the Internet. But we must now begin to move forward with clearer intention. Moffett's image of the new foundation stones also resonates with the perspective *The Urantia Book* offers on our period. In this view, when human society is challenged to fuel the evolutionary forces working to displace the old economic *profit motive* (nationalism and economics) with the oncoming *service motive* (culture and consciousness) in the emerging global orientation to life and work. The poem at the front of this book, by poet David Whyte, "bard of the bottom-line world," comes from a book whose title bears the mark of this evolutionary shift: *Crossing the Unknown Sea: Work as a Pilgrimage of Identity,* as does the title of Whyte's bestselling business book, *The Heart Aroused: Poetry and the Preservation of Soul in Corporate America.*

However we view this transitional period, few continue to argue its reality. The transition is proving to be long and arduous, and is bringing about terrific dislocation. The period is also fraught with the understandable tendency at every level to retreat from this disruptive process and return to more orderly approaches rooted in periods in which order was enforced in *dominator* hierarchies and decisions were made on the simpler industrial-age priorities of *profit motivation.* We see this in the reflexes of the current administration as it responds to world and national events. And these reflexes are particularly evident in the current policies on education.

The Height of the Stakes

Given a new awareness of the central role of learning in determining our ability to make progress—a beginning appreciation that learning is *the* primary means of human advancement—we must realize we are about to be left at the station watching the train disappear. Few educators or policy makers, having considered the view of learning described in Part Two of this book that learning is most fundamentally a process of individual unfolding, would argue seriously against its truth. Few willing to think it through would even dispute Moffett's analysis that education continues to rest on industrial-age underpinnings of nationalism and economics that are inadequate to support a truer and more useful vision of learning and are in dire need of replacement. Yet, rather than consider how such new perspectives might be understood and applied in schools, the present administration implements an education policy reflecting a view of learning that is essentially a view of business. It is the same view that guides the forces of business and commerce to attempt at all costs—through war when necessary—to keep outmoded national and international systems of competition and hierarchy in place. The education policies deriving from this motivation in effect force what Moffett goes on to suggest may rightfully become the central societal institution in the coming period—education—to become accountable to an industrial-age view of learning that is passing from the scene. What can teachers do in the face of this retrogression? Two-Legged Curriculum attempts to equip us to carry Moffett's image of the new foundation stones of culture and consciousness into the conceiving and designing of learning experiences, possibly even of entire schools, for children. Writing a decade before they became obvious to the world, Moffett explains the true height of the stakes involved:

> Unless the raising of *consciousness* and *culture* is the primary goal of education, people eventually betray their practical goals such as material improvement and social amelioration. *Americans are losing both prosperity and democracy because they are too undeveloped to make freedom work.* (my emphasis, 331)

In reality, the primary threat to homeland security is our own lack of development. How can we salvage prosperity and democracy? One long-term answer is to insist that our leaders (and if not the present ones, then the ones we elect in their places) participate in a national conversation on the nature of learning, and how what we call school can begin to serve a truer idea of learning that is capable of sustaining American democracy. Reexamining an insight from Chapter Six in a different context, we can again listen to Moffett as he thinks through the rightful purpose of education:

> I argue that personal development must be central, because all solutions to public problems, no matter how collective the action, depend on mature, enlightened individuals to call for and indeed insist on these solutions. (xvi)

This national conversation must revolve around the necessity to establish in schools approaches to learning that provide learners with opportunities to develop themselves into the "mature, enlightened individuals" who only can make and preserve democracy. What does this kind of learning look like? Moffett has given us the outlines. It entails a twin purpose: to raise culture and raise consciousness.

Two Legs

Because those who have recently been charting the course of U.S. education are unlikely to be impressed by ideas as subtle as *culture* and *consciousness*, I use more recognizable terms: *academic* and *personal*. What I call *personal learning* links directly to Moffett's notion of the growth of *consciousness*. *Academic* in my usage may not be exactly synonymous with *culture* in Moffett's, but I see the translation, at least for the time being, as workable. (Academic skills equip learners, through the various disciplines, to become conversant with the knowledge and skills of society—loosely, with key aspects of *culture*.) In Two-Legged Curriculum, then, school communities—teachers and administrators, students and parents—work together to complete the ongoing retrofitting of education's foundation. A Two-Legged approach begins with the intention to balance the academic and the personal at every stage of classroom and curricular planning. A Two-Legged classroom or school is as much devoted to the care and unfolding of persons as to the acquisition and honing of skills.

A note on how this twin goal relates to the Beginning Model of Twenty-First-Century Education you find at the front of this book and again at the end of Part Two. The Beginning Model centers on the notion from Moffett and other sources that personal development is the true purpose, the central aim, of learning. Why, then, advocate a *twin* goal in the Two-Legged approach? I see two reasons.

First, I separate the academic and personal in order to remind myself of the present need for a greater emphasis on personal learning in my students' experience in school and of the need to continue designing this kind of learning into the courses I teach. In reality, of course, academic and personal learning are both aspects of personal unfolding.

The second reason has more to do with how to make this really happen. Because we have become so invested in creating and holding ourselves accountable to academic standards, it makes little sense to advocate throwing academics and standards off the bridge and suddenly reinvesting everything in personal learning. Such talk would raise unworkable logistical and political barriers, and wouldn't go far. Perhaps the greatest impediment to educational progress during the twentieth century was the destructive pendulum swings as opposing education trends came and went, reversing policies, wasting resources, and breeding cynicism. So it makes sense to build on existing momentum rather than radically change direction; I see the Two-Legged idea as a way to stabilize the pendulum swings and move in a forward direction. If adopted in a sensible manner that sought to find approaches to integrate the two aspects, a Two-Legged plan could help make peace in education circles, since it makes room for a broad range of viewpoints in the conversation, giving both those who call for accountability and those who call for personal meaning a place to stand and work. How, then, have I applied the idea in my classroom?

Designing a Two-Legged English Course

Figure 14–1 shows a statement of purpose I wrote several years ago to guide my own decisions in planning and teaching my sophomore English course. I wrote this statement (a bit cheekily) as if it were intended to guide our entire sophomore English program. While I could not then and cannot now make this claim, I wrote it mainly to keep my own sights set on a clear purpose. Still, I have been surprised at the developments of the past two years at the school. The embracing of the Creed Project by three English colleagues in the sophomore program—this past year including first-year teacher Patty Baca, who handily took four of our eight sections through the experience, allowing well over half the sophomore class to participate—makes me wonder if perhaps there was a reason I wrote the Statement of Purpose this way.

Finding a Course Theme/Title

Reaching this two-pronged goal, I soon realized, meant not creating alternating chunks of curriculum but *intertwining* experiences to promote academic and personal growth in my classes (see the discussion of Scheduling in Chapter Nine). But first I needed a guiding concept, an overarching course theme. This is something I had been considering for a number of years, and this thinking eventually led to the proposed schoolwide thematic curriculum we'll explore later in this chapter. As you may recall from the kickoff section of Chapter Ten, I eventually chose "Envisioning a Life" for our course theme/title. It's funny how resistance to change so often governs us. One day after I'd been using this title a few years on handouts as a way of reminding us what the course was about, a colleague, having noticed the title on a set of copies for my students by the copy machine, stopped me in the hall. "You *name* your courses?" he asked, incredulously. "You can't do that!" "Sure I can," I shot back, mischievously. "Don't you?"

Among other things, I want the course theme to serve as an umbrella for the various thematic studies that make up our year. These

Sophomore English at American High School

Statement of Twin Purpose

The purpose of sophomore English at American High School is to help students develop themselves in two major areas:

1. to promote their progress in reading, writing, language, thinking and learning skills. [Beyond the personal benefits these skills bring, they are also *culture-orienting* skills.] To this end, we teachers find reasonable and effective ways to use standards and assessments in our classrooms;

2. to begin building a personal vision for their lives. [This is one means of bringing about Moffett's "raising of *consciousness*."] To this end, we teachers select themes and literature, design a writing program, and create other activities to encourage and inspire our sophomores to begin envisioning life concepts for themselves.

Our goal is to balance students' time and energies between these two essential areas of development.

Figure 14-1 Statement of Twin Purpose

studies and their themes, by the way, are not set in curricular stone. At least I don't think so. In the same way our notions of secondary English curriculum can center too rigidly on skill development, I believe that oftentimes they center too inflexibly on literature. This leads to a narrowing rather than an expansion of possibilities. I prefer to center my idea of a course on a *conversation* I want our classroom to have through the year. Then I want to choose literature that stimulates this conversation at the same time it helps students acquire the needed academic skills and knowledge. This conversation helps address personal and academic learning goals alike, but ultimately the substance and tenor of the conversation at the center should be guided most of all by personal learning goals set by the school community. Democratically determined personal learning goals, as we'll discuss later in this chapter, should condition the substance and tenor of the conversation that guides learning. The Cross Section of Twenty-First Century English Curriculum at the end of Chapter Eight came out of a conversation with student thinking-partner David Xu on how to help more students *care* about learning. It is a beginning attempt to conceive a more fruitful relationship between academic and personal learning, with personal learning becoming the curricular core that integrates and brings meaning to the academic parts. More conversation is needed to develop this approach.

My idea for the overarching theme of our course crystallized sometime during the first two years I "piloted" Zora Neale Hurston's *Their Eyes Were Watching God* as a replacement novel for Golding's *Lord of the Flies*. After teaching Golding's book for eight years, I had come to the end of the trail. While Golding's novel is clearly a work of genius, I could find no way to construe the view of humanity it so powerfully puts forward in any light that could assist my students to reflect on their lives and purpose in a post–Cold War world. What I want for my students is to facilitate a class conversation that can help them find answers for themselves to their own big questions about their lives, the universe, and what really matters to them. I am not willing to impose my answers, Golding's answers, or someone else's conviction that there are no answers. Since everyone in Golding's story who even asks questions is hunted and/or murdered, for the sake of my students I needed reverently to toss this novel over my shoulder and find one that could help them figure out their lives. Following an inkling, I got permission from my department chair to pilot Hurston's book.

I have discovered in the several years since then not only that *Their Eyes* is a work of genius on a par with the greatest of literary works, but that the novel fits the course I dreamt of creating in a way that is nothing short of uncanny. In the article I eventually wrote for *California English,* I discussed the main character, Janie Crawford:

> Though it may not be immediately apparent, Janie's growth in the novel echoes the remarkable expansion of horizons so characteristic of a developing 15 or 16 year-old. My impression is that Janie's growth as a person, more than that of most literary characters, can incite personal growth in young adult readers. (22)

Sometimes I wonder if, as she created Janie more than sixty years earlier, Zora Neale Hurston had the Creed Project in mind. In *Their Eyes*, Hurston gives us a character who, despite not having known her parents, and being raised by her grandmother, a former slave, conceives a vision for her life—at the age of sixteen. As the novel resolves, with Janie ripened into her forties, fifteen- and sixteen-year-old students can see her reaping the personal rewards of having *achieved* some of that vision:

> Here was peace. She pulled in her horizon like a great fish-net. Pulled it from around the waist of the world and draped it over her shoulder. So much of life in its meshes! She called in her soul to come and see. (184)

It was Duron Aldredge, my student thinking-partner you may recall from Chapter One, who first pointed out to me how perfectly the novel

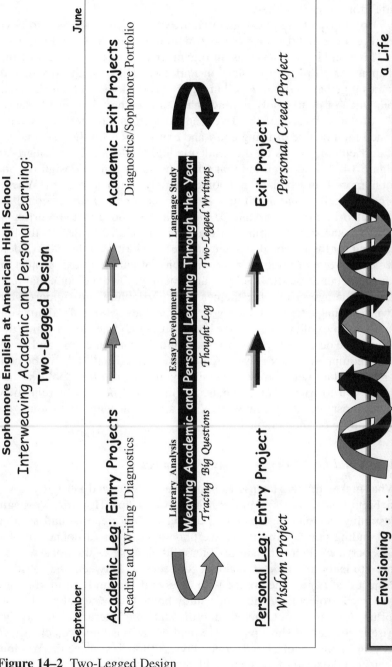

Figure 14–2 Two-Legged Design

fit the Creed Project. It was about then that I settled on "Envisioning a Life" for our course theme.

To represent the two-legged nature of the course I was also envisioning, I created the not-very-artistic graphic you'll see in Figure 14-2. This graphic will serve as an organizer for most of the rest of this chapter. As I did for the ideas in Part Two, I'll explain how this all comes together as if things fell in place in some logical and linear fashion, when of course only in hindsight can I see how it all made sense.

In the overview of the Two-Legged idea in Chapter Ten, I mentioned the practice of using entry and exit projects on the personal leg of curriculum, just as on the academic leg. You can see this clearly in Figure 14–2. Keep in mind that what you see is only a design for one sophomore English class, not some divinely ordained pattern. When I began thinking that Moffett's *culture* and *consciousness* could be translated into *academic* and *personal,* and the idea of two curricular legs took shape in my mind, I already had the Creed Project as the natural exit for the personal leg, and had been working on the fall Wisdom Project for two or three years. Your choice of entry and exit project, of course, depends on the level you are teaching, the developmental realities of the age group, the themes your curriculum can support, your own personal interests (since you want to feel passionate about your course), any colleagues with whom you collaborate in teaching this course, the degree of freedom you are granted or can claim, and more. Little equipped to advise you in all these areas, I will have to be content to explain what I have done, give you a flavor of my process, and invite you to trust your instincts, inklings, and powers of reflection. Since most teacher training revolves around academic learning, I'll concentrate on the personal leg.

A Personal Leg Entry: The Wisdom Project

What makes the most sense to me in the Two-Legged Design you see in Figure 14–2 is the entry-exit design concept. How do we begin designing personal learning into a course? We create sound starting and ending points. And then? We find sound ways of connecting the dots between them. It's simple but solid. Course evaluations suggest that students are indeed making connections between the Wisdom Project that begins the course with a generalized study in the fall and the Creed Project that brings this study home to a personal level in the spring. As it turns out, themes, motifs, and other literary elements that arise in the varied short pieces we read in the Wisdom Project surface all year in our novels, poetry, and plays. Although you see the Wisdom Project at the head of the personal leg in Figure 14–2, in reality it is not strictly a personal learning experience. It is a *two-legged* project, because it provides good supplies of both personal and academic learning. At this point, you may want to read over the student instructions for the Wisdom Project (see Appendix II).

Until 1997, Holt, Rinehart, and Winston's *Elements of Literature* at the sophomore level included only a half dozen selections from the Bible that one could say fit the category of wisdom literature. In their 1997 edition, suddenly the anthology sported an entire section called Sources of Wisdom. Containing five selections from the Bible, two from the Qur'an, five short sayings and one longer tale from the Sufi tradition, one from Omar Khayyam (making nine selections in all from the Islamic world), three Taoist anecdotes, two Zen parables, and a beast fable from the Hindu Panchatantra, plus a number of excellent supplementary selections from around the world, the section actually represented a cross section of world wisdom. It was an enormous advance, and makes it possible for me, supplementing with a few additional pieces, most of which I can find in the anthology itself, to offer my students at the beginning of the year at least one piece of literature that connects in some way with most of their global backgrounds. This new material has enabled me to transform a limping effort at exploring wisdom with my students into what Atticus Finch might call "a living, breathing reality."

To emphasize that we are addressing academic standards, I have begun adding a page of state standards to instruction packets for this and other projects to indicate specific academic skills the project helps students develop. It's a pretty impressive list for this month-long project, as you can see in Appendix II. As the project develops, I'll stop and refer students to the list; for example, we'll look over the Speaking Applications skills when we embark on one of the project's most engaging activities, the Wisdom Project interviews. And in the project we'll thoroughly address most of the reading and writing standards.

Thanks to a May 2000 *Newsweek* devoted to what it called the "Millennial Generation," I got the idea to make the study not only a general exploration of wisdom—addressing essential questions like What is wisdom? How do we know when a person is wise? How can we learn from the wisdom of the past? The Wisdom Project has also become an inquiry that asks students to explore what their generation appears to stand for. In a sense, this aspect of the Wisdom Project is a Creed Project prequel, on a generational rather than a personal level. Now that the *Newsweek* material is getting a little dated, we'll need more current data to gain perspective on this generation, and may need to do some Internet research this fall.

I re-tailor the project every year to reflect current events as well, and you'll see the invitation to consider the Bush administration's War on Terrorism and contemplate, based on our exploration of wisdom, to what extent the administration's actions can be called wise. Students appreciate the opportunity to ground such a discussion in our study of wisdom, rather than to let the usual crosscurrents of unfounded political opinions run loose. As you see in the instructions, the project includes a set of criteria (adapted from *The Urantia Book*) for three Levels of Wisdom, providing a way to judge whether a given action can be regarded as *wise* on ground, intermediate, or higher levels. (Did I really just refer to a set of *standards* for wisdom?)

The project culminates with students writing an essay on wisdom, basing their ideas on a series of prewriting activities, including the interviews, which I collect in a separate packet, and three brainstorms. The entire project, which I think is increasingly helping students develop both academically and personally, now includes more materials than I am able to touch on here. You can find additional materials relating to this project at www.universeWired.com.

Weaving the Personal Through the Year

Because our existing programs are for the most part designed around academic learning, it is not possible to move suddenly to programs perfectly balanced between academic and personal learning. In fact, as with most worthwhile changes, the transition is best when it is deliberate yet gradual. Connie White, our wise, funny, and beautiful principal, reminds us that any change worth making takes at least three years to bear fruit worthy of the name. Rather than the two legs of equivalent weight I aim for ultimately, I think first in terms of beginnings. Figure 14–2 suggests that as we move through the year's labor of developing students' academic skills, we weave "personal strands" around and through the various academic activities that develop students' reading, writing, conversing, and thinking skills. To carry their personal growth through the more skill-oriented work, students develop and revisit their Big Questions, react to and converse about expanded perspectives on course themes and topics using their Thought Logs, and engage in self-discovery through Two-Legged writings. Descriptions follow, along with student insights into each of these approaches.

All this begins in my classes with a course introduction in which I attempt to convey the two-legged nature of the course. In fact the first handout students get from me is itself "two-legged," since it contains two different colored double-sided sheets, the top one in which I try to introduce the personal elements of the course, the bottom one the academic requirements. Below you can see the top page of the personal introduction sheet. We read this together on Day One in the fall:

Envisioning a Life
Course Introduction

ENGLISH 10cp   WORLD LITERATURE
2002-2003   Mr. Creger

Without the vision and the power, this learning will do no good.
Lame Deer, seeker of visions

What students want to learn is as important
as what teachers want to teach.
Lois E. LeBar

What I do is me.
For that I came.
Gerard Manley Hopkins

Welcome to your second year of high school English! I 'd like to begin by wishing you a fun and challenging experience in this class. I hope you will let your hopes run high. For one of my main goals this year is to rely as much as possible on your ideas and input in decisions about how we run this class—and even what we study. I thank you in advance for your involvement and for the pleasure of being your teacher. —Cheers, Mr. C.

I. What This Class Is About

ONCE upon a time, human beings thought the world was a flat disk at the center of the universe. The planets, moon, sun, and stars, people thought, revolved around the earth. Life revolved around families, clans, and villages. Today we know the world is a sphere, a spinning ball not at the center of anything really, and that it orbits a star we call the sun. The countless millions of stars we see on a clear night away from city lights are only a small fraction, a tiny slice, of the actual number of stars in the universe. Recent discoveries suggest that most stars are in fact *suns*, centers of their own solar systems, each sun orbited like ours by its own planets. So the number of planets in the universe *far exceeds* the number of stars, probably reaching into trillions.

During the first half of the twentieth century, people had even less idea of the true size of the universe. Most scientists assumed the conditions necessary for life had come together on earth only by chance, and so it was highly unlikely that life as we know it existed on any other planet. But today, the odds seem slim indeed that among all those trillions of worlds, living creatures have appeared on only one—this one. More and more of us today look beyond villages, cities, even beyond nations. Peering beyond this small world, some of us even prepare to meet neighbors among the stars. As our lives on earth get increasingly complicated, we reach for an *enlarged vision* of life and the universe in which life unfolds.

What does it *mean* to live in a universe as vast as this one now appears to be? What has been said, what is being thought about such things? What exactly *is* the universe, anyway? Does it exist only outside us, or also inside us? Is it like the earth, only bigger—endless galaxies of injustice and suffering, loneliness, greed, and war? Will we always be cut off from it, lost, abandoned? Or is it a place of love, of compassion? Does the universe somehow *care*, and speak quietly in each of our hearts as a loving parent to a treasured child? Is *American High School* part of the universe? What are our lives *for*? What does it mean to live in a way that is *wise*? What does it mean to *serve others*? The reading and discussions, the thinking and artwork, the drama and writing we will do together this year will be about helping each other ask and explore questions like these.

Big Questions

Students begin the course by identifying and writing about "Big Questions"—questions about life, the world, the universe—that they sometimes think about. As new studies commence through the year, I try to remember to invite them to revisit and possibly revise or update these questions. The goal is for students as much as possible to navigate the curriculum of this World Literature and writing course using their own genuine deep interests—well-developed in some students, of course, and just emerging in others—as compasses. Students are regularly encouraged to bring their Big Questions to the year's work of developing reading, writing, thinking, speaking, listening, and study skills. Students relate them to our studies when possible, incorporating them as feasible into essays and final exams. This *strand*, if you will, of weaving the personal through the year begins with the homework assigned on Day One, "Inquiry 1: Big Questions." (I describe the getting acquainted activity we use on Day Two, the Big Question Meet, at the beginning of Chapter Ten.) Following are the instructions for Inquiry 1, the Big Questions writing:

English 10cp   Instructions for Inquiries 1 & 2

Introduction
Big Questions and You

Dear Student,

In order to help me choose literature, writing assignments, and discussion topics that make this an interesting class for all of us, I'd like to know what kinds of things *actually interest you*. Please carefully read the instructions below and write a thoughtful response to the one you are assigned tonight. Carefully and thoroughly answer the questions you are asked. Each of your responses should be well-developed. By "well-developed," I mean that it contains examples and is at least *one full page* in length. If you are unsure how to write more, try adding another example or two. If you still need help, try rereading the instructions and letting ideas come.

Inquiry I - Big Questions

A. *Make a list* of big questions—about life, the world, reality, the universe—that you sometimes think about. Let your mind stay on this as long as you can, and make this list as long as possible. Try a few deep breaths when you get stuck, or do something else for a while. You may find it helpful to reread the first page of our Course Introduction that we read together in class. If you give it time, ideas will flow, and surprising new ones may suddenly come to you. Write each question in a complete sentence, ending in a question mark. Once you have a long, satisfying list, choose *ONE* of these questions that most interests you.

B. *Write a paragraph* explaining why this particular question holds your interest most of all. Try to come up with several reasons for your interest in this question. Why do you think it matters more to you than other questions? Say as much as you feel comfortable sharing. Which question might come in *second* for you? Why?

C. On a separate sheet of paper that you will keep in your binder after you turn in Inquiry I, copy your list of Big Questions, with your first and second most interesting questions marked.

I collect students' responses to Inquiry 1 on Day Two, and try to return them as soon as possible, with comments complimenting the questions they are asking and encouraging them to keep asking them through the year. If and when I am feeling especially ambitious and enthused, in the second or third week I assign Inquiry 2, "Dear Universe," which turns into what amounts to a creative writing assignment for me. Though it takes a powerfully long time, some years I've actually written each student a response signed "Your Friend, The Universe," in which I freewrite what I imagine a friendly, compassionate universe would have to say in response to his or her Dear Universe letter. Well, it's one way for a teacher to get in a little writing! And have you ever imagined the voice of the universe coming through you?

Inquiry 2—Dear Universe

A. Take another look at your Big Question, from Inquiry I. Let your mind *think further* about this question. Does anything about it especially bother you? Confuse you? Mystify you?

B. Make a list of things about your question that puzzle you. In other words, what are some of the hardest parts of your question to answer? *[If nothing about your question puzzles you, you may want to try another question from your list.]*

C. Imagine that the universe has a *personality,* that it is a person you can talk with. Imagine you've recently learned that the universe especially *enjoys* getting letters from its creatures. Imagine that the universe can actually answer any question you ask, and is *glad* to do so. *Write a letter to the universe* in which you ask for help undertanding some of the things about your question that puzzle you. Simply begin with the salutation, "Dear Universe. . . ."

D. Optional: Search the web to explore your Big Question. In your letter, incorporate any information from your web search you think might be interesting to share with your correspondent, the universe. You may want to start by going to Ask Jeeves (ask.com) or Google (google.com).

It is also possible, I've found, for teachers to use students' Big Questions in designing courses. When time permits (and that has only happened twice in the first years I was developing the Big Question approach), I tally and group students' Big Questions for a given year into categories and report results to classes. In Figure 14–3 you can see my tally of one year's Big Questions. Figure 14–4 shows how I then used these results in choosing themes and literature for whole-class study, as well as titles for Literature Circles, which I then called the Outside Book Project. (If you are unfamiliar with Literature Circles, a team reading activity that often helps turn non-readers into readers, see Harvey Daniels's *Literature Circles.* It's a great resource on an activity that certainly deserves to be called two-legged, since it helps students develop reading skills at the same time it helps them learn to share responses and perception on what they read with classmates, which in turn builds enthusiasm for reading; to have students talk about books in a natural way is the very natural goal of the activity.)

My purpose in analyzing the students' Big Questions was to get a sense of what *kinds* of questions they were asking, and then see whether I could use these *kinds* of questions to actually design our course. I first grouped the questions in categories while tallying them, as you see in Figure 14–5. Their questions do not come from a completely blue sky, of course, since on Day One students read the Course Introduction with me in class, and then read the instructions for Inquiry 1 that evening. Both of these pieces I intend to stimulate students to think in the most expansive terms they can as they ask these questions. So the questions they create may not reflect students' average daily states of mind (a definite blessing in many cases). Still, you can see

Big Questions Tally 1998–1999

The Big Questions 112 students in three English 10cp and one English 10general classes asked in response to the course description and instructions for the Inquiry 1 writing assignment break into the following categories. Listed by number of questions per class, in order of frequency asked.

		period 1	period 2	period 4	period 5	total / %
1)	Questions about life in the universe beyond earth.	10	2	6	2	20 / 18%
2)	Questions about afterlife (including soul and reincarnation)	9	3	3	2	17 / 15%
3)	Questions about destiny (incl. end of world, eternity, personal)	3	5	–	4	12 / 11%
4)	Questions about existence of God (creation vs. evolution)	1	2	3	3	9 / 8%
4)	Questions about personal future/career	3	–	2	4	9 / 8%
5)	Questions about (the nature of /relations with) the universe	1	2	2	1	6 / 5%
5)	Questions about individual life purpose/uniqueness	–	1	2	3	6 / 5%
5)	Questions about the challenges of life	2	2	1	1	6 / 5%
6)	Questions about racism, prejudice, respect	3	1	1	–	5 / 4%
7)	Questions about beginnings, origins	1	–	–	3	4 / 3.6%
7)	Questions about humanity's future, millennium	–	1	1	2	4 / 3.6%
7)	Questions about the impact of science/technology	2	–	1	1	4 / 3.6%
7)	Questions about the problems of greed, money, war	–	2	–	2	4 / 3.6%
8)	Questions about love	–	2	–	–	2 / 2%
9)	Questions about "true religion" (Truth?)	1	–	–	–	1 / 0.9%
9)	Questions about beauty	–	1	–	–	1 / 0.9%
9)	Questions about gender issues	1	–	–	–	1 / 0.9%
9)	Questions about the limits of human knowledge	–	1	–	–	1 / 0.9%

Figure 14–3 Big Questions Tally 1998–1999

English 10cp Course Plan Derived From Student Big Questions 1998–99

Changing Visions of Life and the Universe

Themes as Focus Questions (with student "Big Question" areas)	Literature	Writing-Thinking Skills/Activities
		invention strategies general <—> specific

What Are Our Origins?
Where do we come from?
Are we created or evolved?
Is there a God?
What is the true religion?
How best to live?
	Bible excerpts
	Koran passages
	Saadi, Khayyam, Rumi
	Taoist Anecdotes / Zen Parables
	Panchatantra
		Wisdom Project
		Simple paragraph:
		  basic assertion & support
		  focus, coherence
		Inquiry journals

What Is Human Destiny?
What is human purpose?
What is humanity's future?
What of Afterlife and Soul?
What of Eternity?
What of personal and planetary destiny?
	Les Miserables
	Selected quotes, poems
		Complex paragraph:
		  subordinate assertions
		  variety of support
		Inquiry journals

What Are the Nature and Limits of the Universe?
Is there life beyond Earth?
What impact science and technology?
What are the limits of human knowledge?
	Outside Book Project:
	Science Fiction/
	Daedalus and Icarus
	Near Death Lit.
		Multiparagraph essay:
		  complex development
		  concessives
		  parallel structure

How to Love? *What is Beauty?* *What is Moral?* *What is Truth?* *What is Male/Female?* *What is Love?*	"Antigone" Cyrano Romantic/Contemporary poetry	Research skills 6–10 page paper
What Is Our Nature and Relationship to the Universe?	*Their Eyes Were Watching God* *Macbeth, Lord of the Flies*	Reflective essay Inquiry journal Multiparagraph essay
How Best to Grow Personally? *What is my purpose?* *How am I unique?* *How will I learn and earn?* *How to survive life challenges?*	Selected poems/songs	*Career Exploration* *Portfolio Project* *Personal Creed Project*

Figure 14-4 English 10cp Course Plan Derived from Student Big Questions 1998–1999

that the top two categories in 1998–1999 were questions about life on other worlds (18%) and questions about afterlife (15%). In 2000–2001 (not included here), the top two kinds were questions about the meaning of life/self-discovery/life-purpose (20%) and questions about students' personal future (13%). It would be interesting to keep this up consistently for five or ten years and see what longer-term trends might be observable.

The course plan you see in Figure 14-4 was an early draft that I didn't follow terribly closely. But it was an interesting experiment, and I think it had a large influence on my commitment to continue using Big Questions. I took the eighteen *kinds* of questions into which I had grouped students' questions (Figure 14–3) and grouped them in turn into just six larger categories, turning each of the six into a Focus Question. These Focus Questions then became thematic studies. I sequenced, added in our course literature where it seemed to fit, and added the course writing development. Of course I claim no scientific accuracy, since I subjectively chose all the categories in both grouping exercises. But the funny thing is how closely the themes this process yielded resemble the themes of the course I had already been teaching. Perhaps there are only so many themes in a universe. At any rate, students seem interested when these charts go up on the screen as we discuss the Big Question emphasis. Here are some insights from students on the value of the process:

> One of my "big" questions was "Why do people believe in a god and put their whole life in a god that no one has seen or know exists?" This question still applies to me, but readings from this course have helped me realize why people do believe in a god. God gives them hope, security, and just to have someone always there to turn to. This quote [She probably means "question."] is still important to me because I have started to want to turn to God for my problems or my "big" questions.
>
> —Melissa Townsend, June 2001

> The Big Questions assignment made me think about how I see the world and what is important to me. My list had questions like "Why are we here?" and those questions made me think about who I am as a person and how I see things. Those questions had a significant impact on my year this year, and without those questions, I don't think that I would have been able to write my Personal Creed or my wisdom essay. They are still meaningful to me because I still want to know if there is an answer to them. If I didn't do those questions, then there is no telling what kind of shape I would have been in now and after the year is over.
>
> —Tony Caraballo, June 2001

Lately, I have thought about many new "Big" Questions: Who made God? What is my destiny? Etc. This course has helped me realize that these questions were in my mind. It has helped to further develop my thinking process. It has brought up questions about destiny, mainly because of *Les Miserables.*

—Danielle Adams, June 2001

If you want a better answer, you've got to ask a better question.

—Anthony Robbins

The Thought Log

The provocative quote from James Baldwin at the beginning of this chapter and the one above from Tony Robbins are a fine way to introduce yourself to this activity for weaving personal learning through the year. Like the Wisdom Project, the Thought Log is Two-Legged. It helps students address numerous academic standards—in close reading skills, thinking skills, speaking and listening skills—*and* asks them to engage in regular personal reflection on "deep" issues. Twice a week or so, students respond in their Thought Logs to quotations intended to offer expanded perspectives on the themes and literature we are engaged in. Thought Log discussions are consistently among the most popular activities of the year. You may want to re-aquaint yourself by rereading the two paragraphs of introduction to the Thought Log at the beginning of Chapter Ten.

In Appendix II you can see some sample quotes we have used during the Wisdom Project to cast our conversations in new galaxies of thought. In the collection of Thought Log quotes I hope one day to offer as a booklet, I organize quotes by topic. Most of the samples you see now come from the section on Level 3 Wisdom (see Wisdom Project instructions in Appendix II for a description of the Levels of Wisdom). Beyond a study on wisdom, these particular sample quotes will fit anywhere in the year, especially as preparation for the Creed Project.

As you read in the Thought Log preview in Chapter Ten, once I've put a quote on the screen the Thought Log process consists of three steps: quiet reflecting on paper, pair or small group discussions, and whole-class conversation. Until recently, my only instructions for the reflecting step entailed the predictable—Paraphrase, Agree-disagree, What does this remind you of? What part is confusing? Then, some time after I began to learn more effective methods of reading instruction through Reading Apprenticeship training, I created Quote-Crackers, which you'll find in Appendix III. It's a two-sided sheet with a wide variety of sentence starters on one side and two approaches to using them to "crack" tough quotes on the other. I like to ham up introducing the QuoteCrackers by throwing a few walnuts out for sleepy or distracted-looking students to catch and asking the class how these folks should go about opening them. Depending on the level of cynicism or inertia in the room, I might get lucky and someone will mention the word "nutcracker." Pulling a nutcracker out of my back pocket, I hold it up and say, "Yes, it's true. To crack a walnut you need a nutcracker. But what tool do you need when your English teacher gives you a tough quote to figure out, as I am about to do?" You see where this is going. In my other hand I hold up the stack of QuoteCracker handouts and up goes a particularly tough quote while a volunteer passes the handouts around.

I've noticed that the pair discussions are a little more active since the advent of the QuoteCrackers, as students make use of the ready-made response options. As the year goes on, I ease off on requiring them to use the quadrants as instructed, since they hopefully have internalized a few more response options. Higher-level classes, of course, have less need of them, though they'll spark even bright minds. Some students report using the QuoteCrackers for tough passages in nightly reading assignments. Once I've finished the joys of roll taking, and the pair discussions are winding down, I'll ask who would like to make the first footprint in the morning sand of a whole-class conversation. And we're off. Before the whole-class discussion winds down, if I've chosen the quote to connect with our class readings or current events and the connection hasn't already come up, I'll simply ask if anyone can make a connection to our reading, or to current events, and let things develop, often to a natural segue into the main lesson. As you can see from some of the sample quotes, the Thought Log can be an effective way to equip students to discover for themselves the deeper values connections (to recall the learning continuum) in our course literature. And it makes for some rich class conversations. Here are some reflections from students on the activity:

> The thought logs were something I looked forward to each week. I didn't always share my views, for fear of being attacked by fellow classmates. But I did when I had something I couldn't hold back. But I always got a kick out of hearing my fellow classmates try to persuade others [of their] view. Towards the end of the year people were less shy in my opinion, so the conversations were much more interesting. The thought logs let us all stand up and fight for what we believe in. It was like little practices for standing up for your rights. . . . It's like we worked on a whole different part of our brain, feelings. Everyone's point of view, no matter how out there, was added to the conversation. Thought Log discussions were like building blocks to the Personal Creed Project. It forced us to look at things

in a different way, and to find a part of us we might have not known existed.

—Beth Stockcamp, June 1999

The thing I will value the most from this class are the thought logs. I learned many new ways to think of things. I learned how to really understand the reading from practicing my skills on the quote logs. It also got me interested in reading poems.

—Ken Magtoto, June 1999

The other part of this course that I really loved was our class discussions. I love arguing with people and the thought logs gave us good ground.

—Monica Gallos, June 1999

Two-Legged Writings

Two-Legged Writing assignments call for academic skills—such as supporting an assertion with carefully chosen, specific evidence and commentary, writing with focus, development, and flow, according to language conventions—to be demonstrated in the writing of a topic created to promote personal discovery. Remember that I separate academic and personal "legs" of curriculum mainly to remind myself of my goal to give as much attention to students' personal learning as to their academic learning. But in practice, the two legs often work together. Below is the prompt for the English 10cp Fall Semester Final Exam Essay:

Sample Two-Legged Writing Assignment

English 10cp Fall Final Exam Essay Prompt

Write about an important *change* you passed through in 2001. As you follow the instructions below, you will select a change to write about, form an opinion about this change—your essay's assertion—and write your essay supporting that opinion. You will learn how to introduce your essay by discussing one of the *themes* we have explored in our reading this semester, as the theme is developed in at least one selection of our literature. The theme you choose should connect to the change you are writing about. Conclude your essay by making an *allusion* to one of these pieces of literature, showing, in a sentence or two, how the theme of this piece of literature relates to your change. *Clinch* your essay with a related *question* to which you'd like to know the answer.

I won't blame you for taking this as hyperbole, but this assignment, even though it is a final exam essay, is one of the most popular activities of the year. As you see from the prompt, it asks students to demonstrate the academic writing skills they've learned in the first semester.

It asks them to develop an assertion and support it with specific evidence and commentary. It asks them to analyze the term's literature, and be conversant with themes and literary allusions. The assignment becomes two-legged when it also asks them to analyze their own lives over the past year, find a significant change they have experienced, characterize that change with the perfect adjective for the essay's assertion, choose a literary theme to connect with this change, and allude in closing to a work of literature. In a sense, this assignment has personal learning at the center with academic strands woven around it.

Students receive carefully scaffolded instructions that take them step-by-step at home through prewriting—generating ideas, brainstorming, visual planning, outlining—and, on the day of the final, drafting in class. As you can see in the sample essays on the website, students write about different sorts of changes such as moving to Fremont, meeting their boyfriend, getting better grades, and on and on. From extensive lists of possible adjectives we brainstorm in class, each chooses the perfect adjective to fit their change. And they form their assertions on the somewhat dramatic pattern: "No change I have experienced during the past year has been more ___ than ___." The adjective, of course, fills the first blank; the change fills in the second. Since sophomores are by definition changing creatures, this assignment is just their cup of tea.

With help from the learning continuum idea, I can now understand more of why this assignment is so popular with students. As they list changes and choose one to write about, students are considering the facts of their lives. As they characterize this change with the perfect adjective and distinguish it from other changes in their lives, they are creating meanings (judgments) from the facts of their lives, as they will next semester during the Creed Project. And, though not specifically asked to do so in this midyear assignment, many students in reflecting also discover that, as a way of dealing with the important change they wrote about, they relied on or discovered something very much resembling a principle or a belief. And they have made a values connection. When this happens, of course, they have connected the three regions of the learning continuum, creating an experience with the potential to be inherently satisfying (see Chapters Seven and Nine for more on the learning continuum). Indeed, as time goes on the Two-Legged idea may well become three-hubbed.

Jamie Phipps would not have been in the college prep class had not the district, fearing lawsuits from parents claiming that Fremont schools failed to prepare their students to pass the new high school exit exam, canceled all remedial English courses, offering no other alternative. Jamie had struggled all semester to keep up with the reading and writing load, and was *not* looking forward to the final exam essay.

Surprised to find that something actually about herself was the final exam, Jamie did well. Later, she reflected:

> For the first time I was interested in doing a test.
>
> —Jamie Phipps, January 2001

As well as other sample two-legged final exam topics, you can find other two-legged prompts on the website. You can also create your own two-legged writing assignments, especially once you've set developmentally appropriate personal learning goals for your students. Although you can begin doing this, as I have, without *grade-level* or *schoolwide* personal learning goals to connect to, making your own choices in the context of a carefully put-together department, grade-level or schoolwide personal learning plan would make the most sense. How to begin making such choices? The following is adapted from my *California English* article on Two-Legged Curriculum (see www.universeWired.com).

Designing a Two-Legged Schoolwide Program

Let's imagine, then, that a given department, grade-level team, or school has decided to begin devoting some time and care to designing personal learning into students' experiences at school. The more democratic the process the better, as long as focus can remain clear. While it may make sense to standardize *academic* goals by community, state, and even nation, *personal learning goals* should be created with the particular students and community in mind. One approach that makes sense to me is to first choose a select number of *key challenges*, issues a given generation of students will face in their lives in this community. Some communities might settle on challenges like preserving traditional values. Here in the East Bay, one of several challenges that will confront every generation for the foreseeable future is the opportunity to bring increasing racial healing and understanding.

Schoolwide grade-level themes—as long as they are arrived at democratically—can make it easier to address such an issue across disciplines and develop it up through grade levels. Such themes focus students' and teachers' attention on finding links between the challenges students face and their growth as persons. Thoughtful Choices for freshmen and Expanding Horizons for sophomores are two potential grade-level themes a number of colleagues agree may make sense at our school. Widely applicable, flexible, and developmentally interconnected grade-level themes could support a healthy curricular conversation, in and beyond the classroom. Figure 14–5 shows a schoolwide thematic curriculum that has been under discussion at American High School.

Proposed Personal Leg of Curriculum

American High School
Possible Grade-Level Themes, 9–12

12th–Making Connections?

11th–Focusing: Personal Future?

10th–Expanding Horizons
society, world, universe

Spring Personal Creed Project—Students undertake mid–high school personal rite of passage: *What do I stand for and how might I choose to serve others?* **(English)**

Fall Project on World Wisdom—Students gather/analyze data on teen lifestyles—nationally, internationally. *What does my generation think about, care about, and believe? How do these qualities compare with previous generations, and with traditional and nontraditional ideas of wisdom?* Student Big Questions as learning guides. **(English/World History/Math)**

9th—Art and Process of Choice-Making
class, school, community, society

Students observe and analyze choices made by: characters in literature, by society, by themselves **(English)**; by individuals, by society in environmental and other science matters **(Science)**. They explore connections between Essential Questions and Choices?

Students gather/analyze data: on student backgrounds, on student choices and choice-making—at class and school levels **(Geography/Health/Math)?**

Figure 14–5 Proposed Personal Leg of Curriculum

Conversations among, say, social studies and English teachers about race and racial healing could lead to freshman social studies classes spotlighting nations that choose to be involved today in the slave trade, or underscoring episodes of "ethnic cleansing" as they pertain to shifting national boundaries, or discussing an article on the challenges of reconciliation in South Africa or creating a homeland for Palestinians. Better yet—and rarer still in the media—students could examine materials that highlight actual (read *positive*) examples of racial healing where it's happening around the world today. At some level, of course, each of these situations involves a *choice*, made or unmade, which freshmen can examine in connection with their year-long study of thoughtful choice making. At the same time, in their English classes, freshmen could explore the issues—and choices—of race and racial healing through a variety of activities, including, for one example, the analysis of poems by contemporary black authors and student poets, and through a study of a novel often used to address such issues, *To Kill a Mockingbird*.

Having enabled students at a given grade level, in this case the freshmen, to consider an issue like racial healing from the perspectives of several disciplines, we could also design the personal legs of our programs to help students continue their exploration of such issues as their minds and hearts develop *up through* the grade levels. To this end, *Mockingbird*, with freshmen, and Hurston's *Their Eyes Were Watching God*, with sophomores, make a powerful sequence.

Told through the eyes of a tolerant white family looking out at racial injustice around them, last spring *Mockingbird* provided my freshmen examples of the kinds of choices that are prerequisites for tolerance. Atticus impresses his children and the reader with the need for such choices: "You never really understand a person until you consider things from his point of view . . . until you climb into his skin and walk around in it" (Lee 34).

This spring, *Their Eyes* will take many of these same students, now sophomores, further along this road to healing, beyond simple tolerance toward true understanding. Told through the eyes of a black woman in a world where color differences dictate relations even among African Americans, the novel helps my nonblack sophomores climb imaginatively into the experiential skins of black Americans. And Hurston helps black sophomores (and all their classmates) understand and appreciate themselves and their special history more fully. On the social studies side, in World History, students could probe more deeply into these issues as they relate to specific topics on the world scene, perhaps elaborating more deeply on those issues touched the previous year in freshman social studies, or exploring the background to the current events that have plunged us into an urgent new need for racial and cultural understanding between the West and the Arab and Muslim world.

This "deep" approach could allow a school community to settle on a small number of core issues students will face in their lives, and create a curriculum around them. Racial healing, gender fairness, societal class issues, environmental challenge, and spiritual unity are only some possibilities. A more conservative community may assemble an altogether different list. Students would approach these issues from several directions:

- across disciplines at a given grade level,
- according to developmental readiness, and
- vertically up through the grade levels.

So, in an "articulated" series of purposes, each grade level could explore an issue with a slightly different focus. For example, when my freshmen explore racial healing, reading *Mockingbird* in connection with the yearlong theme Thoughtful Choices, they essentially study a sub-issue of racial healing—*tolerance*. At the end of the following year, now as sophomores preparing to begin creating their own visions of life in their Creed Projects, these same students, assisted by the insights Hurston weaves so brilliantly into *Their Eyes,* are taking the next step in their multiyear study of racial healing—toward *understanding*. And, in light of Riane Eisler's notion of an emerging global culture based increasingly on the linking of partnership rather than the ranking of domination, if slavery is considered one of the ultimate expressions of the dominator model of society (along with genocide and war), students can see racial healing as part of the transition to a world based increasingly on partnership. This is just one example from the first two years of high school. Further development of racial healing or other issues could be designed into the junior and senior years, beginning with developmentally appropriate, democratically determined grade-level themes created for the second half of high school. In addressing these themes, of course, students would at the same time be engaged in reading literature, writing, and speaking, developing specific skills in these areas to meet the standards of the academic legs of their programs. See Figure 14-2 for a picture of this interweaving.

Walking on Two Legs

The dust of exploded beliefs may make a fine sunset.

—Geoffrey Madam

Just as bipedalism has worked effectively to carry our bodies, carefully conceived Two-Legged approaches to teaching and learning can work to carry twenty-first century children into the world more ready to cope and contribute. It is the kind of learning experience that inspired Frank to write in the preface to his end-of-year portfolio:

> For me, this course was about finding who I am and my purpose here on Earth, but to the Board of Education this course was about improving my ability to read and write. I believe that they have succeeded in their goal, and as you read these works, I hope you will see that I have met mine as well.
>
> —Frank Whipple, June 2000

Frank's words suggest that a concerted, long-term effort to bring such an approach into widespread practice would do much to stabilize the wild swings of the education pendulum—from today's "objectively measurable data only" end of its travels, to the various equally unwise experiments at the opposite "it's all personal growth" end of the swing. Stacey, reflecting in her portfolio, offers one of many student insights that validate the intuitions that lead me to persist in developing this Two-Legged approach:

> The class as a whole was one of the best experiences I have been through in school. The class was based on something beyond the education of English and I really enjoyed myself.
>
> —Stacey Teixeira, June 2000

Frank and Stacey also echo James Moffett's vision of twenty-first-century education, an approach to learning that rests on two new foundation stones: culture, and consciousness. Such a vision, and the approaches and practices that flow from it, including those I hope to have shared in this book, lead beyond the destructive ranking of a former age, to learning that prepares learners to grapple with the world that is, and create the world that's coming.

 # Afterword

Further Weaving Options
for the Two-Legged at Heart

> The life of a person who fully embraces transformation from
> within will follow a course impossible to predict from a
> knowledge of its beginnings.
>
> —Unknown

To supplement the approaches and activities described in this book
proper, some may be interested in exploring additional possibilities.
This is a kind of bootleg section. Indeed, these further options I use for
Two-Legged Design are more the behind-the-scenes variety; hence
their place in the afterword. Most of them aim in one way or another
to suggest gently to students that the universe may be less cold and
hostile than popularly assumed, that meaning and purpose may indeed
exist, by design, on and beyond the earth.

Cosmos-Friendly Themes

Once I've found an overarching theme/title for a course I'll be teaching, I want to put myself on a three-year plan to create a sequence of
themes we can wrap personal learning strands around as the year pro-
gresses. A few years ago, I assembled a collection of themes I called
"Cosmos-Friendly" because designing a course with such themes
helps students formulate what my experience tells me are more *realistic* visions of life and the universe, and may help them expand their
own sense of purpose. It is customary to bow to the weight of current
evidence of human violence and depravity and regard such visions as
Golding's as *realistic,* and to dismiss visions of the brighter sort as
wishful. Yet evidence to the contary, though admittedly less tangible
and certainly less "newsworthy," is available. Kantor's spectrum, for
one example, appears to reflect a universe capable of design.
Experience indeed shows that hope and faith do not fall from the sky
but are rewards of efforts driven by ideals. Experience also verifies that
doubt moves rapidly toward despair through the progressive domina-

tion of fear; even the terminally ill can choose to live without fear and bypass seemingly inevitable despair. The learning continuum is another ready instance: to learn by cataloguing facts, creating meaning from those facts, and employing those facts and meanings in the search for sound values indeed appears to spark a joy in learning that hints at design. The Personal Creed presentations are evidence of this. I try to create a thematic framework that, without coercion, honors the possibility in student's imaginations of a larger design abroad in the cosmos. On the website you'll find the "Cosmos-Friendly" themes I brainstormed around a central hub (Love) and three ancillary hubs (Truth, Beauty, and Goodness). The themes you'll see in parentheses on this graphic are intended to remind me that any of these themes can be used in conjunction with its opposite. An English course I took at UC Berkeley was designed around the themes Love and War. This, of course, is an especially powerful way to explore a theme, and to learn.

Lighting Up the Dark Canon

The idea here is simple: Use more literature presenting students an inviting, well-lighted universe, a prospect that helps put earthbound tragedies in perspective. Figure A–1 shows a few cosmos-friendly works of literature I find especially effective among my students at lighting the place up.

Below are some passages from *Les Miserables* and *Their Eyes Were Watching God* that give you a flavor of what I mean by visions of a more "well-lighted" universe.

Well-lighted passages from Les Miserables *(page numbers from Washington Square Press/Pocket edition):*

The book which the reader now has before his eyes is, from one end to the other, in its whole and in its details, whatever may be the intermissions, the exceptions, or the defaults, the march from evil to good, from injustice to justice, from the false to the true, from night to day, from appetite to conscience, from rottenness to life, from brutality to duty, from Hell to Heaven, from nothingness to God. Starting point: matter; goal: the soul. Hydra at the beginning, angel at the end. (436)

Courage and forward! Citizens, whither are we tending? We are tending toward the union of the peoples; we are tending toward the unity of man. (Enjolras at the barricade, 416)

The human race will fulfill its law as the terrestrial globe fulfills us; harmony will be reestablished between the soul and the star; the soul

Lighting up the Dark Canon
sample titles

Les Miserables (secondary)
> a vision of a compassionate universe, beginning amid suffering on earth, attained through powerful growth and progress

Jane Eyre (secondary, college)
> a vision of spiritual growth assisted by nature, heaven, and prayer in a responsive universe

Their Eyes Were Watching God (secondary, college)
> a vision of a universe in which love and goodness of heart can transcend even the legacy of earthly slavery

Poetry of Rumi
> arguably the greatest spiritual poet in world history, Rumi remains widely read today in the U.S. Effortlessly blends Muslim, Jewish, and Christian themes and images. Certain poems such as "The Guest House" work with teens.

The Alchemist (secondary, college)
> a millennial fable about finding one's relationship to the world and to others. Universal appeal, international connections

Any and all in the Harry Potter series (all ages)
> filled with rich, surprisingly subtle spiritual messages for a world on the brink of discovering the rich multilayered variety of life in the universe

Figure A-1 Lighting up the Dark Canon

---

will gravitate about the truth like the star about the light. Friends, the hour in which we live, in which I speak to you, is a gloomy hour, but of such is the terrible price of the future. A revolution is a tollgate. Oh! The human race shall be delivered, uplifted, and consoled. We affirm it on this barricade. (Enjolras at the barricade, 417–8)

Until order, which is nothing more than universal peace, be established, until harmony and unity reign, progress will have revolutions for stations. (434)

"'Does she still come to the Luxembourg?' 'No, monsieur.' 'She hears mass in this church, does she not?' 'She comes here no more.' 'Does she still live in this house?' 'She has moved away!' 'Whither has she gone to live?' 'She did not say!' What a gloomy thing, not to know the address of one's soul!"

Student Comments on **Les Miserables:**

> If I were to re-write this story, I would not change one thing or event
> in the ending. It was the most attention-grabbing and soul-moving
> ending that a hero can have. It made Jean Valjean's pilgrimage to
> enlightenment fulfilled and perfection was accomplished. From a
> selfish thief, he had become a selfless saint. I think that Hugo is
> indeed saying that a human being's quest in life is to strive toward
> perfection. . . .
>
> —Monica Yun, January 2000

> The part of Marius' letter I choose to write about reminded me that I
> am a romantic; always have been, always will be. . . . True love does
> come from the soul. When you fall in love with someone you don't
> fall in love with their looks. You fall in love with their soul, the one
> thing that is unique, the way they look at life, their personality, that's
> their soul. . . . So I think that this is not only the most beautiful part
> of Marius' letter. It is also the most deep and insightful thing I've ever
> read about love.
>
> —Megan Irwin, January 2000

> Victor Hugo is saying (in "English") that the heart gets stronger as
> you love someone. You get feelings you've never had for anyone else
> and it's all pure. I think Victor Hugo is oh-so-romantic and this is so
> great!
>
> —Angela Solon, January 2000

Well-lighted passages from Zora Neale Hurston's **Their Eyes Were Watching God**

(Note: The final two quotes may require familiarity with Hurston's use
of dialect.)

> There are years that ask questions and years that answer. Janie had
> had no chance to know things, so she had to ask. Did marriage end
> the cosmic loneliness of the unmated? Did marriage compel love like
> the sun the day? (21)

> All next day in the store she thought resisting thoughts about Tea Cake.
> She even ridiculed him in her mind and was a little ashamed of the
> association. But every hour or two the battle had to be fought all over
> again. She couldn't make him look just like any other man to her. He
> looked like the love thoughts of women. He could be a bee to a blos-
> som—a pear tree blossom in the spring. He seemed to be crushing scent
> out of the world with his footsteps. Crushing aromatic herbs with every
> step he took. Spices hung about him. He was a glance from God. (106)

Of course he wasn't dead. He could never be dead until she herself had finished feeling and thinking. The kiss of his memory made pictures of love and light against the wall. Here was peace. She pulled in her horizon like a great fish-net. Pulled it from around the waist of the world and draped it over her shoulder. So much of life in its meshes! She called in her soul to come and see. (193)

"It's uh known fact, Pheoby, you got tuh *go* there tuh *know* there. Yo' papa and yo' mama and nobody else can't tell yuh and show yuh. Two things everybody's got tuh do fuh theyselves. They got tuh go tuh God, and they got tuh find out about livin' fuh theyselves." (192)

"Love is lak de sea. It's a movin' thing, but still and all, it takes its shape from de shore it meets, and it's different with every shore." (191)

With literary geniuses like Hugo and Hurston as spokespeople, the cosmos—and thereby life itself—sounds like a place of goodness by design. Students need to listen to these messages. Some will actually hear them.

Sharing Personal Growth with Students

One of the great benefits for me in trying to help my students learn in a way that is more personal and satisfying is that as the year goes on I have a different sort of relationship with classes and with individual students than I would otherwise. Since the climate becomes more friendly to personal sharing, even I get involved, thanks sometimes to the gentle prodding of students like Michael Febo, who got me personally involved in the Creed Project by asking me what my creed was. Once in a while, especially when students ask, I feel more comfortable than in the past sharing pieces of the little wisdom I've been able to gather over the years of my life so far. Of course, I have much to learn from everything that happens in the classroom. This sharing adds a special luster to the quality of learning in the class.

Meditating

It was one Friday in Duron's class, sixth period during the 1999–2000 school year, that this little tradition began. For me, it had been a week of less than four hours' sleep a night, and by the end of this week I was toasted. All day I'd been handing out grade reports and listening to students asking about their missing points. You might know the kind of day it was. Well, my patience was gone. My civility was going. Handing out the grades to the day's last class, I muttered something like, "So here are your grades. If you have any questions, don't ask me. If you find any mistakes, I don't want to hear about it."

The class was stunned. This was an especially sweet group, and most days we had a friendly rapport. They'd never seen me even remotely like this. But there I was, unapologetic.

"Uh, Mr. Creger . . ."

"Yeah, Jonna." I lifted my head to gaze toward her seat in the back corner by the teacher's desk.

"Uh, Mr. Creger. Do . . . you meditate?

I scratched my head. "Funny you should ask. This is the first morning I haven't meditated this week. I usually take ten minutes at least in the early morning. That's funny . . . now that you mention it." The class was quiet.

"Uh, Mr. Creger . . . ." It was Jonna again.

"Yeah, Jonna."

"Maybe you should do some meditating this weekend."

"That's a good idea. Think I'll take you up on that, Jonna."

By the next week I must have been back to normal. Midweek, someone in sixth period asked if I would teach the class to meditate. Friday we took a few minutes of breathing exercises and a few more of mental relaxation. The following week my second- and third-period classes asked why sixth period got to meditate and they didn't. Two weeks later my freshman class got into the act, and ever since then word has gotten around and by the end of the year most of my classes insist on meditating once a week. Sometimes I'll call it "mindchillin'" or some other oddball term, just to keep the idea fresh.

To take at least five minutes a week for physical and mental relaxation has become a tradition in most of my classes. In fact, quite a few times this past year I thanked a class for insisting we meditate on a day when I had not managed my morning routine and needed the refreshment. At times it seems that meditating has almost become part of our class approach to mental hygiene. I don't like to push meditation on students; and of course it is an optional activity. I think many get interested at first because of the intriguing time-wasting possibilities it presents. Others enjoy it because a few minutes' nap comes in handy. It's difficult to describe the various tangible and intangible benefits of this practice in a short space. Since several students have chosen to write about this class activity, I'll defer to them. You can read these statements at the website.

Praying for Students

This is obviously not something all teachers will feel comfortable trying. I first began the occasional practice during my second year of teaching after listening to a tape a colleague lent me of an address by Guy Dowd, 1988 National Teacher of the Year. I'll conclude this section by describing a practice Guy Dowd developed for his troubled students. Getting to school before anyone else in the morning, he would sit at his desk and take a few moments to let his mind quiet down. Then he'd allow his mind to call up any student he happened to know was dealing with particularly difficult challenges this week or just needed more love and support than the world was offering. He would get up, and go sit in this student's desk. For however long he could manage before anyone else arrived, he would simply hold this student in his thoughts, and, sitting right where the student would soon be sitting, ask for any guidance on how best to help him or her on this particular day. That has always impressed me.

Appendix I: Creed Project Materials

Initial Step V Packet, Item 1: Option A— Creative Visual Presentations

ENGLISH 10cp   ENVISIONING A LIFE

Personal Creed Project Step V
Option A: Creative Visual Presentation Guidelines

> "I felt this project was a way for each person to say,
> 'This is who I am, and this is what I value, and enjoy.'"
> —Maria Martinez (98-99)

The purpose of your presentation is to present to your classmates your best understanding of

- how you've come to be who you now are,

- what you stand for (your creed),

- the kind of person you see yourself becoming in ten years, and

- how, in as large or small a community as you envision, you might want to make your life count for others.

Grading criteria include the following:

- How well you appear to have prepared

- How clearly you articulate your creed itself

- How well you have suited your presentation style to what you are saying

- The degree to which you seem genuine and sincere, and creativity (See Evaluation Sheet.)

Important: If you choose to be part of a team presentation, at some point each member of your team must stand (or sit) apart from the others and present his or her own personal creed.

Some Possibilities

Poster

cartoon	metaphorical representation
caricature	photo gallery
illustrated timeline	flow chart
facial expression	artwork or music inspired by nature
Venn diagram	chart, map, or graph
report cards on ?	sensory figures
commendatory (award) plaque [for positive influences or inspirations]	
wanted poster [for negative influences]	

Other Artwork

drawing, illustration	sketch	mobile
painting	sculpture	

Dramatic Performance

Song	Skit
Rap	Dramatic reading
Poem	Dance
Puppet show	Dialogue
Sock puppet show	Big Question dialogue
Talk show	Monologue
Parable	Big Question monologue
Story	Fable / Myth
True story (memoir)	
Interview with celebrity (your inspiration, yourself)	
Interview with criminal (your poor influence, Arch Critic, yourself)	

Interactive

Peer interview around campus
Survey of students/friends/family members
Improvisational creed conversation (On the Spot approach):
"If you all have anything you'd like to say about me that might help me understand myself better, please feel free." (an option for the bold at heart)

Techno

PowerPoint
Video project

Other

Initial Step V Packet, Item 2:
Presentation Quadrant Graphic

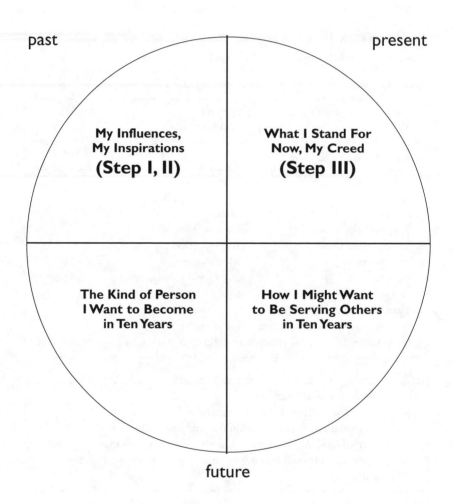

past   present

**My Influences,
My Inspirations
(Step I, II)**

**What I Stand For
Now, My Creed
(Step III)**

**The Kind of Person
I Want to Become
in Ten Years**

**How I Might Want
to Be Serving Others
in Ten Years**

future

Appendix I: Creed Project Materials

Initial Step V Packet, Item 3:
Presentation Tree Graphic

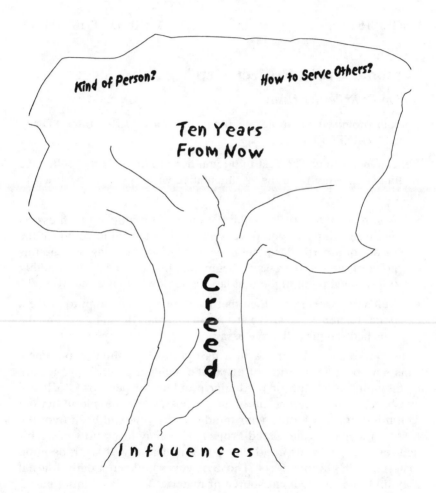

 **Appendix I: Creed Project Materials**

Initial Step V Packet, Item 4:
Instructions for Option B—Reflective Essay

ENGLISH 10 cp   WORLD LITERATURE

Personal Creed Project Step V

Option B: Reflective Essay

Here, as promised, are more specific instructions. PLEASE READ and reread CAREFULLY!

Reflective Writing: The first thing you need to know is that reflective writing is different from the argumentative writing you've been working on all year. Here's how:

- Argumentative writing—like the one- and multiparagraph essays and research paper you have written—is intended to convince the reader of a particular point of view. You are learning to state this point of view at the essay's beginning, prove it point by smoothly transitioned point in the middle, and review it at the end. Right?

- Reflective writing, on the other hand, does not attempt to prove a point. It attempts to arrive at a *personal truth*. Begin by reading the attached sample reflective essay.

A reflective essay begins with a narration of personal experience. This may be a description of a specific incident or scene, of a train of thought, a concept, or particular problem, or perhaps you'll use an observation of nature, an object, a possession, people in action. You might try just letting your mind drift as you read back over the first four steps of your Creed Project. This may bring up some incident or scene in your mind that you might find will work as good material to begin this essay. Those of you who keep a daily journal may find this an excellent source of material for this opening narration, or occasion for reflection. See "Some Occasions for Reflection" (attached).

The essay then embarks into reflection, *reflecting on the possible meaning of the experience just related*. Reflection continues throughout the middle of the essay, exploring connections between the opening experience and your life, and probing still further to reach your ideas about life. Ideas flow naturally one into the next, with minimal transitions, none formal or clunky.

Reflection finally leads to *a realization or discovery of personal or universal truth*. A reflective essay, then, has (1) a beginning, an opening occasion for reflection, (2) a middle reflecting on that experience, and (3) some final truth discovered at the end.

The Assignment: Follow the instructions below.

Beginning: Occasion for Reflection
Look over your Creed Step III. Can you imagine a personal experience to open your essay? This opening—an observation, thought, concept, description, incident, or narration—should lend itself to a series of following reflections having something to do with your values. Look through your writings in your binder, in your writing folder, or in your journal if you keep one. Look over your Thought Logs. Spend a few minutes thinking about your Big Questions. Anything come to mind? If not, let your mind drift into the sunny horizons of divergent thinking (in short, brainstorm). If still no luck, think over your Step IV. And take one more look at the Occasions for Reflection handout. Does anything there jog your mind? If not, take a walk and smell the spring air. Alright already! Rough out a draft beginning. It could last a paragraph or two.

Middle: Your Reflections
Begin reflecting on what you have written. Let your reflections come naturally. Your essay will be more satisfying and successful if you connect the experience to your daily life, and only then to your ideas about life.

Somewhere along the way, consider an influence or two (more if you like) whose values you wrote about in Step I or II. Can you make a connection to your life by reflecting on this person? Let your reflections continue, one flowing from another. At some appropriate point—whether in this middle part, or later at the end—raise possible objections to your values or personal vision (from Step IV), and discuss why you persist in holding them, or it. Let your reflections develop, moving toward a representation of your values (your creed) to come in the next, final section. This middle section should last three to four paragraphs at least.

Conclusion: Reflections as They Lead Naturally
to Your Personal Creed
The ending section of this essay should contain an expression of your personal creed as a natural extension of what you have been reflecting

on. If you haven't done so in your middle section, this section should also incorporate possible objections to your values (Step IV), and show why you persist in holding them. Close the essay with some realization of a personal truth to which this entire process has led you. This concluding section could run from one to three paragraphs.

Requirements

Your essay will be graded on the sincerity with which you attempt and complete this project. The tone, style, and form of writing should be consistent with the content. For further help, reread the attached sample reflective essay and its instructions, and the two essays written by former students. See me with any remaining questions.

Brainstorm: optional   Outline: *not recommended*
Rough draft: in ink, double spaced, clear margins sides and bottoms
Final draft: typed and double spaced   Length: 2 1/2 to 4 pages

 # Appendix I: Creed Project Materials

Initial Step V Packet, Item 5:
Some Occasions for Reflection

Aesthetic Experience

This is that feeling of being lifted by a work of art, literature, film, or music. As well as by experiencing another's work of art, some of our most memorable aesthetic experiences come when we create works ourselves, even if these works don't exactly reach the level of masterful. Many of us have known the joy of reaching some aesthetic peak, the joy of expression, whether our own or another's.

Person-to-Person Contact

Most of us have had experiences of deep love for, and close communication with another person, or with a sports team, musical, choral, or other group. Such experiences—with parents, guardians, siblings, or friends—sometimes take us beyond the concerns of our own egos. Occasionally, such experiences of connecting to another person or group even occur in class situations: in elementary school when a class delights in the story their teacher reads with a dramatic flare; in one of those class discussions in junior high or high school when the class feels strangely connected by an unseen web of understanding or affection. Even a phone conversation with a loved one can bring on such an experience.

Inner Experience

Although these are not experiences all of us have as teenagers, some of us by nature tend more toward reflection and awareness of our inner lives. Some have made self-discoveries through such practices as prayer, meditation, worship, or simply sitting alone in expansive thought. Experiences like these can lead us to flashes of insight into how to solve problems we face, or to sudden truths about our lives, or a deep sense of refreshment, or spaciousness.

Connections with Nature

To be impressed with the beauty of natural surroundings is often to be transported beyond our normal state of awareness. This can happen as readily when gazing from the window of a city bus at the hills silhouetted against a blazing sunset as it can while hiking a rugged trail through purple autumn mountains with a backpack. Sunsets, mountain trails, coastal beaches and cliffs, forests, even hurricanes and snowstorms—all can bring us special feelings of connectedness to something larger than ourselves.

Sensory or Physical Experience

Our bodies don't serve only to distract us from what is going on deep inside our minds and hearts. The experience of running or swimming in a race, playing as a member of a team in an intense competition, engaging in an aikido or karate competition—these things can move us beyond purely physical awareness into a "peak experience."

Appendix I: Creed Project Materials

Initial Step V Packet, Item 6:
Creed Presentation Rubric

ENGLISH 10   ENVISIONING A LIFE

Personal Creed Step V

Option A: Creative Visual Presentation
Evaluation Sheet

Name(s):   _____   _____

_____   _____

Preparation	**/10**
Content / Expression	**/20**

    Influences, inspirations
    What you stand for (your creed)
    Who you are becoming
    How you might serve others

    Eye Contact
    Voice Projection
    Posture (no hands in pockets)

Presentation style fits content	**/10**
How **you present fits** *what* **you present**	

Genuineness, sincerity	**/5**

Creativity	**/5**

Total:	**/50**

Comments:

Personal Creed Project Step V

Option B: Reflective Essay
Scoring Rubric

Missing/Needs work:

Opening Occasion   **/10**
an observation, thought, description,
incident, narration, or other personal experience
- effectively sets up reflections to follow   __ / __
- includes concrete or sensory details as
  appropriate   __ / __
- appropriate length (1–2 paragraphs of
  half page or more)   __ / __

Reflections   **/20**
a series of explorations reaching for personal meaning
- contemplate possible meaning of the
  opening occasion   __ / __
- explore connections between opening
  and your life   __ / __
- explore new ideas as they arise, probing
  for meaning   __ / __
- connect to influence(s) from Step I or II   __ / __
- incorporate objections to your values   __ / __
- ideas flow naturally—minimal
  formal transitions   __ / __
- length: this is the main section of your
  essay (2 to 3 pages)   __ / __

Realization   **/10**
a culmination in a new awareness or discovery
- flows naturally from reflections to realization   __ / __
- realization connects to your life   __ / __
- realization incorporates your personal
  creed or values   __ / __
- length: half page to page and a half   __ / __

- sincerity of whole effort   __ / __

Correctness   **/10**
Spelling: ___ *Errors*   Capitalization: ___ *Errors*
Punctuation: ____   _____ *(kind of error)* ___   _____
Grammar: ___ *Fragments* ___ *Run-on sentences*
     ___ *Subject-verb errors*
Formatting: ___ *1 inch margins sides and bottom*
     ___ *Paragraphing*
                    Must be typed—double spaced
Comments: **Total:**   **/50**

 # Appendix I: Creed Project Materials

Second Step V Packet: Detailed, Annotated Reflective Essay Instructions

Characteristics

Although the style of the Reflective Essay is often open, natural, and intimate, and its subject is often stimulated by a small incident, its reasoning is thoughtfully analytical and its intentions philosophical. The writer's skill in balancing these apparent opposites determines the quality of the reflective writing.

Reflection derives from personal experience. But beyond the description and narration involved in communicating that experience, reflection requires probing into what it can show about the writer's life in particular, and, more importantly, about the writer's ideas about life.

A reflective writer always works to see connections between experience and idea, to test out that idea in the light of other experiences, and to arrive at new dimensions of the original thought. Reflective writing shows a process as much as a product, achieving for the writer, and often for the reader, a sort of epiphany, an "ah ha!"

Characteristics of reflective writing include the use of a concrete occasion, the reflection that extends the meaning of this occasion, and the final awareness reached by the writer. Throughout, the voice and style of the writing are consistent and with writer's intent.

1. Occasion

Reflective essays are grounded in the concrete. An ordinary thing seen, done, read, or overheard can trigger the writer to explore what that occasion might say about the human condition. Occasions for reflection might stem from the observation of a natural phenomenon to a musing over the meaning of a familiar proverb. These occasions then become stimuli for the writer to interpret the world in microcosm.

2. Reflection

The best reflective writing is exploratory. It uses the specific occasion to explore an abstraction which becomes evident to the reader as the subject of the paper. Writers try to figure out this abstraction, turning it over to see it from several angles, thinking about it long enough to probe its meanings.

Because of the exploratory nature of the Reflective Essay, a pattern of thinking emerges as the reader reads and the writer writes. Analysis of hundreds of student essays shows that several patterns seem to be typical of the flow of thinking in and out of the following areas.

Patterns of Reflection

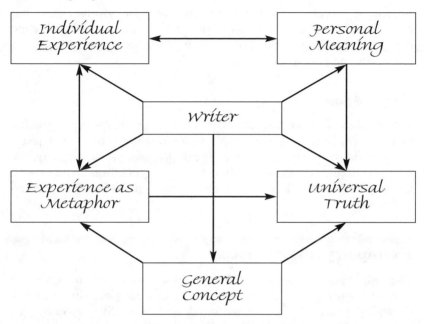

Examples of How Various Patterns Work

- Narrate a *single experience* and move in and out of it along the way, reflecting on the meaning of the various details. The experience becomes a metaphor for the universal truth of statement about life.

- Focus on the *meaning of a general concept*, and use a variety of examples as a base to reflect on different aspects of its significance.

- First *narrate a full incident,* choosing details and images carefully to portray the personal meaning that is then expanded to the universal truth.

- Focus *first on a single occasion* and then *draw associations between it and other related experiences* which build to universal truth.

- *Begin* with a *general concept* (a quotation, proverb, or general experience, and *test personal experience* against it, reflecting on how each experience relates to the general concept. The reflection is refined more fully with each incident it is tested against.

Whatever organization or thought pattern emerges, the writer's reflections give meaning to the narration and focus to the essay.

3. Final Awareness

Reflection creates insights—perhaps not *new* awarenesses, but reawakened ones, or deeper ones. In the best papers, there is a clear change in chemistry of the writer's view of the world, an epiphany for the writer and perhaps the reader.

Voice and Style

Writers show a commitment to the subject. Readers sense a genuine involvement in the ideas the topic generates; the paper is not just a "report" on the topic. The writers speak personally and naturally. We hear a thoughtful voice, almost in conversation with itself. Consequently, the style and presentation of the paper may be open and personal.

Exemplary Student Essay

The following exemplary Reflective Essay was written during an intensive writing workshop. The student has adequate time to work through the various stages of writing development. She began by narrating a full incident, focusing on its personal meaning, moving to its meaning for others, and arriving at a final awareness.

I struggle to pedal uphill as the sun beats down on my squinting and determined brow. I am going to make it this time, I decide. And the right leg pushes. And the left. And pedalling, and pedalling, and harder and harder and—Damn. I look around. Is anyone watching? Millions, it seems, as I lumber onto solid, stolid ground ad crouch with false concern next to the curb. I pretend to examine the gears, muttering hasty insanities. "Don't know why it didn't shift. Could be a problem with the gears. . . ." As if anyone is listening. I sigh and know that passing motorists can't hear my feeble excuses. They only see me, and the bicycle. My face turns brighter red. I slowly stand, right the bike, and face the truth. I will have to push it. Again. I have failed.

Gives reader a presence in the incident by using specific narrative action: details, interior dialogue, specific word choice.

As I walk, I curse myself forcibly, reaffirming not only my physical ineptitude, but my utter lack of stamina, dignity, and character. Finally, I reach the top of the seemingly endless stretch where pedestrianism is paramount to inadequacy. I mount the bike again and heave a sigh of relief to be in control once more.

Why is it so wrenchingly painful to walk my bike? Why does this action lead me to such depths of self loathing? For me, cycling is a humbling experience; I am routinely set face to face (or leg to leg) with failure. In general, I tend to avoid situations where I know I will not be successful. I do not play volleyball. I avoid singing in public. I watch while others bowl. Yet, somehow, I climb back onto a bicycle, knowing that I will never win a major race, ride across America, or even avoid walking the cursed machine.

Reflection begins. Writer ponders what the experience means, questions and explores answers at a personal level.

Uses specific examples to illustrate her idea.

Being mediocre, even terrible, satisfies a deep yearning. My quest for failure? Perhaps. Often, my downfalls bring me joy as I reflect on them. Walking instead of riding up a hill signifies not only imperfection, but a recognition of it as such, and as an acceptance of myself as a person who fails. Such a public statement of my weakness takes courage for me. Much more typical behavior for myself, and perhaps for others, comes in *avoiding* failure.

Continues to question ideas as they occur and to explore answers. She is reflecting upon her first reflection.

Very early in life, we are channeled into activities where we will succeed. Tall boys are taught basketball, strong boys practice football, runts learn piano. If a child shows true aptitude in an area, s/he is encouraged to pursue it to the neglect of other, less promising interests. To the contrary, encouragement dies fast once Peter shows a lack of coordination while shooting baskets. Our society is geared towards success; parents desire highly achieving children. Thus, they applaud successes and steer little ones away from less glorious situations which they see as potentially traumatic. Ironically, even when these efforts are effective and produce skillful athletes, students, or performers, they do not reinforce basic self esteem. Fear of this failure looms largest when it

As she explores a contrasting idea, she moves from the personal "I" to the universal "we." Provides specific examples of society's emphasis on success.

The consequence of this idea brings her to an insight into the human condition that supports her earlier idea of the need for failure.

has been experienced least often.

As children approach adulthood, they steer themselves towards "safe" pursuits. It seems a waste of time to pursue something if one cannot excel, and the possibility of failure grows more drastic. The very words "success" and "failure" cease to refer to specific incidents; they become instead basic evaluations of self.

Now she reflects on the consequence of emphasizing success, fear of failure.

Getting off my bike to walk up a hill is, in effect, a failure. The real pain, though, occurs in the instant when I transfer this incident onto myself. I become the failure. Yet, as I climb back on and pedal once more, I realize that my underdeveloped thigh muscles do not reflect the demise of my general character. Neither, for that matter, do my other failures. Unfortunately, I am not sure enough to lay myself on this probing line very often. I have doubt that I will be able to shift the burden of failing from myself to my action; it is much more comfortable to avoid such painful situations entirely. Such denial of my faults, though is not only impossible, it is undesirable.

Returns to her original occasion to strengthen her observation about failure.

I freely admit that my most valiant efforts at various pursuits have proven to be, if not in vain, also not exactly aesthetically pleasing. I am slowly learning to accept these hideously public embarrassments, and am delving deeper into my private feelings.

It would be a lie to claim that I no longer pretend my bike is malfunctioning when I am too weak to pedal. But with each quick glance for snickering acquaintances, I smile more broadly at my own imperfections. Even more serious failures serve as humbling but joyous blows at the notion that my achievements alone comprise worth. My failures are my freedom.

A surprising conclusion that follows logically the evolution of the thinking

Special thanks to all who worked to develop this and other writing modes in the California Assessment Program during the 1980s.

Appendix I: Creed Project Materials

Additional Creed Project Materials:
Life Chart—Blank Student

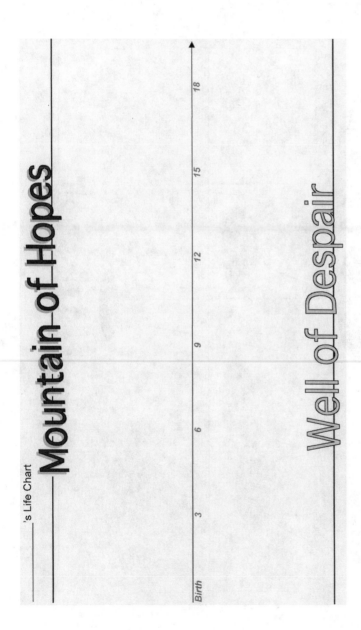

's Life Chart

Mountain of Hopes

Well of Despair

Birth | 3 | 6 | 9 | 12 | 15 | 18

Additional Creed Project Materials:
Mr. C's Life Chart

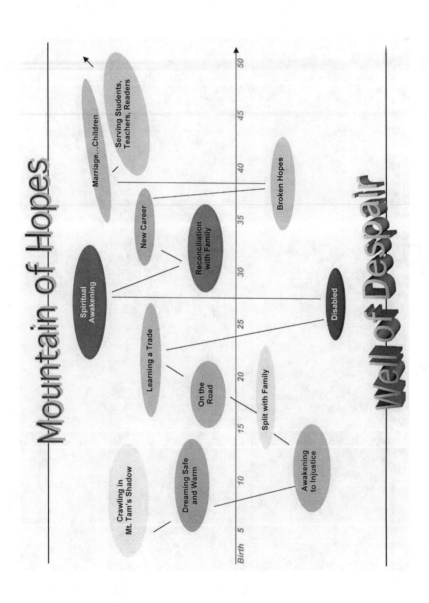

 Appendix I: Creed Project Materials

Mr. C's Personal Creed

Note: Because I've lived more than three times as long as my students now, my creed is more involved. This current version has three sections, each slightly different in emphasis: vision, creed, mission. I explain that a creed is unique to a person, and each may take a unique form. Theirs will probably be fairly simple for now.

My Personal Vision, Creed, and Mission

John Creger

Thanks to my sixth-period sophomores (class of 2000),
for asking me to share <u>my</u> creed with <u>them</u> for a change!

Vision

The universe
is a mountain

Life's goal is to ascend it

There are as many *p*aths up the mountain
as *p*eople to walk them

I came here to climb
the universe mountain

Creed

Religion may nourish me
it may repel me
but *I* must bring my soul to flower.

By my choices
Souls bloom or droop in my footsteps

I stand
open to the gifts inside me
learning to unfold them
helping others find and unfold
the gifts inside themselves.

Mission

To do my work well, with a calm, grateful heart

Seeking guidance and wisdom daily
from the source of universe gifts

To love the climb
loving the mountain
and every day loving one more climber

John Creger
June 2003

With thanks to ALL *my sophomores*

from the classes of 1992, 1993, 1994,
1995, 1996, 1997, 2000, 2001,
2002, 2003, 2004, 2005, and 2006.

American High School
Fremont, California
USA, Earth,
slopes of the
universe mountain

Additional Creed Project Materials:
The Role of Ideals (Graphic for Classroom Use)

The Role of Ideals

How ideals govern our moment-to-moment attitude toward life

Adapted from "An Essay on Hope"
By David Kantor

Despair - Doubt - Hope - Faith

Fear   Ideals

Ideas vs. Ideals?

Today the nations of the world are directed by men who have a superabundance of ideas, but they are poverty-stricken in *ideals*. That is the explanation of poverty, divorce, war, and racial hatreds.

—S. M. Essenger

And there can be no peace in the heart or progress in the mind unless you fall wholeheartedly in love with truth, the *ideals* of eternal realities.

—M. D. Wayer

Only those who face facts and adjust them to *ideals* can achieve wisdom.

—Rodan of Alexandria

(emphasis added, all three quotes)

Appendix II: Wisdom Project Materials

Wisdom Project Instruction Packet

Note: Literature cited is from *Elements of Literature,* Fourth Course (Holt, Rhinehart and Winston, 1997)

ENGLISH 10cp/Hrs   WORLD LITERATURE
Origins and Wisdom   Mr. Creger

World Wisdom Project

Fall 2002

> Failure is simply an educational episode—a cultural experiment in the acquirement of wisdom.
>
> —M. D. Wayer

As we do with hurricanes, we give each generation a name. Out of the First World War came the Lost Generation. My generation, born as our parents' generation (your grandparents) made an energetic new beginning after the horrors of the Second World War, grew into the largest in U.S. history. So large, in fact, that we became known as the Baby Boomers. But all did not go as our parents hoped. Feeling isolated, at times suffocated, by the safety and security our parents wanted for us, many of us early left the sometimes insulated communities where we grew up, to strike out on our own. To connect with the world beyond, we Boomers did unpredictable things: the civil rights struggle, culture-rocking music, a generation on the march—whether as soldiers or war protesters, flower children or spiritual seekers. These were a few of our ways to reach beyond the limitations we felt. After the Boomers, partly in reaction against the excesses of my generation, came a Me Generation, a Gen X, and others. In time, the stage was set for you. Enter the *Millennial Generation!*

And what are you "Millennials" about? A good way to answer this question might be to ask what challenges you face. What challenges set you apart from other generations? Well, your parents work more, leaving you on your own more. The Internet provides you more opportunities to find trouble, as events like Columbine show. Yet these same two factors also mean that you are more connected to each other than previous generations were. "Boomers may be bowling alone," says one observer, "but Millennials are playing soccer in teams." Another challenge may also be shaping you more than it did previous generations: More of you grow up around peers from different backgrounds or cultures. As a result, more of you learn early to become *tolerant*, to accept those who are different from yourselves. Some of you, already having learned not to judge others just for being different, are moving beyond merely tolerating others, and learning to truly *understand* them. How are tolerance and understanding connected to *wisdom*? How can we *apply* wisdom from the past to learn to *live wisely* today? If we acquire wisdom through the *challenges* we face, what other challenges might be shaping your generation? Is the nation's continuing response to the events of September 2001 being guided by wisdom? Is it wise to believe our leaders simply because they are in charge? What wisdom is coming into the world *through you*, the Millennial Generation? What does it mean, anyway, to live in a way that is wise? These are only some of the questions that guide this project.

In completing the project to the best of your ability, you will build your skills by addressing standards in several areas of the *California English–Language Arts Standards:*

Reading Comprehension:

- bring together content from several sources dealing with a single issue (2.4)
- extend ideas presented in primary or secondary sources through original analysis, evaluation, elaboration (2.5)
- evaluate the credibility of an author's argument (2.8).

Literary Response and Analysis:

- analyze the relationship between main and subordinate characters in a literary text (3.3)
- compare works that express a universal theme and offer evidence to support ideas expressed in each work (3.5)
- interpret and evaluate the impact of ambiguities, subtleties, contradictions, ironies, and incongruities in a text (3.8).

Speaking Applications:

Apply appropriate interviewing techniques:

- prepare and ask relevant questions, make notes of responses
- use language that conveys maturity, sensitivity, and respect

- respond correctly and effectively to questions, demonstrate knowledge of the topic
- compile and report responses, evaluate the effectiveness of the interview (2.3 a–d).

Writing Strategies:

- establish a controlling impression or coherent thesis that conveys a clear and distinctive perspective on the subject and maintain a consistent tone and focus throughout a piece of writing (1.1)
- use precise language, action verbs, sensory details, appropriate modifiers, active rather than passive voice (1.2)
- develop the main ideas within the body of the composition through supporting evidence (1.4)
- integrate quotations and citations while maintaining the flow of ideas (1.6).

Writing Applications:

- demonstrate a comprehensive grasp of the significant ideas of literary works (2.2a)
- support important ideas and viewpoints through accurate and detailed references to the text or to other works (2.2b)
- marshall evidence in support of a thesis and related claims (2.3a)
- structure ideas and arguments in a sustained and logical fashion (2.4a)
- clarify and defend positions with precise and relevant evidence— including facts, expert opinions, quotations, and expressions of commonly held beliefs and logical reasoning (2.4c).

Written Language Conventions:

- identify and correctly use mechanics of punctuation (e.g. semicolons, colons, ellipses, hyphens) (1.1)
- understand sentence construction (e.g. parallel structure, subordination, proper placement of modifiers) (1.2)
- demonstrate an understanding of proper English usage (e.g. consistency of verb tenses) and control of grammar,

  paragraph and sentence structure, diction, and syntax (1.3)
- produce legible work that shows accurate spelling and correct use of the conventions of punctuation and capitalization (1.4)
- reflect appropriate manuscript requirements, including title page presentation, pagination, spacing and margins, and integration of source and support material (1.5).

The following seven steps will assist you in this project *(You will include each step when you turn in your completed project; be prepared for spot checks of your progress):*

1) Write the heading "World Wisdom Project Brainstorm #1: Questions and Hopes" at the top of a sheet of paper. After completing steps (a) and (b), respond—in at least one full page—to the questions in (c) and (d). Use paragraph, not list, form.

   a. Get out your list of Big Questions from Inquiry I. Look over your list and try to recall what you thought and felt as you wrote about your Big Question(s).

   b. Get out all the Reading Journals (RJs) that have been returned to you. With your Big Questions in mind (any of them), read through your RJs.

   c. Write several paragraphs in response to the following questions. Which piece of literature we have read so far connects in some way to one of your Big Questions? Which Big Question? How does it relate? Does the piece of literature connect to your question in a way you find satisfying, interesting, confusing, inspiring, frustrating, or what? Does more than one piece of literature connect to your questions? If so, which piece, and which question? If none of the literature connects to any of your questions, please explain why you think this might be the case.

   d. What do you hope to learn in completing this project? Remember: full page = full credit. No dark ink = no credit.

2. Write the heading "Wisdom Project Interviews" at the top of a sheet of paper. Using instructions and interview questions we'll create in class, conduct five interviews—two with peers, two with adults, one with a senior citizen (roughly over 65). Two of your interviews must be with people from a different cultural or religious background than yours. Working from your interview notes, record the main points of each interview. Use additional sheets if necessary. Create your interview questions for the following three purposes:

   a. According to a recent *Newsweek* cover story, Millennials are "ambitious, optimistic, and spiritual." Design a number of interview questions to learn what your interviewees feel are your generation's *greatest strengths* and *greatest challenges*.

   b. You also want to learn what qualities your interviewees think show that a person is wise.

   c. Finally, design some questions that ask your interviewees to reflect on whether they feel the various actions our government has taken in the War on Terrorism have been guided by wisdom. In conducting your interviews, follow the appropriate interviewing techniques from the California Standards.

3. On a fresh sheet of paper, write "Brainstorm #2: Wisdom from Literature" as your next heading. Choose the three or four selections we have read in the text and/or discussed in class that have been most meaningful to you (choices below). For each of your choices, write a paragraph in which you *summarize the selection's essential wisdom* as you see it. The selections and their page numbers:

    Abraham and Isaac, p. 905
    Taoist Anecdotes, p. 936
    Psalm 23, p. 910
    Poems of Lao Tzu, p. 937
    To Everything There Is a Season, p. 912
    Zen Parables, p. 942
    The Parable of the Prodigal Son, p. 916
    from *The Panchatantra,* p. 945
    Passages from the Koran, p. 926
    "The Man to Send Rain Clouds," p. 185
    Sayings of Saadi, p. 928
    "Mother to Son," p. 508 (poem)
    Tale of the Sands, p. 929
    "I Am Offering This Poem," p. 551
    "The Guest House," Rumi (poem, handout)
    "By Any Other Name" (p. 367)
    A favorite quote (or two) from your Thought Log
    "Yacqui Deer Dance" (poem, handout)
    Poems from West Africa (handout)
    "God: the Changing Literary Character" (handout)
    (*Other ideas? See me, please.*)

4. Write "Brainstorm #3: Levels of Wisdom" as your next heading. First, look over your Brainstorm #1 (step 1 above) and your background interviews. Now consider that one may think of three levels of wisdom:

    Wisdom at the ground level we can think of as closer to material knowledge, or cleverness—one has a knowledge of things, is wise to the ways of the world, knows how to get what one wants. We can call this ***Level 1 Wisdom.***

    In its intermediate levels, wisdom helps us to decide how to interact with others, what we should regard as our duty, what is right and wrong, a moral and intellectual perspective. Let's term this ***Level 2 Wisdom.***

Wisdom in its higher forms gives us the desire to serve others, the urge to understand the universe on a spiritual level, to love and be loved, to balance the needs of body, mind, heart, and spirit. This we will call ***Level 3 Wisdom***.

    a.   Write a paragraph responding to the following questions: In general, how do you react to your interviewees' ideas about wisdom? Which do you agree with? Disagree with? Why? What levels of wisdom (see above) have each of your interviewees expressed? Has conducting the interviews led you to change or expand on any ideas you have held previously? If so, which ones? How? If not, why not, do you think?

    b.   In a second paragraph, consider the wisdom from the literature you have summarized in Brainstorm #2 (step 3). Do this by responding to these questions: Which one or two of these selections most strongly impresses you? Why do you think they do so? What level(s) of wisdom does each seem to you to represent? As you consider the wisdom in the literature, do you find yourself changing or expanding on any of your ideas? If so, explain how. If not, please explain why not, if you can.

    c.   Reread everything you've written so far for this project. Reflecting on these things in a third paragraph, write your own personal definition of wisdom. You could begin your definition, "Wisdom is . . ." Or you could begin, "A wise person is . . ." Feel free, if you wish, to incorporate insights from the three levels of wisdom in your definition.

5.   A topic sentence, the assertion in a paragraph, is the paragraph's controlling idea. Check the one Topic Sentence option below that most interests you. Circle your choice of *"reflects"* or *"does not reflect"* wisdom. *(See step 3 of these instructions for page numbers in the text if you need to reread.)*

    a.   The biblical story of Abraham and Isaac *reflects/does not reflect* wisdom.

    b.   Psalm 23, from the Old Testament Book of Psalms, *reflects/does not reflect* wisdom.

    c.   "To Everything There Is a Season," a poem from the biblical book of Ecclesiastes, *reflects/does not reflect* wisdom.

    d.   The Parable of the Prodigal Son, from the New Testament, *reflects/does not reflect* wisdom.

    e.   "Daylight" and/or "Comfort" [choose one or both], a passage from the Koran, *reflects/does not reflect* wisdom.

    f.   "The Pearl," "Relative," "Information and Knowledge," "The Thief and the Blanket," "The Destiny of a Wolf Cub" [choose one or, at most, two], brief tales from Saadi's Gulistan, *reflects/does not reflect* wisdom.

    g.   The Sufi story "The Tale of the Sands" *reflects/does not reflect* wisdom.

    h.   Rumi's poem "The Guest House" [or "Yacqui Deer Dance" or a poem from West Africa—choose one] *reflects/does not reflect* wisdom.

    i.   The Taoist anecdote(s) "Wagging My Tale in the Mud," "The Missing Ax," "The Lost Horse" [choose one, or at most two] *reflects/does not reflect* wisdom.

    j.   The Zen parable(s) "Muddy Road" [and/or] "The Thief Who Became a Disciple" *reflects/does not reflect* wisdom.

    k.   "The Tiger, the Brahman, and the Jackal," from the Panchatantra, *reflects/does not reflect* wisdom.

    l.   Leslie Marmon Silko's story, "The Man to Send Rain Clouds," *reflects/does not reflect* wisdom.

    m.   Santha Rama Rau's story "By Any Other Name," *reflects/does not reflect* wisdom. Langston Hughes' poem "Mother to Son" or Jimmy Santiago Baca's poem "I Am Offering This Poem" *reflects/does not reflect* wisdom.

    n.   The wisdom found in (a given work of literature we have read) can be helpfully applied in (a given social or political situation).

    o.   The wisdom found in (a given work of literature we have read) can be considered (Level 1, 2, or 3) Wisdom.

    p.   Certain elements contribute to making a person wise. (In your argument, use 1–3 of our literary works.)

    q.   Certain factors are involved in the process of becoming wise. (Use 1–3 of our literature works.)

    r.   In different traditions from different periods and parts of the world, wisdom appears with similar themes. (Use 2–3 of our works.)

    s.   The policies of our government since the attacks of September 2001 *do/do not* appear to be grounded in wisdom. (Use 2-3 of our works.)

6.   Turn a new sheet of binder paper horizontally, and write along the long edge (now on top): "Essay #2, Visual Plan."At the center of this sheet, copy your choice of Topic Sentence (from step 5). Draw a rectangle around it. In a moment, using a pencil, you will be adding General Supports to support your assertion (Topic Sentence). Group these ideas around your rectangle, and enclose them in ovals. Before you do this:

    a.   Look back at your ideas about what makes a person wise (step 4c).

    b.   With these ideas in mind, read back over your reading selection, and find general ways in which the reading selection supports your Topic Sentence. You are not looking yet for specific supports (such as examples or quotations).

c. With your pencil, jot down as many of these general ideas as you can think of (four to six is a good number). Group them around your rectangle.

d. Choose what you think are the three best general supports you have. Draw ovals around these. Save the other general supports by jotting them down on the back of your emerging Visual Plan. You may need them again! Once you have saved these spare ideas on the back, erase them on the front.

e. From each General Support (oval), in a direction where you have some room, draw a line outward. On each of these lines you will be writing a specific support to support the general idea that is inside the oval. In this essay, specific supports will be examples or quotations from your selection that support what's inside the oval. *See your class notes for more on Visual Plans.*

Appendix II: Wisdom Project Materials

Rubric for Wisdom Project Prewriting

World Wisdom Project

Steps 1–4
Scoring Rubric

Note: This scoring rubric is based directly on the Wisdom Project instructions. If you read and followed them carefully in completing the assignment, you are more likely to earn full credit.

Step 1   **/10**
(c) Several paragraphs relating literature you read in the Wisdom Project to the Big Question(s) you wrote in Inquiry I. You were asked to explore connections between the literature and your Question(s). Even if you found no direct connections, you were asked to explore and explain possible connections, explaining the connections or why you may have had difficulty making them. (7 pts. possible)
(d) A paragraph on what you hope to learn in this project (3 pts.)

Step 2   **/20**
At least five interviews, each with at least six questions, each question including a response from an interviewee. Four points for each interview as above, with responses.

Step 3   **/10**
Three or four paragraphs, each on a selection that has been meaningful to you. Each paragraph should summarize the essential wisdom of the piece as you see it.

Step 4   **/10**
(a) A paragraph evaluating your interviewees' ideas about wisdom, in relation to the three levels of wisdom
(b) A paragraph evaluating our literature on wisdom, mentioning the one or two selections that most strongly impress you
(c) A paragraph on your own personal definition of wisdom, incorporating the three levels of wisdom if you like

Total score   **/50**

Wise Sayings: What's the Point?

An Experiment

Purpose: To determine what value, if any, can be found in collecting and sharing wise sayings as an exercise in class.

Procedure:

1. Each student will bring to class on the due date a wise saying—a phrase, a sentence, a short poem or epigram. If possible, bring a wise saying from your own cultural, racial, or national background. You can find this wise saying at home, among friends or neighbors, at the library, on the Internet. If, in a rare case, you are not able to ask others, you may create your own. However, the saying needs to be one that a sizable number of people in the world might agree is indeed a wise saying.

2. Write your saying a few lines below the heading line on a sheet of paper.

3. Write a paraphrase of your saying (put it in your own words).

4. Make a hypothesis: How do you predict this assignment will come out? Will it create any learning that is of value?

5. Create teams of four. Each team chooses the following:

    a. Notetaker: notes down the team's decisions and main discussion points

    b. Discussion Leader: ensures that everyone has a turn to speak

    c. Presenter: takes responsibility for the quality of the team's presentation

    d. Artistic Director: in charge of getting all teammates involved in creating the team's poster

6. Take turns sharing your sayings with your teammates:

    a. Members take turns reading their own sayings aloud.

    b. After reading, the reader asks each teammate to paraphrase the saying. When each has attempted a paraphrase, the reader reads his or her own paraphrase, and the team discusses these questions:

        1. How accurate were the team's paraphrases?

2. Are there any similarities among your team's wise say-
    ings? If so, make a note of any similarities you find.
3. Are the sayings interesting? How? Why?

7. Update, refine, or completely change your hypothesis: How do you
    predict this assignment will come out? Will it create any learning
    that is of value?

8. Each team chooses one of the sayings that the greatest number of
    teammates agree is an especially interesting one. Team presents
    saying to the class with a poster and explanation. Requirements:

    Artistic Director: Your job is to make sure your team's poster is in
    bold, visible letters, including the saying, author's name (if any),
    and an illustration (optional).

    Discussion Director: Your team will be depending on you to make
    sure everyone gets the chance to speak, both in your discussions
    and in your presentation, when your team explains your poster.
    Your team should take turns explaining the following:
    a. Why your team selected this particular saying
    b. What it means
    c. How your team's saying connects to at least three of these:
        •   Your lives
        •   Our class
        •   Our school
        •   Your friends
        •   Home
        •   The news
        •   Other countries
        •   The universe

9. Teacher Shares "Wisdom Without Boundaries" (a PowerPoint
    presentation).

10. Each class nominates and votes for one wise saying to become our
    adopted Wise Saying.

Inquiry Journal 3: What did this activity help you learn? Give specific
examples please. And remember, with Inquiry Journals it's full page =
full credit.

Wise Sayings Presentation

Scoring Guide

Notetaker: _____   **/20**

quality and completeness of notes   /10
- written according to class guidelines: dark ink, with margins, etc.
- covers major team decisions (see step 8a, b, c in instructions)
- (see step 6, questions 1, 2, 3 in instructions)

presenting skills   /10
- eye contact with audience (not just teacher)
- comfortable posture, hands at sides (not in pockets)
- contributes to team speaking effort
- Voice quality: volume, clarity, projection

Discussion Director: _____   **/20**

quality and completeness of information presented   /10
- covers major team decisions (see step 8a, b, c in instructions)
- (see step 6, questions 1, 2, 3 in instructions)

presenting skills   /10
- eye contact with audience (not just teacher)
- comfortable posture, hands at sides (not in pockets)
- contributes to team speaking effort
- Voice quality: volume, clarity, projection

Presenter: _____   **/20**

quality of presentation   /10
- each team member plays a meaningful part in presentation
- each team member has spoken part to play
- presentation effectively organized ahead of time

presenting skills   **/10**
- eye contact with audience (not just teacher)
- comfortable posture, hands at sides (not in pockets)
- contributes to team speaking effort
- Voice quality: volume, clarity, projection

Artistic Director: _____   **/20**

quality of poster   **/10**
- saying clearly visible in block letters
- attractive design

presenting skills   **/10**
- eye contact with audience (not just teacher)
- comfortable posture, hands at sides (not in pockets)
- contributes to team speaking effort
- Voice quality: volume, clarity, projection

Appendix III: Materials for Weaving Personal Learning Through the Year

Sample Thought Log Quotes

Sample Thought Log Quotes

Seek the inner life and its ideals, so that when the realistic outer life falls apart, you will not be in a blizzard but in a gentle rain shower that quickly passes. —T. Daniel

A search for happiness is a formula for misery; a search for meaning often produces happiness as a by-product. —Betty Stone

How many of us reason, "If I am not perfect, then I must be worthless"? —T. Rayson

People know what they want to be, not what they are. —Nuri Lundy, 1998–99

Some people go fishing all their lives without realizing it's not fish they're after. —Henry David Thoreau

Without a vision, a people perish. —Bible

Hope is only a four letter word, only with all the power of the universe. —Matt Vivian, 2000–01

If you keep your destiny in mind, every moment in life becomes an opportunity for moving closer to it. —Arthur Golden, *Memoirs of a Geisha*

What a privilege it is to have self-conscious life, and to begin to perceive our part in the evolution and creation of the cosmos. —T. Andrew

Wisdom guides the mother and father to feed the child one spoonful at a time. —T. Gabriel

If you bring forth what is within you, what you bring forth will save you. If you do not bring forth what is within you, what you do not bring forth will destroy you. —T. Tomas

Fear of a name increases fear of the thing itself. —Albus Dumbledore

Much of human life consists in learning that your life is only a
transition.   —T. Ham

What a wise man can see from the top of a tall tree, a fool cannot see
from close range.   —Anthony Mbanugo, 2001–02

The ignorant are awed by show; the wise are awed by what is not
seen, by thought.   —*Letters of the Scattered Brotherhood*

The noblest of all memories are the treasured recollections of the
great moments of a superb friendship.   —Rodan of Alexandria

A society is built upon the quality of its relationships.   —T. Redona

A person is wise when he is able to use his past experiences to make
the right decisions considering the needs of the body, mind, heart and
spirit.   —Rudy Gagernon, 2001–02

There is only one Wisdom; it is to understand the thought by which
all things are steered through all things.   —Heraclitus, 500 B.C.

Live as if you were to die tomorrow. Learn as if you were to live forever.   —Mahatma Gandhi

In the end, we will remember not the words of our enemies, but the
silence of our friends.   —Martin Luther King, Jr.

The true test of character is not how much we know how to do, but
how we behave when we don't know what to do.   —John Holt

What the caterpillar calls the end of the world, the rest of the world
calls a butterfly.   —Richard Bach

It's not the knowing of the truth that is important, but the searching
for it.   —T. Tarkas

Wisdom is not contained in cleverness, any more than knowledge is
contained in facts.   —teaching proverb

Appendix III: Materials for Weaving Personal Learning Through the Year

QuoteCrackers

Thought Log QuoteCrackers

- The "Shining Phrase" in this quote that jumps right out at me is . . .
- This phrase catches my attention because . . .

- The part of this quote I don't understand is . . .
- One way this part might connect to the rest of the quote is that . . .

- I would paraphrase this quote:
- I agree / disagree with this quote, because . . .

- This quote makes me feel . . .
- This quote makes me ponder . . .

- This quote makes me visualize . . . (describe in words or draw)
- This quote inspires me to sing, write, draw, dance, play music . . .

- I think the author's purpose in writing the quote was . . .
- A question I'd like to ask the author is . . .
- I'd ask this question because . . .

- This quote connects with our theme of . . .
- This quote relates to our reading or literature when . . .
- I think my teacher chose this quote for us because . . .
- This quote connects with the part of my own life that . . .

- This quote reminds me of . . .
  - a person, writer, public figure

- another quote
- a particular piece of literature
- a song, music, dance, film, other work of art

- The dominant impression this quote leaves me with is . . .
- If I were to change this quote into a question, I would write . . .
- What this quote needs is . . .

Quote Cracking: Quadrant Style

Option A
A Quadrant for quotes you have a clue about

Date: Today's Quote	
• *QuoteCracker* . . .	• *QuoteCracker* . . .
• *Free response* . . .	

Option B

A Quadrant for quotes or passages that are difficult *to crack*

Date: Today's Quote	
• *QuoteCracker* . . .	• *QuoteCracker* . . .
• *QuoteCracker* . . .	• *QuoteCracker* . . .

References and Recommended Reading

Bronte, Charlotte. 1847. *Jane Eyre*.

Burke, Jim. 1999. *The English Teacher's Companion*. Portsmouth, NH: Heinemann.

———. 2002. *Tools for Thought*. Portsmouth, NH: Heinemann.

Coehlo, Paulo. 1994, 2003. *The Alchemist*. San Francisco: HarperSanFrancisco.

Covey, Stephen A. 1989. *The Seven Habits of Highly Effective People*. New York: Simon and Schuster.

Creger, John. 2002. "Zora Neale Hurston's Janie: Pointing the Way to Two-Legged Curriculum." *California English* 7 (February): 22–27.

Daniels, Harvey. 2002. *Literature Circles: Voice and Choice in Book Clubs and Reading Groups*. York, ME: Stenhouse.

Daniels, Harvey, and Marilyn Bizar. 1998. *Methods That Matter: Six Structures for Best Practice Classrooms*. York, ME: Stenhouse.

Daniels, Harvey, Marilyn Bizar, and Steven Zemelman. 2001. *Rethinking High School: Best Practice in Teaching, Learning, and Leadership*. Portsmouth, NH: Heinemann.

Darwin, Charles. 1871/1981. *The Descent of Man*. Princeton, NJ: Princeton University Press.

Davis, Gary. 1983. *Educational Psychology: Theory and Practice*. New York: Random House.

Davis, Wade. 2002. "We Need a Global Declaration of Interdependence." *Toronto Globe and Mail* (6 July). www.commondreams.org/views02/0706-01.htm.

Dryden, Gordon, and Jeannette Vos. 1999. *The Learning Revolution*. Torrance, CA: The Learning Web. *Orders: www.thelearningweb.net.*

Einstein, Albert. 1956. *Ideas and Opinions*. New York: Crown.

Eisler, Riane. 1987. *The Chalice and the Blade: Our History, Our Future*. New York: HarperCollins.

———. 2000. *Tomorrow's Children: A Blueprint for Partnership Education in the Twenty-first Century*. Boulder, CO: Westview Press.

Golding, William, *Lord of the Flies*. 1954. New York: Putnam.

Halloran, S. Michael. 1982. "Rhetoric in the American College Curriculum: The Decline of Public Discourse." *Composition in Four Keys: Inquiring into the Field*. Ed. Mark Wiley, et al. Mountain View, CA: Mayfield. 184–97.

Hawkens, Paul, Amory Lovins, and L. Hunter Lovins. 1999. *Natural Capitalism: Creating the Next Industrial Revolution*. Boston: Little, Brown.

Hugo, Victor. 1862. *Les Miserables.*

Hurston, Zora Neale. 1998. *Their Eyes Were Watching God.* New York: HarperCollins.

———. 1939. *Moses, Man of the Mountain.* New York: Lippincott.

Kantor, David. 2002. "An Essay on Hope."
www.urantiabook.org//archive/readers/Hope_website.htm.

Kohn, Alfie. 1990. *The Brighter Side of Human Nature: Altruism and Empathy in Everyday Life.* New York: HarperCollins.

———. *The Case Against Standardized Testing.* 2001. Portsmouth, NH: Heinemann.

Lee, Harper. 1960. *To Kill a Mockingbird.*

Ladson-Billings, Gloria. 1994. *The Dreamkeepers: Successful Teachers of African American Children.* San Francisco: Jossey-Bass.

Loye, David. 2000. *Darwin's Lost Theory of Love.* Lincoln, NE: toExcel.

Moffett, James. 1994. *The Universal Schoolhouse: Spiritual Awakening Through Education.* San Francisco: Jossey-Bass.

Nord, Warren A., and Charles C. Haynes. 1998. *Taking Religion Seriously Across the Curriculum.* Alexandria, VA: Association for Supervision and Curriculum Development.

Patterson, David. 1988. *Literature and Spirit: Essays on Bakhtin and His Contemporaries.* Lexington: University Press of Kentucky.

Phifer, Nan. 2002. *Memoir of the Soul: Writing Your Spiritual Autobiography.* Writer's Digest Books.

Popham, W. James. 2001. *The Truth About Testing: An Educator's Call to Action.* Alexandria, VA: Association for Supervision and Curriculum Development.

Postman, Neil, and Charles Weingartner. 1969. *Teaching as a Subversive Activity.* New York: Dell.

Probst, Robert, et al. 1997. *Elements of Literature, Fourth Course.* Orlando, FL: Holt, Rinehart and Winston.

Roland, Allen L. 2002. *Radical Therapy.* Novato, CA: Origin Press.

Rowling, J. K. any and all in the Harry Potter series.

Rumi. *The Essential Rumi.* 1995. Trans. Coleman Barks. New York: HarperCollins.

———. *The Soul of Rumi.* 2001. Trans. Coleman Barks. New York: HarperCollins.

Whyte, David. 2001. *Crossing the Unknown Sea: Work as a Pilgrimage of Identity.* New York: Riverhead Books.

———. 1996. *The Heart Aroused: Poetry and the Preservation of Soul in Corporate America.* New York: Doubleday.

———. 1998. *The House of Belonging.* Langley, WA: Many Rivers Press.

The Urantia Book. 1995. Chicago: Urantia Foundation.

Zemelman, Steven, Harvey Daniels, and Arthur Hyde. 1993, 1998. *Best Practice: New Standards for Teaching and Learning in America's Schools.* Portsmouth, NH: Heinemann.

Zinsser, William. 1988. *Writing to Learn.* New York: Harper and Row.

Index